Beer & Philoso

Please see the other books in the Epicurean Trilogy
Conceived by Fritz Allhoff:

 Food & Philosophy
Eat, Think, and Be Merry
Edited by Fritz Allhoff and Dave Monroe

 Wine & Philosophy
A Symposium on Thinking and Drinking
Edited by Fritz Allhoff

Beer & Philosophy

The Unexamined Beer Isn't Worth Drinking

Edited by Steven D. Hales

BLACKWELL PUBLISHING
350 Main Street, Malden, MA 02148-5020, USA
9600 Garsington Road, Oxford OX4 2DQ, UK
550 Swanston Street, Carlton, Victoria 3053, Australia

First published 2007 by Blackwell Publishing Ltd

2   2008

Library of Congress Cataloging-in-Publication Data

Beer & philosophy : the unexamined beer isn't worth drinking /
edited by Steven D. Hales.
     p. cm.
   Includes bibliographical references.
   ISBN-13: 978-1-4051-5430-7 (pbk. : alk. paper)   1. Beer–Philosophy.
I. Hales, Steven D.   II. Title: Beer and philosophy.
   TP577.B37 2008
   641.2′3—dc22

                                                              2007014518

A catalogue record for this title is available from the British Library.
Set in 10.5/13pt Sabon
by Graphicraft Limited, Hong Kong
Printed and bound in the United States of America
by Sheridan Books, Inc., Chelsea, MI

The publisher's policy is to use permanent paper from mills that operate
a sustainable forestry policy, and which has been manufactured from
pulp processed using acid-free and elementary chlorine-free practices.
Furthermore, the publisher ensures that the text paper and cover board
used have met acceptable environmental accreditation standards.

For further information on
Blackwell Publishing, visit our website:
www.blackwellpublishing.com

What's on Tap

Foreword
I Wink, Therefore I Am

Michael Jackson

To be a respected intellectual is no guarantee of being right. The most famous editor of *The Manchester Guardian*, C. P. Scott, pronounced that television would never be a success, because the word itself mixed Greek and Latin. Philosophy is all Greek to me, but I studied Latin. *Timeo Danaos et dona ferentes . . .*[1]

Among the gifts of the Greeks were translations of the Christian gospels from the original Aramaic scrolls. The Greeks interpreted "strong drink" as "wine." I wonder, did they think Jesus turned water into Retsina or Riesling? The Saxons were in no doubt. Their version of the miracle is much more exciting: "Suddenly, the room was filled with barrels of beer." Lest you suspect my own theological agenda, I should make clear that the translation from the Saxon was provided by a Jesuit priest, Ron Murphy, who was at the time Dean of Georgetown University and Head of its Department of Germanic Languages. Ron and I have a pint of Salvator together now and then, but I am sure my certainties have not influenced his verities.

Do we have the Greeks to blame for the elevation of wine and the subjugation of beer? It seems to me that they started it, but the Romans followed; Tacitus said that the Germanic peoples drank beer, and that it made their breath smell. I don't suppose he ever rode the Paris metro.

In my experience, true lovers of wine respect and enjoy beer. I have been encouraged in my writing by James Beard, M. F. K. Fisher, Robert Lawrence Balzer, Robert Finegan, Robert Parker and Jancis Robinson, among many others.

---

[1] I fear the Greeks, even when they bring gifts . . .

A Hellenophile who grows renowned Cabernet and Merlot in Napa, as well as cultivating olives and making cheese, is one of my favorite brewers. His name is Fritz Maytag, and his Anchor Steam Beer has a worldwide reputation. Maytag and his brew crew were the central characters in a film I made a few years ago. The film was about the renaissance – now more of a revolution – in the world of beer.

It was a road movie. We started in San Francisco, and headed through the wine country of Northern California to a farm at Tule Lake, hard against the state line by Klamath Falls, Oregon. There, the crew would ride the combines as the farmer harvested the barley for the brewery's vintage-dated Anchor Holiday Ale. "Getting in touch with the roots of your beer" sounds a definitively Californian concept, but I wish more brewers and states would do something similar.

The grape and the grain should be companions of honor. People enjoy going to Napa and Sonoma to visit vineyards, yet they pass through North Dakota, East Anglia (England), the Munich Basin (Bavaria, Germany) and the Hana region of Moravia (in the Czech Republic) without even noticing the fields of malting barley. Beer is being grown.

The grape needs only oak to modify its aromas and flavors. Only the biggest beers in palate and potency can deal with the flavor compounds and microflora given by oak, though it's used as one of many elements in the revolution. Most beers are much lower in alcohol and more delicate in constitution than wine. Their natural preservative is hops, the dried flowers of the hop plant, which also add a powerfully fragrant aroma and an intensely appetizing bitterness. The hop is a beautiful aromatic plant, often growing in the same regions as apples and cherries. Look for the cones ripening on the vines in late summer in the Willamette Valley of Oregon, the Yakima Valley of Washington State and the Snake River Valley of Idaho.

I asked Maytag to compare winemaking and brewing, given that he does both. "Winemaking is like painting in oils; brewing is like being a water colorist," he proposed. Maytag was studying American and Japanese literature and enjoying the bars and restaurants of North Beach, San Francisco, when he was told that his favorite beer was to cease production. Gradually, he became the owner of the brewery. The way he tells it, he might have been the Good Soldier Schweick, an innocent overtaken by the fates. I shall not attempt to explain to you his reference to oils and water colors. It sounded whimsical but it was a metaphor perfect to the last detail. Please think about it, and work it out for yourself.

"What is there to say about beer?" is a refrain that has burrowed into my head like an earwig for the past 30 years. My resistance and persistence may encourage these irritating ignoramuses in their belief that beer lovers are blockheads. "They can't read," I am assured, though no evidence is proffered. If this were true, the literary petits bourgeois would not have met any beer lovers on whom to base their conclusions. Those whom I have encountered in the last few days seem to be obsessed with philosophy.

Go to any decent beer festival and you will see at least one person wearing a tee shirt announcing: "I drink. Therefore I am." This poses one of the most intractable questions known to humankind: Are the old jokes the best? Perhaps we could let that one stretch its laughing gear in the pub tonight.

A pub is not a restaurant. Nor is it a bar. It is neither a table at which to sit and eat nor a counter at which to perch and drink. Proper pubs are havens in which one can anchor the soul, and hope. They have pockets of peace and conversational corners. They offer the possibility to think-and-drink or talk-and-drink.

It is the ability to think that distinguishes us as human individuals, if I understand Descartes. It is hardly an original thought, but he filed it down to a sound bite.

If that is all he achieved, why is he thought to have been such a clever chap? The brilliance of philosophers, it seems to me, is to massage one or two bons mots into a schtick and be remembered for it as a life's work. It's a good gig.

Still, there are certain requirements. The end result should be in "the language of the people" (a phrase imparted to me by my boss on a small-town evening paper when I was 17 years old). It should appear to resonate with wisdom, yet be impenetrable.

"Write out of the side of your mouth," a later editor told me. I was working on a vaguely disreputable tabloid then. The editor wanted his writers to engage their readers with a nudge and a wink before offering them tidbits of dubious gossip. Does the wink automatically tarnish the words? Perhaps their integrity could be better maintained by a twinkle in the eye.

"Listen to your beer" is a brilliant example from Fred Eckhardt, one of the beer movement's own philosophers. Fred, an early writer on beer, caught my ear with that line. He does not identify himself as a philosopher on his business card. "Shaman" is the term he uses, if I remember right.

When Fred and I first met, his home town, Portland, Oregon, had one brewery. Today, its metro area has more than two dozen breweries. Portland's rival at the opposite end of the West coast, San Diego, has a similar number. Their contest is turning semantic: one city's total is delineated by its zip code; the other by its county line. At stake is the title "City With the Most Breweries": not just on the West Coast, nor in the United States or North America, but in the whole world.

When I started writing about beer, the United States had about 50 brewing companies. Back then, you could count on two hands the beers that were not standard golden lagers. Apart from the Anchor products, you would finger the odd Porter (from Pennsylvania, Stegmaier and Yuengling); an outstanding amber ale (Ballantine's IPA, being chased by a man with a sickle from Albany, NY; to Newark, NJ; to Providence, RI . . . well, you get the idea). Yes, I also quite liked Tiger Head Ale and Rainier Ale and Prior Double Dark, but the rest were barely distinguishable from golden lagers.

When the baby boomers began to vacation in Europe, go to college there, or serve in the military, they developed tastes that Milwaukee didn't meet, and St Louis didn't satisfy. Nor was Rocky Mountain Spring Water the answer, though there was an oracle in Boulder.

"Relax. Don't worry. Have a home brew," counseled Charlie Papazian. When President Carter signed Alan Cranston's bill federally legalizing homebrewing, no one could have imagined the outcome. Papazian, a nuclear physicist who preferred teaching, began holding classes. Before long, he was running a national association. When the amateurs started to turn professional, he even started a magazine with the Greek name *Zymurgy*.

Today, there are between 50 and 100 styles of beer being produced in the US, by about 1,500 breweries. That is a far greater choice of beers than can be found in any other country. It includes some of the world's best beers and a whole new category of "extreme" beers.

Faced with this astonishing diversity, I began my 1993 *Beer Companion* with the words "Never ask for 'a beer'." It's sharp and snappy, wise even, but how do you pronounce those quotation marks? I'm still working on it.

When I grow up, I want to be a philosopher.

Editor's Introduction

Steven D. Hales

The mouth of a perfectly contented man is filled with beer.
Egyptian proverb, c.2200 BCE

Beer: the cause of, and the solution to, all of life's problems.
Homer Simpson, 1997 CE

Beer, in all its vast variety from simple barley mash accidentally fermented by wild yeasts to modern lagers, ales, stouts, bocks, and triples, is the most democratic of beverages, drunk by the plebeians and the patricians alike. Bud Lite may be on tap in the most disreputable dive and Andelot Cuvee Diabolique served in the most upscale restaurant, but throughout the whole gamut: beer.

Unlike wine, which in ancient times was an elite drink for the wealthy nobility and considered a divine gift from the god Dionysus, beer has long been a drink available to every citizen. Indeed, beer has long been a food staple, part of one's daily life. The stonecutters and laborers who built the Egyptian pyramids were paid in beer and bread, with a gallon per day their standard wage. Three thousand years later empires had risen and fallen, religions had failed and new ones been born, yet beer was a constant. In 1249 the Adam and Eve pub was built in Norwich, England, to serve the Norman masons who constructed Norwich Cathedral. Like their ancient forebears, the men were paid in beer and bread. And one can still enjoy a well-earned pint at the Adam and Eve to this very day. Beer is still the modestly priced beverage of the people. Beer – not wine or liquor – is what's packed in the cooler

1

on the bass boat, the perfect beverage to wash down ballpark hot dogs, the thirst-quencher after mowing the lawn on a hot summer day.

Increasingly, connoisseurs have come to realize that beer is every bit the equal of its snooty sister wine when it comes to pairing a fine drink with a meal. In the past quarter century in the United States, beer has undergone a considerable revival, with brewers returning not only to the historic brewing traditions inherited from Germany and the Czech Republic, but also to the inventiveness and flavor components of Belgium, and the styles of Britain and Ireland. Even the major corporate breweries in the US have felt the pressure and produce at least some beers brewed by craft methods.

Beer is a great uniter of human beings from every epoch in time, from every place on earth, and this very ubiquity of beer in our lives makes it a vehicle by which we can examine our lives – and that, dear reader, is the beginning of philosophy. Beer drives the human condition, even if the human is in no condition to drive. Yet what can sober *philosophy* have to tell us about ourselves as we hoist another pint? The beer lovers and scholars in this book have a great deal to say about how you can strengthen your mind through 16 ounce curls.

You have no doubt gotten into plenty of disagreements about whether this beer tastes better than that one, whether those who disagree with your tastes are just dopes, or whether deliciousness really is in the mouth of the beholder. Yet just what constitutes a good beer? Are there objective criteria that pick out the delectable from the vile, or is it truly *de gustibus non est disputatum*?[1] Why do beer aficionados revile Pabst Blue Ribbon but revere Chimay Blue Grande Réserve? Is ale fresh from the cask and served in a glass really better than an ice-cold aluminum can? Is it just plain snobbery, or are there real truths about beer and taste? Philosophers collect such questions together as *aesthetic* ones. In the first part of the book, *The Art of the Beer*, your thinking companions consider just these issues.

In his archly funny "Thirst for Authenticity: an Aesthetics of the Brewer's Art," Dale Jacquette considers that to consume beer properly is to participate in an art form, from the moment that one's ale is tapped from the keg and pulled from the unformed sloshy void into a solid pint of existence, to the instant that the last trail of foam passes from the glass. But can you really brew authentic beer in Portland

---

[1] In matters of taste there is no disputing.

or San Diego, or is it more like "authentic Navaho beads" made in Taiwan? Jacquette argues that a German brewery that adheres to the Beer Purity Law (*Reinheitsgebot*) of 1516 produces a product that is authentic in a way that a Belgian or American brewery consciously abiding by a medieval German law does not. Still, just as jazz and blues are America's unique musical forms, maybe there can be culturally authentic beer coming out of Pittsburgh, too.

Even if a product arises out of a specific cultural tradition, it may nevertheless be dishonest, a fraud. Garrett Oliver, in "The Beer Matrix: Reality vs Facsimile in Brewing," discusses products that are not what they appear to be, or are marketed as being. "American cheese," for example, is more of an edible plastic than it is actual cheese, and soft, mass-produced bread has little in common with crusty home-baked loaves. At a certain point, we might no longer call such things cheese or bread, but mere facsimiles of the real thing. The same is true of beer. A lightly fermented beverage made mostly of corn and rice, with a little hop extract thrown in, and filtered through activated charcoal to be made palatable . . . is it *beer*? Oliver thinks not, and while he calls for a renewed understanding and appreciation of the real thing, as a brewer he fully understands the forces that press against the craft methods, and towards the slippery slope that leads to a warm, sticky pool of near beer.

Still, even if there is good sense to be made of authentic, genuine beer, what of the taste of beer itself? "Authentic" does not mean "excellent." Yet is it reasonable for a drinker of Czech Budweiser Budvar to criticize the drinker of Anheuser-Busch Budweiser? Is there a real truth about taste? Michael Lynch, in "The Truth about Beer" tackles this question head-on. He contrasts what he calls *beer realism*, the view that folks like a certain beer because it really is a good beer, with *beer relativism*, the view that if you like it, it is good beer – and just because you like it. Lynch argues for a *via media*: that the quality of a beer is broader than any individual's idiosyncratic taste, but at the same time quality is inextricably linked to the judgments of reasonable beer drinkers, ideal beer-tasting conditions, and socially shared standards of beer excellence. There is a real truth, maintains Lynch, that Smuttynose IPA is superior to Schmaltz Lite, but it is not a truth wholly divorced from the human palate.

Peter Machamer, in "Good Beer, or How to Properly Dispute Taste," is also concerned with how one might evaluate beers. He is in perfect

3

sympathy with Lynch that no account of beer quality is satisfactory without understanding the human palate. Before we can proceed to questions of evaluation, he claims, we must first have the right vocabulary. A beer vocabulary can become quite complex. Simple descriptors include sweet–dry, alcohol (as burn), hops (as bitter bite), malt (as molasses-like sweet, heavy flavor), added flavors (fruits, herbs, honey), light to heavy body, effervescence/bubble feel, etc. At the extreme, tasters can identify the components of beer by their chemical names. But what of evaluation? Machamer argues that what makes a beer a good one is so strongly connected to the context of drinking that Lynch's notion of ideal beer-tasting conditions makes no sense. A Sam Adams Honey Porter is lousy when sitting in the hot sun on a summer picnic, but fabulous in front of the fire on a snowy winter's evening. The essentiality of context may even mean that the best beer is in fact a free beer.

No matter what the context, there are certain absolute limitations on what a beer can be. In "Quality, Schmality: Talking Naturally about the Aesthetics of Beer; or Why is American Beer So Lousy?" Martin Stack and George Gale note that no human beverage can be as basic as Drano, as acidic as battery acid, or as bitter as chokecherry. Other constraints on beer are set by tradition and the necessities of the artisanal processes that produce it. They discuss the methods of beer production, and what these mean to the styles and flavors of beer. Stack and Gale argue that the universal derision of mass-produced corporate American beer is directly connected to the cost-cutting measures of the major breweries. Prices are kept low by minimizing the raw materials of beer, even though ironically it is these materials out of which flavors are made. In other words, mass-produced American beer may be bad, but breweries have made a conscious decision to give you less beer per bottle. That way they can afford to buy more Clydesdales and cigarette boats.

Sam Calagione, in "Extreme Brewing in America," agrees wholeheartedly with Stack and Gale's assessment of corporate American beer. He notes that only three breweries make over 80% of the beer Americans drink, and that this has happened in a country that supposedly champions individuality and freedom of choice. Yet bucking this hegemony is what Calagione calls the "outsider art" of craft brewing. He sees the craft beer movement – local, small, independent, adventuresome breweries – as garage bands in a Clear Channel world, the punk rockers or electric Dylan of ale. Emerson-like, Calagione argues that the experimentalism and risk taking of the artisanal brewers is much truer to the spirit of America than the mass-market homogenization of American culture.

Beer may be commodified, but it isn't just any commodity, like a refrigerator or a pair of shoes. Ancient societies treated beer as a civilizing, morally uplifting drink, in stark contrast to the puritan thread of abstinence that still runs deep in the Western world. The importance of beer is reflected in many of the world's creation myths, and is one of the oldest, most persistent ideas in human history. For instance *The Kalevala*, the national epic of Finland, devotes many more verses to the creation of beer than the nominally more momentous creation of the world. In its Preamble, the bard sings of beer's rejuvenating pleasures:

> Let me sing an old-time legend,
> That shall echo forth the praises
> Of the beer that I have tasted,
> Of the sparkling beer of barley.
> Bring to me a foaming goblet
> Of the barley of my fathers,
> Lest my singing grow too weary,
> Singing from the water only.
> Bring me too a cup of strong-beer,
> It will add to our enchantment,
> To the pleasure of the evening.
> (*The Kalevala*. Translated by
> J. M. Crawford. New York:
> J. B. Alden, 1888.)

In the 4,000-year-old Babylonian epic of *Gilgamesh* (tablet 2), the savage wildman Enkidu is civilized by the potent humanizing power of beer:

Enkidu knew nothing about eating bread for food,
And of drinking beer he had not been taught.
The harlot spoke to Enkidu, saying:
"Eat the food, Enkidu, it is the way one lives.
Drink the beer, as is the custom of the land."
Enkidu ate the food until he was sated,
He drank the beer – seven jugs! – and became expansive and sang
 with joy!
He was elated and his face glowed.

5

> He splashed his shaggy body with water,
> And rubbed himself with oil, and turned into a human.
> (*Gilgamesh*. Translated by C. F. Horne. New York:
> Parke, Austin, and Lipscomb, 1915.)

After seven jugs of beer sufficiently refine Enkidu, he becomes the boon companion of the king Gilgamesh, and they fight many battles together.

There can be little doubt of the pleasures of beer, just as there can be no doubt as to the displeasures of overindulgence. Several of the writers in the first part of the book argue that there is a meaningful way to order beers by quality. Yet should we always pursue the higher quality? Is this a moral question or merely a practical one? And just how is the fellowship of sharing a beer together connected to abiding and genuine friendship? The second part of the book, *The Ethics of Beer: Pleasures, Freedom, and Character*, looks at just such issues.

If you had $30 to spend on beer, would you spend it on one case of really good beer, or two cases of cheap beer that tastes half as good? In "*Mill v. Miller*, or Higher and Lower Pleasures," your devoted editor considers just this question in the context of the moral philosophy of the nineteenth-century thinker John Stuart Mill. Mill argued that one would lead a better life learning to appreciate the finer qualities of things than simply amassing vast quantities of low-quality pleasures. Mill would advocate buying the one case with your $30. Yet, as I argue, there are risks in this approach; the more appreciative one is of high quality, the less satisfied one is with low quality. A fan of Stoudt's Double IPA will be unlikely to stomach Miller Lite. Unfortunately, the latter is far more available and cheaper than the former. When it comes to the pursuit of pleasure, Mill's theory is subtle, provocative, and well worth pondering.

In *De Moralia*, the first-century Greek writer Plutarch wrote, "the end of drinking is to nourish and increase friendship." Plutarch is certainly onto something. Nevertheless, Jason Kawall asks, in "Another Pitcher? On Beer, Friendship, and Character," whether friendships that are centered around the act of drinking beer together are especially deep or worthwhile ones. Drawing on reflections on friendship from Aristotle to modern thinkers, Kawall maintains that sharing a few pints leads to self-disclosure, further shared activities, trust, and the sort of shared stories that are the touchstones of rich and authentic friendship. While beer (and the alcohol it fortunately contains!) is the catalyst for making friends, it is not the foundation of the subsequent friendship. Kawall considers the question of whether other things might serve as well as beer – why not coffee friendships, for example? – and concludes that indeed, the conviviality and social ritual of beer drinking is unique.

Beer has always been regarded as an essential product; it was regulated in the first written laws, the Code of Hammurabi. The Code regulated the price of beer and laid out the penalties for dishonest beer sellers. The law continues to take an intense interest in beer 4,000 years later, as Alan McLeod discusses in "Beer and Autonomy." A practicing Canadian attorney, McLeod examines the wildly variable and flatly strange Canadian laws regulating the homebrewing of beer, the commercial production of beer, traveling with beer, beer advertising and packaging, and the taxes and duties on beer. McLeod is not simply concerned to call beer-loving Canucks to arms, but to explore the vital concept of autonomy. If there is a value for citizens in being free from unjust government interference in how they conduct their private lives, then surely citizens would experience great liberty when it comes to the enjoyment of a humble beer. But as McLeod disturbingly and convincingly shows, this freedom is severely curtailed.

Beer's role in the good life is not limited to appreciating its aesthetics or even ethical reflection upon its consumption. There is also an ancient tradition according to which the drinking of beer brings a kind of wisdom. In the thirteenth-century Norse *Poetic Edda*, the hero Sigurth asks Sigrdrifa (Brunhild) to teach him wisdom, and if she knew of what took place in all the worlds. In reply, Sigrdrifa says:

> Beer I bring thee, | tree of battle,
> Mingled of strength | and mighty fame;
> Charms it holds | and healing signs,
> Spells full good, | and gladness-runes.
> (*Eddas*. Translated by H. A. Bellows.
> Princeton University Press, 1923.)

Not books, not Google, not a team of professors. Sigrdrifa brings beer – and so perhaps the famous love that students have for beer is not so remote from their studies as one might think. But what sort of wisdom is to be had in altered states? The *Edda* is cryptic on this point, mentioning "ale-runes" and their power to aid mortal men even "till the gods are gone." The third part of the book, *The Metaphysics and Epistemology of Beer*, explores such issues.

In "Beer and Gnosis: the Mead of Inspiration," Ted Schick observes that there is no question that beer is psychoactive because ingesting it alters our state of consciousness. But is it also revelatory? Does it give us a special sort of knowledge? Some philosophers, such as the great Harvard scholar William James have thought so. Schick argues that even if the altered states brought on by beer do not provide us with any new facts, they do acquaint us with a particular state of consciousness. Some forms of knowledge require certain experiences; knowing what anger, love, and hate are like requires that we experience those emotions. No mere description will suffice. The same is true of beer; to know what it is like, one must drink a few. Furthermore, Schick maintains, having done so may alter the value or meaning we attach to the ordinary facts of everyday experience.

Neil Manson also addresses questions of knowledge in his dialogue "The Unreasonable Effectiveness of Beer." Manson takes as his starting point the line attributed to Ben Franklin, that beer is proof that God loves us and wants us to be happy.[2] Inspired by David Hume's *Dialogues Concerning Natural Religion*, Manson's characters Demi, Phil, and Clem debate the legitimacy of intelligent design, cosmic fine-tuning, and irreducible complexity. Over beers in a tavern, they examine the issue of whether the miracle of yeast's converting the sugars in malted barley to alcohol – precisely the chemical that produces great pleasure – is truly evidence of a beneficent deity. Of course, if the deity is perfectly benevolent, what about hangovers?

The final chapter in this part, "What's a Beer Style?" by Matt Dunn, deals with a metaphysical issue: what are the *styles* of beer? This might sound initially trivial, as if one might just buy a good reference book and look it up: there are pilseners, ales, lagers, stouts, bières de garde, dubbels, weizenbier, altbiers, lambics, bitters, milds, porters . . . Nevertheless somebody had to write that reference book, and how did *they* decide? Is there a natural classification of beer into a sort of periodic table of the beers, or are our classification schemes formed by convenience,

---

[2] It causes me great pain to note (as a devoted scholar nevertheless must) that Franklin's line is almost certainly apocryphal. He did write something similar about wine, though. In a 1779 letter to the Abbé André Morellet, Franklin wrote, "We hear of the conversion of water into wine at the marriage in Cana as a miracle, but this conversion is, through the goodness of God, made every day before our eyes. Behold the rain which descends from heaven upon our vineyards; there it enters the roots of the vines, to be changed into wine – a constant proof that God loves us, and loves us to be happy."

idiosyncratic interests, or tradition? The sorts of questions Dunn raises are similar to those biologists ask when they try to decide how many species there are in the world and what, exactly, divides them.

Modest thought on beer and the drinking of it gives rise to a host of philosophical issues, as we have already seen. Yet what about the great historical philosophers? Did they ever reflect upon the glass? There is, of course, the testimony of Monty Python's "The Philosophers' Drinking Song."

> Immanuel Kant was a real pissant
> Who was very rarely stable.
> Heidegger, Heidegger was a boozy beggar
> Who could think you under the table.
> David Hume could out-consume
> Wilhelm Friedrich Hegel.
> And Wittgenstein was a beery swine
> Who was just as schloshed as Schlegel.
> There's nothing Nietzsche couldn't teach ya
> 'Bout the raising of the wrist.
> Socrates, himself, was permanently pissed.
> John Stuart Mill, of his own free will,
> On half a pint of shandy was particularly ill.
> Plato, they say, could stick it away –
> Half a crate of whisky every day.
> Aristotle, Aristotle was a bugger for the bottle.
> Hobbes was fond of his dram,
> And René Descartes was a drunken fart.
> 'I drink, therefore I am.'
> Yes, Socrates, himself, is particularly missed,
> A lovely little thinker,
> But a bugger when he's pissed.
>> (Composed by Eric Idle. First heard on
>> *Monty Python's Flying Circus, The Second
>> Series*, aired from September 15 to
>> December 22, 1970, episode 22: "How
>> To Recognize Different Parts Of The Body.")

While it may be true that Hume and Socrates were guys that you might want to bend an elbow with, in general Monty Python overstates the case. Nevertheless, there are philosophers who had an interest in brewing and intoxication and those whose theories can be brought to bear directly on the concerns of beer lovers. The final part of the book, *Beer in the History of Philosophy* addresses these matters.

In "Drink On, the Jolly Prelate Cries," David Hilbert considers the thought of the eighteenth-century philosopher and Anglican bishop, George Berkeley, who is chiefly known to posterity for advocating the radical thesis that there is no unthinking stuff in the world. According to Berkeley, bar stools, kegs, mugs and the all paraphernalia of ordinary life (plus everything else) are merely ideas and have no existence outside the mind of those seated on the stools, tapping the kegs, and drinking from the mugs. What is less well known is that Berkeley devoted much of his energy in later life to promoting the use of a concoction he called tar-water for the treatment of a wide variety of health ailments. Fortunately, Berkeley thought that many of the same virtues were found in some beers. It may seem paradoxical that one and the same man could claim both that beer only exists as an idea in the minds of those consuming it and also that it could cure all known afflictions. Hilbert explores Berkeley's resolution of this paradox, demonstrating that it is possible to both appreciate and benefit from beer even if it is only an idea.

Immanuel Kant, far from being a real pissant, was probably not the most entertaining tippling companion. He led a quiet, uneventful life in the small town of Königsberg, Prussia, and was noted primarily for punctuality and deference. However, as Steven M. Bayne shows in "Beer Goggles and Transcendental Idealism," Kant's thoughts about perception and reality have considerable relevance for beer enthusiasts. Many have noted that after a few pints their drinking partners become more beautiful – but is this beauty genuine and objective, or should it be construed as a purely subjective artifact of beer goggles? Kant has a very interesting story to tell about how human cognition helps shape the facts of the world.

In the final chapter of the book, "Beyond Grolsch and Orval: Beer, Intoxication, and Power in Nietzsche's Thought," Rex Welshon explores a seeming contradiction in the thought of the famous wildman of philosophy. On the one hand, Nietzsche blames beer-loving Germans for "the alcohol poisoning of Europe, which has hitherto gone strictly in step with the political and racial hegemony of the Teutons," but on the other hand he lavishly praises the intoxication he associates with power, divination, sensuality, levity, strength, and creativity – and aligns under the Greek god Dionysus. Nietzsche insists that the most spiritual and sublime intoxications are Dionysian, while complaining about "how much dreary heaviness, dampness, sloppiness, how much *beer* there is in the German intellect!" Welshon sorts all this out, arguing that for Nietzsche psychological transformations are not effected by beer alone, but come from the great health and spirit within.

The ancient themes and concerns connected to beer – revitalizing pleasure, fellowship, regulation, knowledge, and spirituality – remain undiminished to the present day. Hopefully *Beer & Philosophy* illustrates how deep waters run just below the surface of our everyday activities, how something as prosaic as quaffing a pint with friends is but a facet of the complex, wonderful, and endlessly fascinating life of the mind.

In the end, philosophy is as much a part of beer as barley, as even the language of brewing reveals. Brewers measure both the sugar content of the wort, or unfermented beer, and that of the finished, fermented beer. Since sucrose is heavy and dense, sugar content determines the density of the beer, which, measured relative to the density of plain water, is called its specific gravity. Along with the length of the fermentation cycle, sugar content also determines the beer's final alcohol content, since the yeast consumes the sugar and produces alcohol as a waste product. Therefore the measure of how much sugar is in the batch is a vital brewing statistic. Yet even here in the science of brewing, the art of philosophy is to be found – sugar levels are measured in degrees Plato. Mere coincidence? I think not.

Part I

The Art of the Beer

1

Thirst for Authenticity
An Aesthetics of the Brewer's Art

Dale Jacquette

Oh, Jerusalem, Jerusalem! Or rather, oh, Zundert, oh, Zundert!
Vincent van Gogh, Letter to Theo, 7/8 February 1877

Liquid Amber

The quest for a satisfying glass of beer can be understood as a metaphor for a deeper thirst for authenticity. A properly poured glass, served at the right temperature, with just the right balance of hops and malted barley, refreshing and fortifying, like truth itself, is something pure and worth pursuing for its own sake.

I speak not of beer in cans or bottles, but of beer fresh from the barrel or keg. It should be draft beer hand pumped into a glass and encouraged to build a creamy head that spills over the rim and comes to the table as a potable work of fine art as noble as any our civilization has produced. The virtues of beer must be contrasted on purely aesthetic grounds with those of wine, distilled liquors, and the moral disgrace of total abstinence.[1] The enjoyment of beer is an ancient

---

[1] Charles Baudelaire, *Artificial Paradises* (translated by Stacy Diamond from *Les Paradis artificiels* (1860), Secaucus, NJ: Citadel, 1994, p. 9): "A man who drinks only water has a secret to keep from his peers." Thomas de Quincey, commenting on Basil Montagu, *Inquiry into the Effects of Fermented Liquors by a Water-Drinker* (London: 1814) in *Tait's Magazine* 1834–5, writes, in an article titled "After the Lakes": "Mr. Montague had published a book against the use of wine and intoxicating liquors of every sort. Not out of parsimony or under any suspicion of inhospitality, but in mere self-consistency and obedience to his own conscientious scruples, Mr. Montagu would not countenance

15

democratic, yea, proletarian pleasure that at its best reflects the natural products of the harvest handcrafted to bring their full potential to fruition. The right beer, the best, most delicious, noble and rewarding beer, is nevertheless as elusive as ultimate philosophical truth, and context and state of mind have as much to do with the experience as the chemical composition of the wort and the process and natural history of its fermentation.

To seek a perfect beer is to open all one's epistemic resources to new discoveries in much the same way as an explorer setting forth to find uncharted islands. There is much to learn, much to savor, and much to avoid as dangerous and unpalatable, where an adventurous discriminating palate is one's only guide.

Metaphysics by the Glassful

Since the work before us is an exercise in phenomenology, the pure empirical description of a distinctive kind of experience, let us consider the sensation of drinking a beer by beginning with the defining moment in the life of any beer. What identity conditions are implied when a glass of beer is served?

A beer, we must observe, exists in a strange kind of world. We human beings exist as individual physical entities. We might also be something more than this, if certain metaphysicians and religious thinkers have been right about the immaterial nature of the soul. At least while we are languishing in this vale of tears, we are nevertheless discrete spatio-temporal beings, our bodies are distinct from one another's. I have my body and you have yours. Mine has a relatively clear-cut visible physical boundary that distinguishes it from yours, occupying a distinct part of space and time. Similarly for all other physical entities in our experience. It is true of chairs, cheese, churches and children. It is true of volleyballs and astrolabs, of candlesticks, solar systems, and the great pyramids of Giza.

---

the use of wine at his table. So far all was right. But doubtless, on such a system, under the known habits of modern life, it should have been made a rule to ask no man to dinner: for to force men, without warning, to a *single* (and, therefore, thoroughly useless) act of painful abstinence, is what neither I nor any man can have a right to do." (*Thomas de Quincey*. Edited by Bonamy Dobrée, New York: Schocken, 1965, p. 136.)

But it is not true of beers. Beers exist communally in a keg all floating indistinguishably around one another in a volume of liquid, until one by one they are called forth into the world to enter a glass and are served to an appreciative drinker. That moment of being poured from the spigot is what I call the defining moment in the life of a beer. It is the exact instant of time when a beer is tapped from the cold darkened depths where it has lived in quiet anonymity like a baby in the womb, inseparably from all its brothers and sisters, until at that moment it finally becomes an entity unto itself, the glass of beer that has just been served.

Phenomenologically, then, we must take our bearings from this defining moment in the emergence of the object that you are proposing to savor. It is a beer. Nothing more or less. But what *is* a beer? Say it is a fermented malt beverage, and, if I were your Zen master, I would break one of your legs with a 2 × 4. (Not really. I mean, as a teacher, how often do you need to create that kind of memory? I think there are insurance problems these days with trying to be a Zen master in the classic sense anyway.) When I ask about the nature of beer, I already know that it is a certain kind of drink made from a specific range of natural ingredients that is fermented with cultivated yeasts in a mash of water, malted barley or other grains, wheat or rice, and hops. I know also that it is a drink that glows with an inner light and life, that sparkles with dancing trails of bubbles when it is poured into a glass. A beer is a most beneficial drink that is intended in moderate amounts for the aid of digestion, the refreshment of the soul and the enrichment of reasoning. As philosophers, we must accordingly try to answer a series of related questions about the *ontology* or theory of *being*, the logical requirements and existence conditions, for a glass of beer. A glass of beer is drawn by the irresistible pull of the tap from a pool of possible glasses of beer. Now let us be clear (remember the 2 × 4): the glass of beer that you are about to savor is an individual thing that was not an individual thing only an instant before. The defining moment of its life is when it has been poured for you. If we don't understand this basic fact, then we shall never make progress in understanding the aesthetics of beer.

Now, imagine, or better, have shimmering before you, a freshly poured beer. It is not *morally* objectionable to drink beer from a bottle or even from an aluminum can. There are some beers, such as Red Dog, that taste better from the can than from the bottle, and on pragmatic grounds are to be preferred especially if cooling in a hurry is a factor;

17

while others, like Corona, that taste better imbibed directly from the bottle, say, with a wedge of key lime. Nevertheless, I teach that we must think of bottled or canned beer only as emergency rations, for a picnic or at an otherwise excellent restaurant where they don't have a drinkable beer on draft, or to sneak into a movie theatre. If you are serious about beer as opposed to any of a tavern's other allures, then you must only frequent those establishments where beer is served sweetly bitter and fresh from the cask. Remember that a beer's defining moment is when it is poured. If it is never poured, but consumed directly from the container in which it was purchased, it never achieves the purpose for which it was intended and toward which all its existence has aimed. If it lives inside a bottle or can it is still waiting to be poured, although, as we say with some reluctance, in extreme circumstances it might be encouraged to enter immediately from the bottle or can into the esophagus. Such a desperate act is itself unfaithful to the nature and calling of an individual beer. We should not be so self-absorbed, even as phenomenologists exploring the horizons of our subjective encounters with fermented malt beverages, as to suppose that the aesthetic experience of beer is somehow more about us as the experiencers than it is about beer as an object of experience. Rather, we must begin with what is truly distinctive about beer, from which we must then acknowledge the complex interplay of experience and its object in our concept and aesthetic expectations for the enjoyment under ideal circumstances of a single freshly poured glass of beer.

Pouring is Enchanting, not Decanting

To proceed, before we can advance our understanding of the concept of authenticity, we must accordingly consider the beer's first appearance. Discounting slugs from tinned or bottled vessels, a beer begins life as an individual thing extracted from the common soup of all the other beers when it issues forth from the cask to the glass.

The first question in judging a beer is therefore its *pour*. *How* does it pour? (I know *why*, and I usually start out knowing *where*.) This comes first for me, because, with a few exceptions, I don't personally care how a beer otherwise looks. Color preferences belong to different categories of beers, and it is hard to generalize. Where a beer's pour is concerned, on the other hand, a few universal principles apply. I usually do not want to see a beer before it is poured, and beer is better protected until its defining moment by an opaque urn. If beer comes in a clear bottle, then I can admire its color and get a sense of its body and bubbles before it is poured. As a general rule, however, I want to *see* the beer poured first-hand, not only to know that it's fresh, but because the pouring of a beer, when it is competently done, can be a highly enjoyable experience in itself, one that tells us a lot about a beer's quality even before we taste it.

There are nice questions of barreling and temperature control and delivery devices that can all make a difference in a beer's pour. Nonetheless, these have become so widely adopted in most of the places an average beer drinker is likely to patronize, however, as the industry has developed and adopted modern technologies, that we might cancel them out of consideration, and focus our attention instead on the immediate user-end. By this I mean the question of how the beer goes from barrel to mouth more specifically by the vehicle of a glass. A beer is poured, and we must judge how it is poured. But it is poured into something from which we are ultimately meant to drink. It is the birth of a beer to be poured, its first view for many months of the outside world. And for this we need to investigate the requirements of a proper beer drinking glass, for which I shall now offer a disquisition amounting to a tirade in which I promise to take no prisoners and spare no one's feelings in the matter. This is emphatically *not* a matter of subjective preference and quirky opinion. There are natural *laws* about these things, and I have made my discoveries only after many years of painful empirical inquiry that I now unstintingly impart.

Beer *must* be drunk from a *glass* designed specifically for beer. This itself, moreover, is not one thing. There are a number of acceptable shapes and dimensions and matters of detail that have culturally evolved in authentic beer-drinking cultures. Nevertheless, there are beer drinking vessels that are incompatible with the dignity of beer and with the aesthetic pleasures of beer served at its best. There are certain things, I am sure we can all agree, from which, other things being equal, one should ordinarily not drink a beer. It is inimical to the *concept* of the freshly poured beer to be ingested from absolutely anything and everything with the appropriate solid geometry to contain a liquid and convey it to the mouth.

For example. I would not drink beer from a skin-diving glove or a condom. Rubber and other soft containers as a rule are forbidden.

19

Nor would I gladly drink beer from an ashtray, a milk carton, a goldfish bowl, a pith-helmet, a soup can, or for that matter a teacup. Tea is okay to drink from a teacup. Hence the name. To drink beer from a teacup on the contrary is an abomination. We are intended by God and nature to drink beer from a relatively small thin-walled glass, ideally with the brewery's coat of arms embossed on the side and a rim of silver or gold. Mugs are not appropriate because they interpose too thick a barrier between the liquid and the lips. As an experiment, try drinking the same beer from a glass and from a mug, and see if you don't prefer the glass. When I espy people in Munich's Biergartens or at the Oktoberfest (held in September, students on the European tour take note), lapping up beer from massive glass Flintstones buckets, I think only of a dog's water dish and a slosh-slosh from bowl to gullet for which we would be hard-pressed to describe an *aesthetics*. Still, if such tankards are used extensively in certain places where good beer is made, doesn't this mean that they are an authentic part of beer-drinking culture?

The answer, as we can say in few areas of philosophy, is unqualifiedly *no*. Big heavy glass mugs are *out*. They are awkward to handle, and, as alluded to above, the thickness of their walls interferes with the introduction of the beer in just the right amount of flow to the right place on the tongue and palate for maximum enjoyment. They are at best a novelty for persons who are otherwise inadequately equipped in their natural sensibilities to enjoy beer drinking as a fine art. This ban includes more especially those big glass boots, meter-long drinking bulbs, and hats advertising your favorite sports team that hold two beer cans accessed by suction through a pair of wide plastic straws.[2] If that is the point of beer drinking, I think you might as well take it intravenously or by gravity-fed enema. Beer is meant to be drunk

---

[2] I recently learned that boot-shaped beer glasses have not been designed simply to embarrass unwary tourists, but have their origin in nineteenth-century German university equestrian fraternities. If you ever have the misfortune to be served beer in a glass boot and you do not want to create an incident by sending it back and demanding a beer glass intended for an adult (which I would not hesitate to do), then I strongly recommend drinking with the toe end of the boot pointing downward. Without this precaution you are almost certain to cause an uprush of beer as you set the boot back down that is as inevitable as the laws of physics to splash your face and clothes with a baptism of foamy brew. Possibly, this is why some establishments offer this type of glass to their detested tourist customers in the first place, for the sake of generating a few good laughs among the overworked and underpaid wait-staff.

from a thin-walled glass, thinner and finer than an average tumbler or water glass. A good beer drinking glass can nevertheless have a variety of shapes, or it can be thistle-shaped or perfectly cylindrical if sufficiently narrow, like those used in authentic Düsseldorf Altbier, such as Diebels Alt or Schumacher Alt. I have seen brandy-snifter beer glasses for specialty beers, and these are often acceptable, if perhaps a little pretentious.

This is also the place to discuss the problem of the German, especially Bavarian and more particularly Munich Biergarten, *Maß*. A Maß is a gigantic glass mug that holds an entire liter of beer. At the Oktoberfest, and again in Munich's famous Biergartens, you do indeed witness Fräuleins charging away from the tap with three or four of these monstrosities in each hand just as seen in the postcards, or magically balanced on a tray, handing them out to beer drinkers seated on wooden benches around long tables in the early autumn sun. The Maß is dear to Bavarians, who know a great deal about beer and as such are dear to me, but it offends my sense of beer-drinking aesthetic for all the reasons mentioned above. It nevertheless poses an interesting philo-sophical challenge to the thesis that authenticity in beer drinking requires what I consider to be the optimal vessel. For I suppose that the Maß is in some sense an authentic part of Munich and thus of the wider Bavarian beer-drinking culture.[3]

How such a practice might have arisen is explainable on the principle that has so often shaped human institutions, in the popular assumption that bigger is better. Kings and lords drink from kingly and lordly sized beer steins, we might imagine. So, for tonight, let us feel like kings and

---

[3] Patrick Lee Fermor, *A Time of Gifts* (London: John Murray, 1977), paints a lively picture of Bavarian beer halls during his 1933 journey from Rotterdam to Istanbul (to Budapest in this first volume of his travels) that still rings true today. See pp. 90–2: "I was back in beer-territory . . . One must travel east for a hundred and eighty miles from the Upper Rhine and seventy north from the Alpine watershed to form an idea of the transforma-tion that beer, in collusion with almost non-stop eating – meals dovetailing so closely during the hours of waking that there is hardly an interprandial moment – can wreak on the human frame . . . Waitresses with the build of weight-lifters and all-in wrestlers whirled this provender along and features dripped and glittered like faces at an ogre's banquet. But all too soon the table was an empty bone-yard once more, sound faltered, a look of bereavement clouded those small eyes and there was a brief hint of sorrow in the air. But succour was always at hand; beldames barged to the rescue at full gallop with new clutches of mugs and fresh plate-loads of consumer goods; and the damp Laestrygonian brows unpuckered again in a happy renewal of clamour and intake."

lords with our giant glass beer steins! If, on the other hand, it should turn out that the Maß was introduced for tourists after World War I, then I would need to qualify even the judgment that the Maß is an authentic part of Munich or greater Bavarian beer-drinking culture, since the culture itself goes back so much further in time. The Maß, I should say, is authentic to this beer-drinking tradition and hence potentially a part of an authentic beer-drinking *Erlebnis*, or anyway to its *Erfahrung*. I would also say that it's an accidental and even regrettable part of the tradition that I think would be better phased out. One goes to these places not so much to enjoy a fine beer but for other social purposes, to sing and turn a wooden tabletop and heavy glass implements into an improvised percussion instrument, to display one's generic manhood by hefting and downing these buckets of suds, and probably other things that I would not be able to penetrate without further funded study. A pity, too, because the beer in these halls is excellent and deserves to be savored from the kind of goblet that best suits its peculiar virtues.

At a busy venue, indoors or out, one advantage of the Maß is that the wait-personnel cannot serve all the guests as frequently as at a more intimate locale. You get a liter or at most two (or three, etc.) to last you the whole evening, or at least until it's time to hit the next *Stammlokal*, and the Ober or Fräulein in the same interval can serve many other patrons. The disadvantage, and in my mind it overwhelms whatever improvements the Maß confers, is that you are at once given so much beer that it cannot possibly be fresh by the time you empty the gigantic schooner. It is flat and dull and stale at the end, even for the speed drinker, which is not the recommended way to consume a fine beer, whereas in a moderately sized glass the entire draft in an average drinking time can be as fresh and frothy as when it was poured. Then, instead of drinking down more deeply from an almost bottomless tank, big as your thigh, in the care of a properly attentive server instead, you simply request another moderately sized glass of freshly poured beer. No, give me a plain handsomely fashioned thin-walled glass that can be held comfortably in one hand; a glass made for an adult that an adult can use to enjoy a beer. I would like to see the fabulous beers of Munich's Biergartens, HB, Augustiner, Hacker-Schorr, Spaten, Gabelsburger, among others of deserved fame, served in elegant glasses of 0.3 (a so-called *null-drei*) or 0.4 (*null-vier*) liters, from which the taste of the beer can be better enjoyed – but realistically I don't expect it to happen (you try to talk to those people).

22

The proper method is to fill the beer glass until it is appropriately topped with liquid and allow the head to cascade over the rim and into the grate on which it stands while being poured. A white plastic knife or spatula (*spatele*) is used in good Dutch bars to level off the foam as it rises. But the foam itself must run freely down the side of the glass to cool it and give it the external gleam that indicates a freshly poured glass of beer. The glass should continue to shed small amounts of liquid as the beer is enjoyed. And that is how it should be, because in evaporating, it continues to keep the glass, and, more importantly, the beer inside it, cool. One needn't worry about the tabletop or tablecloth, however, because (a) where are your priorities? and (b), for the anally retentive, that is what paper pulp coasters or *Bierdeckel* are for.

When the beer is poured, if you witness the process, it should roil in the bottom of the glass at first and produce a stream of bubbles that are engulfed by the swirling beer as it continues to enter. There are exceptions, to be sure, and I am obviously speaking specifically of a Helles or bright beer, lager or pale ale, say, a Heineken, Brand, Oranjeboom, Grolsch, Hertog Jan, or Murauer, Mönkshof, Thurn und Taxis, Radelberger, an Alsacian Meteor, Fischer, or Cardinal, a Ruppaner, Fürstenberg, Nordbräu (pride of Ingolstadt), an Austrian Gösser, Ottakringer, or Czech Krusovice or Slovakian Zlaty Bazant, and not, say, of a stout, like Guinness, or Weizenbier, for which the pouring rules and criteria of pour again are altogether different.

What is Authenticity?

We have now said enough and sufficiently plumbed the metaphysics, ontology and phenomenology of beer at the defining moment of its pour to raise again the problem of authenticity. What makes a beer-making and beer-drinking experience *authentic*, and why, if we want to appreciate and understand its aesthetics, should we care?

The concept of authenticity, in its most general terms, applies specifically to cultural products. We do not describe rocks, trees, insects or sunsets as authentic or inauthentic. To characterize something as authentic is additionally a term of praise. We do not refer to authentic artifacts that are completely unsuited to their purpose, that are bungling or incompetent, shoddy, disdainful or distasteful. Among cultural products, moreover, we inexorably speak of authenticity only from an external perspective, as outsiders judging the faithfulness of a certain cultural entity in relation to its originating market or tradition. We can only judge that something is authentic if and when we have experienced disappointing imitations that do not measure up to whatever qualities contribute to make something that people produce particularly enjoyable or that lend it a special occasion for appreciation and celebration. To be authentic is something good, something positive, valuable and worthwhile. Still, there are many qualities of which the same can truthfully be said, of which authenticity is only one among several attributes that has yet to be precisely distinguished.

Whatever we consider to be authentic assumes a level of perfection in an indigenous context that is expressive of aesthetic values as distinctive, original, or characteristic rather than imitative, derivative or contrived. There is a kind of rightness about what is authentic, of fitting into or recalling its context of origin, and possessing an aura of appropriateness and satisfaction. Even within this already circumscribed category, we do not apply the authentic–inauthentic distinction to any and every cultural product of a specific type. We do not usually refer to authentic or inauthentic tables, knives, or shoes as such; although we might do so in the case, for example of Chippendale deal tables, Bowie or Swiss Army Victorinox™ knives, Mexican, Texan, or New Mexican cowboy boots or Greek sandals. Typically, when we do so, we mean to emphasize their relation to inferior knockoffs made outside the defining context of their respective crafts by persons who are not part of the way of life from which these products originate. Thus, an inauthentic life or way of life is alienated or otherwise dissociated from essential human needs and wants, that is, often commercialized or commoditized for the sake of values that are adopted for inauspicious reasons.

Deutsches Reinheitsgebot

The historical Eurocentricity of so much of what we have characterized as authentic beer invites discussion of the German *Reinheitsgebot* or purity law for brewing beer.

The *Reinheitsgebot* was enacted by the Bavarian ruler Wilhelm IV in 1516, although breweries in Germany and elsewhere presumably if not universally must have followed similar practices for hundreds of years before. The key passage of the law states:

> *Ganz besonders wollen wir, daß forthin allenthalben in unseren Städten, Märkten und auf dem Lande zu keinem Bier mehr Stücke als allein Gersten, Hopfen und Wasser verwendet und gebraucht werden sollen.*
> In translation:
> Most particularly we want it to be the case from now on in all of our cities, towns, and in the provinces [of Bavaria] that no beer should be made [transformed and used] from ingredients other than malt, hops and water only.

Nor was the *Reinheitsgebot* the first effort in German law to codify the requirements for brewing excellence. A previously unknown document, the *Wirtshausverordnung* or "Statuta thaberna" of Runneburg (1434), discovered in Weißensee (Thüringen) in 1998, states in its Artikel 12: "*dass Bier nur aus Hopfen, Malz und Wasser gebraut werden darf*" (beer may only be brewed from hops, malt and water). In 1906, the need to include yeast (*Hefe*) was recognized in the German *Biersteuergesetz* (beer tax law). To make beer only from water, malted barley and hops (plus yeast), these three (four) ingredients, neatly summarizes many of the elements we have already described as essential to authenticity in beer making. There is noble tradition and history in such a proposal, simplicity, a sense of limiting the brewmaster's art and in a way thus forestalling the kinds of excesses that quickly lead to decadence in any art form and are incompatible with the highest standards of authenticity.

Philosophical Pleasures of Authentic Beer

Suppose now for the sake of argument that there is such a thing as an authentic beer or type of beer or method of making, serving or drinking beer. Then we could not legitimately refer to a delicious contemporary Egyptian beer like Sakara Gold, for example, as an authentic *Egyptian* beer, or Efes as an authentic *Turkish* beer, fine specimens of the brewer's art though they are, because these cultures do not happen to have an original beer-making tradition.

Discounting for the moment the fermented grain mash beverages of the ancient Near East, the above-mentioned beers are currently produced under the direction of a Dutch or German rather than Egyptian

25

or Turkish Braumeister. These beers are made and sold in Egypt and Turkey; fair enough, but in a certain sense they might as well be made in Hanover or Eindhoven. If an Egyptian or Turkish brewer of these excellent beers there should someday be, then of necessity they must depart from their European training to satisfy their own culturally indigenous tastes in order to create an authentic Egyptian or authentic Turkish beer. What is different, of course, and this is vital, is that while Sakara and Efes brew their beer from local grain (presumably) and water (almost certainly), the beer is, culturally speaking, an imported German beer that is not in any distinctive way a reflection of local culture.

Beer gets much of its special flavor from the water and yeast from which it is brewed. Water, chemically considered, as important as it is to beer making, is obviously not a cultural entity. We never speak, unless we are trying to be funny, of authentic or inauthentic H_2O, even with the trace elements that give water from a particular place its particular taste. A beer, considered as a cultural product, therefore, if made by a characteristically European process, especially if it involves other imported substances, on the present assumption, could never be an *authentic* Egyptian or Turkish beer. Even if it is made from uniquely characteristic Egyptian or Turkish water, malted grains, hops and yeast, it will then at most constitute an excellent German (or Dutch, Belgian, Austrian, or the like) beer made from Egyptian or Turkish ingredients.

The only way for there to be an authentic Egyptian or Turkish beer is for an Egyptian or Turkish brewer to produce a kind of beer that specially satisfies native Egyptian or Turkish tastes. The issue is more complex than this idealization suggests, because those Egyptians and Turks who drink beer – and many abstain for religious reasons – in the meantime will have had their taste expectations molded to a certain extent by the availability of European-style beers, including those made from at least some local natural ingredients. There can only be an authentic Egyptian or Turkish beer, cross-culturally influenced by the German tradition, as historically it must be, if Egyptian or Turkish brewers make beer that appeals to a distinctive trend in taste preferences among national Egyptian and Turkish beer drinkers. Authenticity on this conception does not necessarily require many long years of beer-making tradition, although these can sometimes recommend a beer as knowing its business. It is conceptually possible, on the proposed understanding of authenticity, for an authentic beer to emerge upon the scene virtually overnight. In practice, this would be a rather remarkable achievement, but it is not excluded by our concept of authenticity in beer making and drinking. As a general thing, it usually requires years for a beer to find its taste target among a particular consumer population, and the good European beers have had in some cases as much as a thousand years, and most at least several hundred, in developing their craft.

To designate an Egyptian or other Near Eastern beer as authentic in the sense we have been considering, one would need to return to the days of dynastic and probably pre-dynastic rule in ancient Egypt when a fermented grain beverage according to surviving documents was included along with coarse bread and onions as part of the daily diet for workers on the great pyramids. This type of lightly alcoholic cereal mash (the alcohol was good for killing waterborne parasites) could perhaps be responsibly designated an authentic Egyptian beer, though only related to what we are prone to think of today as an authentic beer irrespective of cultural venue by the most tenuous of family resemblance associations. There is thus a fine line between what is to count as a beer in the first place and what is to count as an authentic beer of its type. We cannot stray so far that we are speaking of something other than a beer as we ordinarily conceive of the category, and yet it must diverge sufficiently from established archetypes so as to exemplify something characteristic of indigenous tastes in order to count as authentic. This is nevertheless a feat that many beers have managed very ably to achieve.

Am I unpatriotic, then, to disdain most American beers? I would not be the first to say that the truest American patriotism supports quality and excellence in all things. To make things better in the good old USA we sometimes have to prefer products made outside our shores until American manufacturing catches up with evolving educated tastes. And, let's face it, American beers for the most part are weighed in the balance and found greatly wanting. I have a German friend who quite likes American beers, but insists that he is able to enjoy them only by not thinking of them *as* beer at all, but as something more like lemonade or soft drinks. Or consider the legendary man who sent his favorite American beer to a German medical laboratory for analysis and several weeks later received the solemn verdict: "Your horse has diabetes." Hamms, Schlitz, Budweiser, Miller, Michelob, Old Milwaukee, Blatz, Hudepohl (possibly the worst beer anywhere, if indeed the outrage is still being perpetrated). Give me a break. The most depressing words I can hear from a waiter or waitress are: "Oh, we have Miller, Miller Lite, Coors, Coors Lite, and Icehouse." If they don't have Bass or something like Anchor Steam, Molson, Labatts, or a small local brew, I usually ask to see the wine list, or, failing that, order bottled water. Among American beers when I have no other choice, I like Rolling Rock (although I think it is perhaps a bit over-rated), Pennsylvania Pilsner, Stoudts, or Yuengling's Black & Tan.

'Twas Prohibition that undid a fine primarily Czech brewing tradition in the United States, and after World War II the trend toward packaging all products for mass distribution and consumption was inimical to the qualities of a good beer, most of which does not travel well. The microbrewery movement is a promising trend that still does not bear comparison with the best European beers, and there are numerous exceptions among small local American breweries to my general complaints. One problem is that many of larger brew houses are financially motivated to buy out their smaller higher quality competitors to everyone's except the stockholders' (short-term) disadvantage. We can only hope that our children and grandchildren will someday inherit a better world of American beers that they will surely deserve.

Finally, we should note that being authentic does not necessarily mean that we enjoy or otherwise approve of the authentic item. There is no contradiction in saying, "X is an authentic Y but personally I do not like it." On the other hand, if enough people did not at some time genuinely enjoy the cultural product in question it is doubtful as an empirical matter that the item would have ever established itself sufficiently firmly in a culture to earn the sobriquet "authentic," or for anyone to much care whether or not a particular exemplar of the relevant sort was or was not authentic or inauthentic. I may not like Belgian kriek (cherry-flavored) beers – indeed, I personally loathe them – but I think I can recognize an authentic kriek, which in the first place I do not consider to be an authentic beer, without appreciating the flavor, enjoying the taste, or approving the concept.[4]

---

[4] Returning to Baudelaire, we discover similar beer prejudices in *Les Fleurs du Mal* (1845, 1857), Bouffonneries – XXI. Sur les débuts d'Amina Boschetti au Théâtre de la Monnaie à Bruxelles:

> Que sur la grâce en feu le Welch edit: 'Haro!'
> Et que, le doux Bacchus lui versant du Bourgogne
> Le monster répondrait: 'J'aime mieux le faro!' (p. 320)

Something must additionally be said about the so-called *real beer movement* originating in the UK. There is much to admire in this trend from the standpoint of promoting authenticity in beer. I must admit in my own case that while I am prepared to judge such efforts as *authentic*, I do not find the result particularly pleasurable when compared with the best Dutch and German product. What is laudatory about the real beer movement is its desire to make beer only from traditional ingredients corresponding more or less to the German *Reinheitsgebot*, using only traditional wooden hand pumps rather than CO_2-driven propulsion units that can distort the flavor and add distracting fizz beyond the natural fermentation of a properly brewed beer. For all its virtues, I nevertheless personally find UK real beer generally too bitter, usually excessively hopped (a problem with much of the microbrew beer locally made also in the United States and Canada), and, above all, in the rightly motivated real beer commitment to serving beer at room temperature, flat and without the benefit of artificial cooling. Here, then, is a perfect example of an authentic beer that, while it must be pleasing to a sufficient market share of the beer-drinking public, does not add up to pleasure or enjoyment for me. A chilled beer is the thing, I say, and the concept of serving beer chilled is no less authentic in principle than the concept of ice or a cold flowing stream or *Keller*, in which beer can be kept and served cold.

On one of the rare occasions when I am prompted to quote Holy Scripture, I am reminded of the Book of Revelation 3:16: "So because thou art lukewarm, and neither hot nor cold, I will spew thee out of my mouth." Christ's first recorded miracle upon returning to the Bible's pages after an unexplained 20-year absence during the

How to a fiery grace the Belgian says: 'Away!'
And how, if Bacchus were to pour a vintage wine,
The monster would respond: 'Some Belgian beer for mine!' (p. 321)

James McGowan, English translator of these lines, explains this verse in a note to the text, p. 382: "Baudelaire treated the Belgian beer, 'faro', with nothing but disgust, explaining that it was brewed from the waters of a river which served as a public sewer; therefore it was 'twice-drunk'." (Charles Baudelaire, *The Flowers of Evil*. Translated with notes by James McGowan; with an Introduction by Jonathan Culler. Oxford: Oxford University Press, 1993). My negative attitude toward kriek notwithstanding, Belgium today and in its distinguished brewing tradition is home to many interesting and hygienically prepared beers, ales, doppels, and lambics, many of them flavored with exotic substances. I still don't like them.

29

so-called lost years is relevant here. Subsequent to his astonishing the priests and rabbis in the temple as a 12-year-old boy, during 20 years of wandering, as some scholars believe, when he may have been studying Buddhism and possibly mastering fakir tricks in India, Jesus astonishes the banqueting guests at the marriage in Cana, changing jars of water into wine. An excellent stunt, and more power to him for the accomplishment. A person could save a lot of money that way. Better by far, however, had it been for the history of our civilization and for the fate of our immortal souls had he made beer instead, and Grolsch in particular.

It is for good reasons that German and Dutch beers have acquired the reputation within Eurocentric cultures, by which I include Scandinavia and Middle and Eastern Europe, the United States, Canada, Australia, New Zealand, and other similarly Euro-colonially influenced regions of the globe, of being authentic and possibly the only truly authentic beers. Think fondly, then, of Pacifico, Dos Equis, Red Stripe, Kingsbury, Little Kings Cream Ale, Schwertbrau of Ehingen, Warteck, Andechser Klosterbiere, Jacob, Czech (*not* American) Budweiser (Budvar), and on and on. From this, however, we cannot, regrettably, assume that any and every beer or pouring of beer in these formerly Celtic lands is automatically authentic. As the twentieth-century Austrian philosopher Ludwig Wittgenstein proclaims in his influential treatise, the *Tractatus Logico-Philosophicus* 2.225: "There are no pictures that are true a priori."[5] As true of authenticity in beer as of anything else, genuinely good beer is a world unto itself, to be pioneered and relished, to irrigate our philosophical reflections. In a lifetime of the most enthusiastic beer connoisseurship, pursuing the god Gambrinus, we can never exhaust the varieties and brands awaiting our discovery and delight.

---

5 Ludwig Wittgenstein, *Tractatus Logico-Philosophicus*. Edited by C. K. Ogden. London: Routledge & Kegan Paul, 1922.

2

The Beer Matrix
Reality vs Facsimile in Brewing

Garrett Oliver

You know, I know this steak doesn't exist. I know that when I put it in my mouth, the Matrix is telling my brain that it is juicy and delicious. After nine years, you know what I realize? [Takes a bite of steak] *Ignorance is bliss.*

Cypher, The Matrix

In the groundbreaking 1999 film *The Matrix*, the lead character discovers that the world he believes he inhabits is in fact an elaborate ruse constructed by computers who have reduced mankind to unwitting subservience. Nothing in waking life is real – people lie asleep in pods for their entire lives, dreaming a "life" that has been concocted for each of them by their computer masters. This computer-generated fake life is called "the matrix," and the film's heroes see through the curtain of lies and seek to free humanity. In one pivotal scene, a man supposedly fighting on behalf of humanity, having been offered a dream of eating a wonderful steak, happily betrays his comrades rather than relinquish that dream. A fake steak, for him, trumped real friends and the future of the human race. The enjoyment of food can be among the greatest pleasures we experience; few of us would give up our sense of taste for all the money in the world.

Now, I'm not a philosopher but a brewmaster. Still, after seeing the film, it was difficult for me to walk through a supermarket without thinking that many of us live in a "matrix" of false food. As we traverse the aisles, we know that there's something wrong, a certain unease, but we rarely come to terms with the problem. From bread to cheese

31

to beer, we are offered facsimiles of foods that were once honestly made. We know in our hearts that they are false, but we eat them anyway. A good example is plain, modern American white bread. Bread traditionally has four or five ingredients, each of which can be pronounced by a five-year-old child. But this "bread" – let's call it "Amazing Bread" – has 25 ingredients, many of which could tongue-tie the average adult who attempted pronunciation. Ask anyone who has ever baked a loaf of bread to tell you how long that loaf will remain fresh. Almost invariably the baker will tell you "a day, maybe two." We all know this.

Well, Amazing Bread stays "fresh" in a bag for two weeks. A slice of it can be rolled into a doughy marble and flicked across a room. Bite into it, and it will collapse and stick to the roof of your mouth like putty. It is blindingly white, with an incredibly even texture of tiny holes. Its "crust," made of sprayed-on food coloring, is not remotely crusty. It is steamed rather than baked. And to top it all off, it has virtually no attributes of bread – it doesn't taste like bread, act like bread, smell like bread or look like bread. It holds mayonnaise and keeps meat from falling to the floor, but its resemblance to bread pretty much ends there. Amazing Bread is in fact an impressive technological achievement, a chemical sponge, a bread facsimile, just as so-called "American cheese" is a cheese facsimile. A food technologist once told me that most pre-sliced "American cheese" is, technically, edible plastic. He said that the first commercially available edible plastic was the Crisco brand of hydrogenated vegetable oil, and that the military is working hard on battle-convenient plastic foods. Amazingly, Kraft recently aired a television commercial crowing that its "pasteurized processed cheese food" – colloquially known as "American cheese" – is made from 70% milk. But wait a minute – cheese is 100% milk! What's the other 30%? Best not to ask – besides, it technically never claimed to be cheese anyway. It's yellow, it melts – why ask upsetting questions?

Beer, a drink once considered not only wholesome but also magical (see, for example, "Beer and Gnosis" in this volume), has been similarly reduced to a pallid ghost in a can. American mass-market beer doesn't look like beer, smell like beer, act like beer, or taste like beer. It is not made, at least not entirely, from traditional beer ingredients. However, in order to discuss this concept, we must discuss what our food actually is, and even more importantly, what we expect it to be.

This is the Only Butter We've Got

What is beer? A thing cannot be considered artificial if there exists no definition of the real object. When we speak of certain foods, the definition is easy – either this is a lamb chop, or it is not. The only question, really, is whether the sheep in question had moved beyond lambdom and the chop become mutton. If the "lamb chop" is in fact made from textured tofu, we can generally agree that it is not a real lamb chop; no actual lambs were injured in the production of the dish. But what about "soy milk"? Last I noticed, soybeans do not lactate and are bereft of teats or even young to suckle – how can there be "soy milk"? Is "soy milk" actually artificial milk?

It can be reasonably argued that soy milk is not artificial milk, because there was no expectation by the consumer that it came from a cow. In fact, the consumer almost certainly desired the soy milk because it did not come from a cow – its cowlessness is perhaps its principal virtue. Margarine, however, moves into a different, grayer realm. Margarine was created as an artificial butter, made from vegetable oil, flavorings and colorings for people who were unable to obtain real butter. Over time, it was claimed that margarine was healthier than real butter, and margarine arguably moved from being "artificial butter" to "genuine margarine." Margarine's cowlessness was deemed virtuous. These days we have become increasingly aware that margarine is not healthier than butter – in fact, it may be less healthy than butter. As a result, margarine, its *raison d'être* stripped, slowly fades from the scene and is once again increasingly seen as artificial.

I was once traveling with a friend near the border of Virginia and North Carolina when we pulled up to a nice-looking roadside diner and went in for breakfast. The friendly waitress extolled the virtue of the diner's pancakes, and knowing decent pancakes to be rare up north, we went for them. When the steaming stacks were brought to the table, they were accompanied by Aunt Jemima's "maple syrup," which is, of course, more than 95% corn syrup. This we expected. What we did not expect was the pats of yellow goo sandwiched between cardboard and wax paper. She'd brought us margarine. We looked out the windows at the cows happily abiding in the adjoining field and called her back over. "Excuse me," we entreated, "do you have any butter?" She pointed to the offending yellow chips and said, "That

33

is butter." "No," we said politely but firmly, "that's margarine." Her friendliness cooled. "Well," she said, "this is the only butter we've got." Thus rebuffed, we soon skedaddled, musing down the road on how it seemed that the likelihood that one would be served real butter was inversely proportional to the proximity of cows.

What Did You Expect?

When it comes to many things that we consume, the expected provenance can be the critical attribute at hand. Artificial flavors and artificial colors are artificial precisely because we might reasonably have expected a different provenance. Red is red – there is no such thing as "artificial red." What there is, however, is "artificial red*ness*," a red color derived from an unexpected source.

If a lollipop is bright red and tastes of cherries, we might expect that its redness came from cherries and so did its flavors. Of course, we would rarely be correct. For this reason, consumer protection law seeks to protect us from subterfuges by making the manufacturer of the lollipop tell us that all is not what it seems.

For reasons that are not clear to me, this is not true of beer. In the United States, beer does not require primary ingredient labeling. If it did, we might be alerted to various ingredients that some would find unappetizing. For example, a popular "Porter" is almost certainly darkened by food coloring. So what do we expect? Many Americans, even those who consume "beer" every day, have no idea what beer is or how it's made. Over time, the expectation or knowledge of the real article has been removed, leaving a ghost, a facsimile in its place. What is beer? Those of us who know what beer is might say something like this:

> Beer is a beverage made from barley and/or wheat, usually malted. When the malted barley and/or wheat is mashed with hot water into a porridge, the natural enzymes in the malted grains break down the grain starches into sugars. These sugars are rinsed away from the grain husk, creating a liquid called the "wort." The wort is boiled, usually along with the flower of the plant *humulus lupulus* – the bitterness and aroma-giving hop – and then cooled. The wort is then inoculated with yeast, which ferments the wort into beer. From that point it is aged for some period of time – anywhere from several days to a full year – and then put into a bottle, can, cask or keg.

This basic definition of beer was codified most famously by Wilhelm IV of Bavaria in 1516 as the *Reinheitsgebot*. It basically said that beer was to be made from nothing other than barley malt, hops and water. Later, provisos were added for yeast and for wheat – after all, only the royal family was allowed to brew wheat. This was the first widely enforced consumer protection law in Europe and was later extended through all of Germany. To this day, the *Reinheitsgebot* has protected German beer from certain adulterations, and German beer is generally considered to be of high quality. However, it has also stifled creativity, and may now prove a disadvantage in the marketplace; Germany makes relatively few types of beer. The *Reinheitsgebot* is still followed by German brewers even though it is no longer technically in force – it was considered a trade restraint by the EU, a way of keeping foreign beers at bay. German brewers stick with it because it's what German consumers expect when they ask for a beer. To them, beers made from other ingredients are not real beers. So perhaps the question of whether a beer is real depends on how the beer drinkers believe and expect it should be made. But what do Belgian, British and American beer drinkers expect?

We Had to Do That

As traditional beer gains traction in the marketplace over mass-produced beer, it's worth asking whose traditions we're talking about. Among craft brewers in the United States, I think it's fair to say that the beers of Belgium are particularly revered. They are often idiosyncratic, complex, hugely flavorful and wonderful with food. However, they rarely conform to Germany's ingredient roster of malt, yeast, hops and water. Many of Belgium's most celebrated beers contain large amounts of sugar, which is added to the kettle to give strength and complexity without concurrent color and residual sweetness (sugar, unlike malt, ferments out completely, leaving the beer drier). They've been made this way for hundreds of years – beer styles such as abbey tripels and dubbels depend on sugar and cannot be properly made without it. Other beers are spiced – coriander, orange peel, star anise, and other spices find their way into traditional Belgian beers. So what would offend the German brewer is proper to the Belgian brewer, who might find all-malt German doppelbocks too sweet. The

35

German brewer would consider the Belgian witbier to be "adulterated" by spices.

It is here that the concept of beer style becomes useful. The style of a beer describes its history, ingredients, production technique, color, aroma, and flavor. Pilsner, for example, is a beer style that originated in the town of Pilsen in Czech Bohemia. The original Pilsner beer was Pilsner Urquell, and the word "Urquell" means "original source." Pilsner is made from 100% barley malt, it is flavored with hops and no other spices, it undergoes a cold fermentation with bottom-fermenting lager yeast, followed by weeks of aging, it has a yellow color, it is clear, it has a sharp bitterness and floral aroma. This is a classic definition of Pilsner-style beer. When beer enthusiasts ask for a Pilsner beer, they expect that it will have these attributes.

In that case, are popular "light beers" real Pilsner beers? One of them says "A True Pilsner Beer" right on the label. They do contain barley malt, but not nearly 100% – a good proportion is corn, which is not a traditional beer ingredient. The "lightness" is achieved with the help of bacteria-derived artificial enzymes. Hops have been replaced by hop extract, sometimes chemically altered to avoid unwanted "skunking" reactions when exposed to light. The bitterness is, on average, 25% that of traditional Pilsner – in fact, it's at the borderline of what the average person can even perceive. Some undergo "wort stripping," the practice of sending the wort through a column of ionized air in order to remove unwanted compounds that might later become flavors. There is little aroma to speak of. Even their "lightness" is suspect – Coors Light has 104 calories in a 12 ounce can, while regular Coors beer has 120 calories per can. The difference is 16 calories, virtually nothing (though in a world where people will willingly consume possibly carcinogenic chemicals in their coffee to avoid the 16 calories in a teaspoon of sugar, maybe they've got a point). The head on a traditional beer is made up largely of protein – the heads on these beers can be enhanced with so-called "heading liquid," essentially a soap-like substance that will make foam appear when a beer can't form its own. Without ingredient labeling, it's hard to say who is using such substances, but the law allows them, and the heading liquid manufacturers are making them for somebody. I once watched someone filtering a brand-name malt liquor (cheap, strong, nasty beer made specifically to be sold to the disadvantaged) and saw that something black was being injected into the beer stream. I asked what it was. The filter operator mumbled an answer, but I couldn't make it out. When I asked again, he told me that it was activated carbon. The beer was made so quickly and from such low-quality ingredients that it was entirely undrinkable unless filtered through activated carbon.

So, then what is this stuff? I think we can decide it isn't Pilsner, even though virtually every mass-market beer in the world – including that malt liquor – can trace its roots to Pilsner. Are these products even beer? If this question strikes you as radical, think harder. I might argue that the average mass-market beer doesn't look like beer, smell like beer, act like beer, is not made from proper beer ingredients, is not made how beer is made and is generally lacking in beer attributes.

There is an old joke among brewers – ask any brewmaster in the country, and he's almost certain to have heard it. It goes like this: four brewmasters went out to a bar, one from each of the big three American mega-breweries and a brewmaster from Munich. When they got to the bar, the brewmaster from Anheuser-Busch said, "I'll have a Bud Light," the brewmaster from Coors said, "I'll have a Coors," and the brewmaster from Miller said, "I'll have a Miller Genuine Draft." The German brewmaster ordered a Pepsi. "You're not drinking with us?" the others cried. "Well," said the German, "if you gentlemen aren't drinking beer, then neither will I."

Even the producers of these beers may not believe they are real. In their book *Under the Influence*,[1] authors Peter Hernon and Terry Ganey quote the respected beer market researcher Robert Weinberg, who was an executive at Anheuser-Busch in the 1950s. Speaking of brewery owner August Busch Jr, known as "Gussie," he said Gussie probably didn't think that their cheap Busch Bavarian brand was really beer. "If you had Gussie on a psychological couch and asked him about beer, he would say that Budweiser was beer but that 'We had to do that' about Busch."

Once, when I posted an opinion on the bloggish bulletin-board website BeerAdvocate.com, I was assailed by another blogger who objected to my assertion that the mass-market American beers weren't real beer. "How could you say that?" he asked. "Millions of people feel that it is beer." As far as I'm concerned, this is not a useful argument – millions of people in India felt that McDonald's fries were just fried

---

[1] P. Hernon and T. Ganey, *Under the Influence: The Unauthorized Story of the Anheuser-Busch Dynasty*. New York: Simon & Schuster, 1991.

potatoes until they learned that they were flavored with beef extract, a substance proscribed by Hinduism. I asked the blogger a seemingly simple question – what has to happen before you don't consider it beer anymore? What proportion of the beer may be made of corn or rice? 50%? 80%? If a "beer" was made entirely from enzymatically converted rice, flavored with isomerized hop extract, and put into a can within less than a week after fermentation, then would you consider it still to be beer? He never did write back to answer the question. Pity.

Are those Real Bubbles?

Over the ages, consumers have had good reason to wonder whether their beers were real, or at least whether they were what they appeared to be. The *Reinheitsgebot* and preceding similar laws were enacted for a reason – beer adulteration has always been common and the people have demanded redress. In the German city of Danzig, the laws enacted in the 1200s were particularly harsh: *Malam cerevisiam facieus in cathedrum stercoris* – "Whoever makes a poor beer shall be tossed onto the town dung heap." You'd think this would be a fairly effective deterrent, but money was involved, so brewers continued to employ tricks. A popular one was the addition of a hot spice, usually a type of chili, to mimic the warming sensation of alcohol. If applied with a judicious (if not honest) hand, chili peppers could allow a brewer to sell a weak beer as a strong one, and stronger beers were considerably more expensive. Apparently the placebo effect of the belief of the drinkers that they were drinking something strong was sufficient to make them feel intoxicated, and careful tricksters were rarely found out.

Traditional British cask-conditioned beer was in many ways unchanged from the Middle Ages right up until the 1970s. Cask-conditioned beer is the stuff you see drawn from hand pumps into pint glasses in British pubs. While Americans and many other non-Britons may see such beer as "warm and flat," when properly served it's lightly chilled and has a nice prickle of natural carbonation. The beer finishes its fermentation in the cask, the yeast settles to the bottom, and the beer is pumped by hand up to the bar – the beer is never filtered. Cask beers, even when they are not strong, can have a remarkable complexity of flavor, and it's something many British people savor. Starting in the 1970s, many breweries came to realize that they could make much more money if they withdrew traditional beer from the market and replaced it with filtered, artificially carbonated fizzy beer – the stuff that the rest of the world seemed to be drinking quite happily. Cask ale was fussy – it required work by a trained cellar master to bring it into proper condition before it was served. Besides, its popularity was declining, partly because unscrupulous or lazy cellarmen either didn't take proper care of the beer or worse, put just about anything into the casks. I've heard many tales of pubs where partially drunk pints left on tables at the end of the evening would end up back in the cask to be served the next day. Cask ale could be wonderful, but it was notoriously unreliable.

When the breweries made their move, they didn't expect the reaction. A group called "Campaign for the Revitalisation of Ale" was soon formed to stage rallies, protests and boycotts against the brewers for taking away traditional beer. The organization set out to define what a real ale was, and then in a stroke of genius changed their name to the Campaign for Real Ale, or CAMRA. By defining "real ale" as beer which undergoes late fermentation or re-fermentation in the container from which it is served, CAMRA was successful for a time at labeling the breweries' new offerings as ersatz. CAMRA won its battle, and they restored "real ale" to the British landscape. Inevitably, though, the brewers fought back. In the 1990s, they started to introduce versions of cask beers that were in fact filtered, artificially lightly carbonated, then pumped full of nitrogen. Their detractors dubbed these beers "nitro-keg" beers, but the breweries gave them more flattering handles such as "smoothflow." When dispensed, often from a fake hand pump, these beers mimicked the mouthfeel and appearance of cask beer. The aficionado would quickly balk, but the casual consumer didn't notice a big difference. And this beer, requiring no skilled cellarmanship, was more reliably drinkable.

Guinness pioneered this neat trick in the 1960s. Until then, Guinness had been a cask-conditioned beer. When cask-conditioned beer is pumped quickly into the glass, the beer mixes with air. Nitrogen forms small stable bubbles and air is mostly nitrogen. So this gives a beer a tight creamy head. I think you can pretty much see where this is going. Nitrogen was dissolved into the beer, which was then forced out of the special new Guinness spigot at high pressure. This caused the nitrogen to break out of solution, and *voila*, a tight creamy head on a very lightly carbonated glass of Guinness. The trick was successful and eventually

39

became iconic unto itself. When Guinness introduced its "draft can" (don't even get me started on so-called "draft beer in a can") in the 1990s, it represented a new level of facsimilitude. The can, which had a nitrogen-containing plastic "widget" floating in it, produced a similar head on the beer as the draft system did. So the can mimicked the draft, which itself mimicked the cask. Dizzy yet?

Just Pour It In

Today, the craft brewer asserts that he is bringing reality back to brewing and sending beer facsimiles packing into the darkness. We are brewing by hand, attempting natural carbonation, and eschewing all manner of easy extracts and ersatz flavorings. But a little knowledge is a dangerous thing, and as craft brewers get bigger and more experienced, temptations are rife. I have resisted the sirens of technology, but I can hear them singing in my head at night.

This year the Brooklyn Brewery bought a new bottling line. The purpose of this bottling line is to produce Belgian-inspired beers in corked champagne bottles. These beers are to be bottle-conditioned, meaning that their carbonation will be derived from a secondary fermentation in the bottle. Or will it? I've been dismayed to find that genuine 100% bottle-conditioning is actually becoming rare. Many beers, even those brewed by monks, now go into the bottle with considerable carbonation; a small dose of yeast and sugar simply provides a final boost of extra carbon dioxide. This form of "bottle-conditioning" is much easier than the old-fashioned method, where the beer goes into the bottle flat. Less yeast is needed, which can make for a less hazy, more commercially acceptable beer. In order to bottle carbonated beer, I would need a pressurized bottling line. In order to bottle flat beer, I would need a non-pressurized bottling line made for wine bottling. I decided upon the latter, because the former offered a temptation I feared I could not resist. I want this beer to be exactly what it appears to be. Will I regret the decision? Quite possibly. But right now I feel good about it.

Last year, I had another stark decision to make. Our Saison de Brooklyn, a Belgian-style farmhouse ale, ceased fermentation well short of its goal, leaving us with a sweet, half-fermented beer. We had won several awards for this beer in the past and considered ourselves proficient in its production. But the saison yeast is famous for foiling the best-laid plans of brewers, and this time it was my turn. The salespeople were waiting for the beer as the weeks dragged on. We tried all sorts of coaxing – the yeast would not go back to work. I consulted colleagues, moaned incessantly about the "evil bastard yeast," pulled my hair out. Then, one day, an esteemed colleague sent me an email. The subject line was "Just pour it in." He had discovered that the addition of a tiny amount of artificial enzyme to the stuck fermentation would miraculously restart it, yielding the result that he wanted. He said he would send me some of this enzyme to test out. The bottle showed up, complete with a hilarious label promising that this "fermentation elixir" would cure all manner of ills. In a flask in our lab, it performed as promised.

The pressure was on. The salespeople were starting to get impatient. The yeast mocked me daily. All it would take was a few drops of this enzyme, this yeast steroid, and I would be instantly saved. I stared at the bottle. In the end, though, the beer was saved through fermentation by other yeast strains borrowed from other brewers. It turned out nicely and won awards. Was I a virtuous brewer, an upstanding righteous person who had turned away the devil? Unfortunately, I don't think so. If I had not been surrounded by my staff, who would have been disappointed in me had I caved, I might well have just poured it in. Is the brewer who offered me this magic bullet less virtuous than I? No, he is an excellent brewer, a realist, and possibly more viable than I am. Romance and reality can become very expensive these days.

If You Only Knew the Power of the Dark Side

Mouse: Do you know what it really reminds me of? Tasty Wheat. Did you ever eat Tasty Wheat?

Switch: No, but technically, neither did you.

Mouse: That's exactly my point. Exactly. Because you have to wonder: how do the machines know what Tasty Wheat tasted like? Maybe they got it wrong. Maybe what I think Tasty Wheat tasted like actually tasted like oatmeal, or tuna fish. That makes you wonder about a lot of things. You take chicken, for example: maybe they couldn't figure out what to make chicken taste like, which is why chicken tastes like everything.

(Scene from *The Matrix*)

41

Garrett Oliver

There's a war on, and it's coming to a supermarket near you. Battle lines are drawn, hearts and minds will be fought for. The question is, how "real" do you want your food to be? Do you mind a tomato with genes transferred from a fish? Suppose the fish gene makes the tomato taste wonderful and last for weeks? Does it matter to you where the bubbles in your beer come from? Whether the bitterness comes from hops or a chemical? Whether the aroma has come from a lab flask or from traditional sources?

A Belgian brewer recently visited me in Brooklyn. He was moving from a small traditional brewery making 100% bottle-conditioned beers to build a large commercial brewery making mass-produced beers. This was to be one of the most technologically advanced breweries in the world, and he relished the challenge. The rolling joke was that he was going over to the Dark Side. "Obi-Wan never told you how he maintained a shelf-stable haze in his witbier," we intoned deeply and chuckled. Very funny – at least to easily amused brewers – but we both knew the ring of truth was getting louder.

In a 2006 article in the *Brewer's Guardian*, Dr Charles Bamforth, the well-respected Anheuser-Busch Endowed Professor of Malting and Brewing Sciences at the University of California at Davis, laid out a likely future for mass-market brewing. Flavor technology has become so advanced, he said, that in the near future beer will not be brewed, but assembled. Water will be combined with ethanol derived from the cheapest sources and then this base will be injected with flavor extracts and colors and finally carbonated. The plant will be entirely automated – there will be no need for people. The result will be indistinguishable from the beers now on the shelf. He points out that this is not a future he desires, but it is one he sees coming. I'd like to think that he is wrong, but my evidence is thinner than his.

Red Bull, the very popular nasty sweet energy drink, is made in a manner similar to that described above. Red Bull is real; it is not a facsimile of anything, it arrives with no history or baggage. We have no expectation that it adheres to any code, nor that it is made in any particular way. If its ingredients or method of production change, there will be no outcry. But part of the beauty of beer is its baggage, carried down these 10,000 years to the present. Those of us who love beer want its heritage respected, its arcane ways adhered to, its flavors derived gently and naturally, its production recognizable to brewers from past centuries. Perhaps, then, it is not simply a matter of flavor if we decide that Saison Dupont is beautiful and Colt 45 Malt Liquor is not beautiful. There is a certain beauty in our belief, expectation and the reality of the truth. Can a beautiful truth be concocted in a flavor lab? A perfumer might say yes. The craft brewer says no.

But still my roof is covered with artificial grass, surrounded by real plants. It's not your father's Astroturf – this stuff is expensive, and it was developed for residential use. I hauled it up there and rolled it out in the spring sunshine. The "grass" looks real; if I take off my shoes, it feels real. It changes my mood in a way that the black tar underneath did not. I don't have to water it, and it's guaranteed for 10 years. And yes, in an odd, cheesy way, it is beautiful. I'm done writing, and I'm going up to the roof to enjoy a real beer.

The Truth about Beer

Michael P. Lynch

You are at a party and your host offers you a choice of beers: a bottle of Smuttynose IPA or a can of Schmaltz Lite.

From where I sit, and I suspect you'll agree with me, this is no choice at all. I'll take tap water – hell, even a wine-spritzer – over bad beer in a can.

But is our preference really tracking an independent fact about beer, or is it – as we can imagine some smart-ass at the party saying – just a "matter of opinion"? Can we really say that if Mr Smart-ass takes the Schmaltz, he is making a mistake? This isn't just an academic question. Given the explosion of interest in beers in the US and the rise of the microbrewery during the past two decades, most beer drinkers have been privy to a conversation that has at least touched on these issues. Are some beers, and some ways of drinking beer, really better than others? Are expensive microbrews worth the cost?

Is there, in other words, a truth about beer?

Reflecting on this question can help us get clear about more than just our thoughts about beer. It can also help us make sense of our attitudes towards a host of things we apply standards to in our daily lives. This is because our question is really just an example of one of philosophy's oldest mysteries.

Like almost every interesting philosophical question, this one was first noticed by Plato. In Plato's dialogue, *Euthyphro*, the title character is a very unlikable busybody on his way to prosecute his own father for murder. Plato's real-life mentor and literary protagonist Socrates can't resist: since Euthyphro seems to think he is so good and pious, Socrates innocently asks whether Euthyphro would mind telling him what piety *is* exactly. Euthyphro sniffs that piety is what the gods love. But, says Socrates, this doesn't answer the question, because this response is itself ambiguous between two very different views, namely:

X is a pious act just because the gods love it.
Or
The gods love X because it is a pious act.

On the first view, the gods *make* things pious or holy by loving them. They determine what is pious and what is not. Socrates, however, rejects this as implausible: for it means that any action whatsoever, no matter how arbitrary or bizarre, could be pious. There are no objective constraints on piety at all. It all stands or falls on the gods' whims. Far better, Socrates suggests, to go with the second interpretation. On this view, the gods are perfect detectors of what is pious and what isn't. Knowing all, they know all the facts about piety. But they don't make those facts. Yet if that is what Euthyphro meant by saying that pious acts are whatever the gods love, then – Socrates points out gleefully – holier-than-thou Euthyphro still hasn't said what piety really is. He has just pointed out the obvious fact that the gods love pious actions. That doesn't tell us what piety is.

Socrates' point can be generalized. Suppose I ask you what good beer is, and you say good beer is beer that people like. This could be read as saying:

X is a good beer because people like it.
Or
People like X because it is a good beer.

Our question about whether there is any truth about beer is a bit like this. If you think that folks like a certain beer because it really is a good beer, then you are what we might call a *beer realist* (because you think there are *real facts* about what makes for a good beer).

You reject beer realism, however, if you say that what makes a good beer a good beer is just that some folks like it. This is what our smart-ass friend is up to when he claims that whether the can of Schmaltz Lite is better or worse than a bottle of Samuel Smith's is a "matter of opinion." He implies that whether something is a good beer depends on your taste. If you like it, it is good beer – and just because you like it. Call this view *beer relativism*.

Michael P. Lynch

A moment's thought shows us that there could be more than one version of beer relativism. For it depends on whose taste one thinks beer quality is relative to. What we might call *radical beer relativism* will hold that beer quality is in the eye of the beholder (not be confused with "*beauty being in the eye of the beer-holder*," an entirely different thesis, let me assure you – see "Beer Goggles and Transcendental Idealism" in this volume). According to radical beer relativism, whether X is a quality beer is relative to a person's taste at any particular time. Since tastes can vary from person to person and time to time, so does the truth about beer quality. If you like Schmaltz Lite (perish the thought) and I don't, then our opinions are both right – relative to our standards of taste.

Radical beer relativism may sound pretty reasonable. After all, we *do* tend to say things like: "There's no accounting for taste" (when someone orders Schmaltz Lite at the bar); and we don't tend to think that the truth about beer is objective like the truth about whether jumping off a 30 floor building might affect whether you can play tennis on Saturday. (It will, by the way.) After all, what would real facts about good beer really amount to anyway? And how could we know about them? These questions seem difficult to answer. So one might think that radical beer relativism, which appears to avoid those tough questions, is the truth about beer.

But things are a bit more complicated – actually they are a lot more complicated. For radical beer relativism (RBR for short) has some pretty weird consequences – consequences that don't square with our actual way of thinking and talking about beer.

First, RBR implies that we really can't disagree about beer. After all, if you say that Old Peculier is a good beer and smart-ass denies it, RBR implies that you are both correct. Old Peculier is a good beer relative to your taste, but not to smart-ass's. All that is really going on is that you are saying that you like Old Peculier and your pal is saying he doesn't. And that is something about which you can both agree. Compare this with the following: you say there is another cooler of beer in the next room and your friend denies it. On this issue, one of you is clearly right: either there is a cooler with beer in it in the next room or there isn't. You are disagreeing over whether the next room has the objective property: *containing a cooler of beer*. Yet if RBR is right, apparent disagreements over beer aren't really like this. For when I assert that "X is a good beer" and you deny it on this view, we aren't disagreeing over whether X has some objective property. I am simply asserting that it has the property "being good according to my taste" and you are asserting the completely compatible property of "being good according to your taste." And of course, we can *agree* that the beer is good according to you but not according to me.

Even worse, not only can't we really disagree about beer if RBR is right, we can't improve our taste in beer either. If what makes good beer is individual taste at any particular time, then my teenage preference for Cheapweiser is no better or worse than my present preference for Sierra Nevada.

In sum, if RBR is right, we are all experts on beer. If I declare that warm Schmaltz Lite in a can is the best damn brew ever made, then so it is. I can't be wrong!

Well so what? After all – some things are just relative, aren't they? And if beer taste isn't just a matter of taste, then what is?

Here's what: on the one hand the advocate of RBR is surely right that beer taste is in some way subjective. Whether one beer is better than another is surely not as objective a matter as whether bullets can kill you. But on the other hand, RBR is clearly *too* subjective a view. After all, the reason that we find the above consequences of RBR a bit odd is that it is a feature of our own practice as beer drinkers that

1   we treat some beers as better than others,
2   we talk about improving our taste in beer,
3   we think there are experts on beer.

As evidence for all three claims, consider the very serious beer tasting competitions held around the globe, including the annual United States Beer Tasting Championship and the Great American Beer Festival. In these sorts of competitions, beers are rated in a number of categories by expert judges. These are serious events. Winning one is seen as something to be touted by a beer company, and the victorious brews are especially worth trying.

In this sense, our attitudes about beer are not much different than our attitudes about wine. Most folks, even those of us who know little about wine, are willing to acknowledge that there is a lot *to* know, and will defer to the experts. For the experts, we believe, can discriminate small differences between wines that the novice cannot. Or again, compare music: the expert musician can discern differences in performances of a single piece that pass the novice right by. So it is with beer. Some folks are perfectly happy with Schmaltz Lite; but those in the know can discern subtle (or in this case, perhaps not so subtle) differences between Schmaltz Lite and other lagers, even others in the (shudder) "light beer" category.

What this tells us is that RBR doesn't match our actual beer-tasting practice. *Our actual beer practice, like our actual practice with regard to almost anything, appeals to certain standards and norms.* Some beers pass those standards, some don't, and some sit in the middle between passing and not. Yet (at least some) people who drink beer do have standards, and our theory of truth in beer should reflect that fact.

But how exactly? Here is an initial suggestion:

> Beer relativism (BR): It is true that X is a good beer just when reasonable beer drinkers would judge it to be a good beer in ideal beer-tasting conditions.

By a "reasonable" beer drinker, I mean someone who likes beer and ain't afraid to toss back a few, but who is also able to restrain his or her appetite when the occasion demands.[1] By "ideal beer-tasting conditions" I mean a hypothetical situation in which one has all the time one wants to sample every beer ever made. (In many cultures, this is called "heaven.") This situation doesn't exist; but *if* it did, then according to our initial suggestion, the beers that most beer drinkers would agree on in that situation would in fact be the good ones. The thought is that given enough time, and enough beers, reasonable beer drinkers would be able to converge on some beers as good. Moreover, bad beers would be those agreed to be bad in ideal situations. The remaining beers, should there be any, would be neither good nor bad. They would be of indeterminate quality.

Like RBR, BR rejects beer realism: what makes for good beer on this view is still determined by what we happen to judge is good beer, not the other way around. However, unlike RBR, BR seems more in line with our actual beer practice.

For one thing, it makes sense of our intuitive idea that we can disagree about whether X is a good beer. According to BR, what we are

---

[1] I'll assume too that reasonable beer drinkers have statistically normal human physiology. The creature from the Alien movies might like beer for all I know, but it is not a reasonable beer drinker in my sense of the term.

disagreeing over is whether X would be judged to be a good beer by reasonable beer drinkers in ideal conditions. It also makes sense of the idea that our taste can improve: it improves the more I end up knowing the truth about beer: that is, the more I agree with what our reasonable beer drinkers would say in ideal beer-drinking conditions. And finally, it makes sense of the idea that I can just be wrong about whether e.g. Schmaltz Lite is a fine beer. I am wrong if it turned out that Schmaltz beer wouldn't be one of those beers hit upon in ideal beer-drinking conditions. In short, BR allows for there to be a moderately objective question whether X is a good beer. It isn't just a "matter of opinion" but it isn't something *really* objective either: we – that is, reasonable beer drinkers in ideal situations – make the facts about beer.

A moment's thought, however, reveals that BR is still a bit simplistic. For it brushes under the rug an obvious question: who are these reasonable beer-drinking yahoos and how the hell did they get so lucky? In other words, BR says nothing about the *initial* standards that the hypothetical reasonable few (sitting around in their hypothetical ideal pub sipping hypothetical beer) are appealing to when making their decisions. More to the point, it seems that given differences in these initial standards, opinions about what is a good beer may differ across groups even in ideal conditions. For example, there may be different standards about whether color should affect the rating of a beer more than smell, or whether the quality of the hops matters over and above the contribution they make to taste. What twenty-first-century reasonable beer-drinking Americans might think, *even in ideal conditions*, is a good beer, a nineteenth-century Belgian might shrug off as little better than schmegma.[2]

Faced with this question, it may seem that we are back where we started. If we say that standards come one to a person, then we end up with RBR again. But if we say there is one and only one real set of standards by which reasonable beer drinkers should measure beers, we end up with something very close to beer realism. And we face its problems too: for how do we know what the real standards are? Ask the big beer drinker in the sky? I don't think so.

The key out of this quandary is common sense. Of course there are standards about what makes something a good beer. And of course they can change. But they don't change at a rapid rate, nor do they

---

[2] A technical term for the last few drops of liquid left in a bottle or can of beer.

differ from person to person. Beer making is a collective enterprise. Even for those many lone wolves out there making beer in their basements, you had to learn the craft somewhere. You didn't invent it yourself – you inherited your initial recipes, and therefore your standards, from other sources: beer-making kits and other beers, to name a likely few.

Moreover, there are reasonable objective constraints on what could count as a standard of beer quality. Objectively speaking, beer standards require that no wine is a beer, for example, and that any beer all samples of which are poisonous and which tastes like gasoline is not exactly a top-notch beer. That is, constraints on beer quality require that beers be made with certain ingredients. Moreover, there are different types of beer, and each type of beer will further impose certain objective "real" standards on what can count as a beer of that type. Consequently, variation on beer standards will be less pervasive than one might think at first, for what appear to be different standards of measurement are often due to the fact that beers in question are of different types. Stout is to light-bodied lager, after all, as apples are to oranges. Obviously, real experts on beer would be people who knew all the facts – subtle and obvious – about what makes one type of beer different from another and are well aware of the tiny differences that constitute a single beer's going astray of the standards that these facts help to impose. And in so far as some of the issues involved are vague – as many clearly will be, the difference between some types of stouts for example – the experts (at least at the ideal limit) would also know which are vague and which can be determinately decided.

With these obvious facts in mind, I propose we revise our initial suggestion as follows:

> The Beer Truth (BT): It is true that X is a good beer relative to initial standards S just when reasonable beer drinkers would judge it, in light of those standards, to be a good beer in ideal beer-tasting conditions.

I suggest that BT, or something like it, is the truth about the truth about beer. Yes, there are facts about what makes a good beer. It isn't just a "matter of opinion" in the simple-minded sense whether one beer is as good as another. But just because it isn't a matter of opinion doesn't mean our opinions don't matter. Expert, ideal opinions do matter, and our opinions improve when they become more expert.

50

It is worth emphasizing that BT is perfectly consistent with the thought that the quality of an individual experience of a particular beer at a particular time may be a completely contextual matter. Cheapweiser tastes simply heavenly after being stranded in the desert for 40 days and nights, and a Dogfish Head IPA may be bitter indeed if your boss announces you are fired while you are drinking it. Yet these facts are distinct from what would be judged to be good or bad in *ideal* beer-tasting conditions as defined.

There is a general lesson here, naturally. Human beings may make certain standards (within the limits imposed by reality). But once made, these standards take on a life of their own; they become part of our daily practice and we sometimes even forget they are there, or how we originally arrived at them. Consider, for example, standards for what constitute a grammatical English sentence, or fine continental cuisine or good acting. In each case, we "make" these standards, but once made, it becomes a real question as to what those standards are, or whether what we do meets them or not. Hence it is not surprising that what makes a good beer, relative to our *shared standards*, is something that some folks have a better grip on than others, just as what makes a good joke is something that some folks have a better understanding of than others. Not everyone knows what is funny, and not everyone knows good beer.

So trust me. Don't choose the Schmaltz Lite. It is bad by any standard.

4

Good Beer, or How to Properly Dispute Taste

Peter Machamer

Why, if 'tis dancing you would be,
There's brisker pipes than poetry.
Say, for what were hop-yards meant,
Or why was Burton built on Trent?
Oh many a peer of England brews
Livelier liquor than the Muse,
And malt does more than Milton can
To justify God's ways to man.
Ale, man, ale's the stuff to drink
For fellows whom it hurts to think:
Look into the pewter pot
To see the world as the world's not.
    A. E. Housman, *A Shropshire Lad*

Were "Guernica" hung in Hell, contemplating it would hardly be worthwhile . . . yet it is not the work that would be at fault, rather the contemplation of the work in the galleries of Hell.
    Paul Ziff, *Reasons in Art Criticism*

Dealing with beer, like dealing with any important kind of object in your life, has a number of possible modes of interaction. First and foremost, what do you do with the object? In the case of beer, the typical activity is to drink it. However, you could just look at it; you could never take it from its bottle, can, or keg; you could simply worship it; you could collect full bottles; so there are many things you could do with beer. Here, being of a practical bent, I'll deal only with drinking.

52

Now when drinking a beer, there are three relevant post-imbibing responses that I shall discuss: describing, evaluating, and enjoying. They are not the only responses of course. Upon drinking one could become ill and vomit; or choke; or laugh and feel the bubbles go up one's nose; or . . . But we won't consider these responses except perhaps in passing.

Note that these activities – describing, evaluating, and enjoying – are the same ways of interacting with any object that one may take an aesthetic attitude towards. So one may describe, evaluate and enjoy a person, a painting, a piece of music, a sunset, or almost anything – given the right occasion. It is probably impossible to demarcate the class of objects towards which one may take an aesthetic attitude, but drawing such lines is not my present goal. As I shall show, these activities are all complex, being comparative and context-dependent.

Two of the activities just listed are quite clearly intellectual or cognitive and require the person engaged in them to have learned certain abilities and concepts. Of course, one does not need to take a beer appreciation course to describe beer, nor to evaluate a beer. However, one does need a vocabulary for describing and some memory of comparable experiences for evaluating, and these are learned cognitive abilities. But, what of enjoyment? Or the sheer pleasure gained from drinking a beer? Well, joy and pleasure may be related to describing and evaluating, and very often is, though it need not be tightly connected. We shall explore this in what follows.

Description

Let's start with *the object*. Every object has certain important properties that may be described. For beer, according to most texts, sensory evaluators and beer snobs, color is described first: blond, amber, brown, black. Then, they say, move on to the tastes and flavors. Here's a typical list, which may be given, at beer tastings, to participants in the form of rating sheet:

- sweet–dry
- alcohol, as burn
- hops, as bitter bite

- malt, as molasses-like sweet, heavy flavor
- added flavors: fruits, herbs, honey, etc.

One is supposed to rate the intensity or degree of presence of these properties of the beer. Often the intensity of the constituent flavors and tastes will correlate with the good properties of the beer, and contrast with the properties of flavors that should not be there (see below).

Finally there are texture (or mouth feel) components:

- light (thin) to heavy (thick) body
- effervescence or bubble feel.

If you get really into descriptions you might avail yourself of the possible descriptors that are learned by studying the beer flavor wheel (Figure 4.1). This device is an attempt to isolate the various flavor components that can be found in some degree in all beers. To use it you just go around the wheel, ticking the properties off as you find them, and rating their intensity, say on a scale of 1 to 10, where 1 is not detectable and 10 is really intense, can't miss it.

If you really get deep into describing beer, then you may have to take some chemistry lessons and learn terms like:

Acetaldehyde = Fresh-cut green apples
Precursor to ethanol in fermentation, sometimes found in young beer; may be formed through the oxidation of ethanol and further oxidized to acetic acid; may also be produced by Gram-negative bacteria.

Diacetyl = Buttery, butterscotch, slickness
Vicinal diketone with a threshold of about 0.1 ppm; is reduced to some extent by yeast but may be at elevated levels if the beer is prematurely separated from the yeast or if the respiratory ability of the yeast is impaired; also may be produced by lactic acid bacteria, in which case it may also be accompanied by sour flavors.

Phenolic = Medicinal, plastic-like, smoky, adhesive strips
Aromatic hydrocarbons produced by yeast, particularly wild strains, but are also associated with coliform bacteria; these compounds may also be extracted from malt, hops, and sanitizer residues. (Bickham, 1997)[1]

---

[1] S. Bickham, Focus on flavor: an introduction to sensory analysis. *Brewing Techniques*, 1997, December.

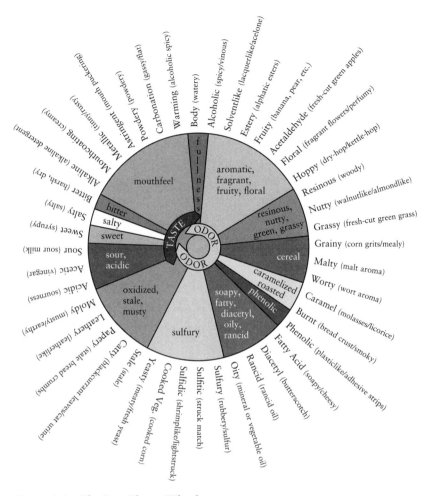

Figure 4.1   The Beer Flavor Wheel
Source: http://brewingtechniques.com/library/backissues/issue5.6/flavorwheel.html.
The Beer Flavor Wheel was developed in the 1970s by Morten Meilgaard.

You may well ask, why do I want to learn all these words? The answer is in order to describe beer precisely and accurately. Still, why would I, you say, want to get to get so technical in my descriptions? You probably don't, and there is certainly no need unless you make your own beer and have to evaluate where and why it goes bad, or you feel the social need to become a beer snob in order to impress other people. I had a wine-writing friend who used to aggressively ask of every winemaker about every wine, what was the acid level, measured as pH. Most winemakers didn't know and, moreover, didn't care.

This is the main point: Descriptions, of anything, are produced by people *for certain purposes*. Descriptions are speech acts. As actions they may accomplish their purpose or not, but the purposes themselves have to be judged as good or bad on independent grounds. One may give a good description for a bad purpose or conversely. One good purpose a beer taster might have is being able to convey information to someone (say, a knowledgeable bartender or beer purveyor) about what kind of beer he or she desires. A bad purpose would be to bore your friends by showing off your knowledge of chemical beer terms, but this could be turned into a good, albeit self-serving, purpose if they leave you alone with many full bottles of beer.

One major purpose served by the kinds of beer descriptions I have laid out is to be able to use them to justify evaluations of different beers. The verbal descriptors provide us with a vocabulary to give reasons why we think one beer is better than another. Yet, as noted, the use of descriptions for reason giving is but one purpose that such words may serve. So purpose is paramount. I shall return to this below.

Evaluation

The second cognitive aspect of beer drinking is evaluation. I asserted above that this is always comparative. For example, you may find a beer intensely hoppy, with a big bitter finish. You wouldn't be able to make this judgment if you had not learned to identify the taste and flavor of hops. Such learning requires prior beer-drinking experience, performed in an attentive manner. You must learn, by dissecting the phenomenology of the drinking experience, how to discriminate among the various properties that a beer presents, and how to refer them to the physical properties of the beer. To be able to do this well, it actually helps to have some training. Moreover you wouldn't be able to judge intensity if you had not attentively tasted beers that, for example, were less hoppy. However, just by ascertaining a comparative rating on the beer with respect to the intensity of one or more characteristics is not yet to evaluate its goodness. This judgment still remains a description, though now a relational, comparative description. Nothing is implied about whether or not hoppy is a good characteristic for a beer to have.

Or, put another way, should one value a beer because it is intensely hoppy?

Once again a question arises. Certainly it is true that if someone desires, say, a strongly malt-flavored beer, then finding one with intensely malty character will fulfill that desire. But again, why value intense malty flavors? One quick answer is that the intensity of flavors exhibits, to a greater degree, the major properties any beer must have by virtue of its component structure. These are a beer's "true" properties, and need to be contrasted with "off" properties such as musty, burnt, moldy, and stale. The off properties are what ruin beer, and they often come from spoiled ingredients or bad brewing techniques.

There are also higher order, more complex properties that are important. These are harder to learn and to apply, and involve more complex judgments (though they are still comparative). Classic examples of such properties are balance, harmony, depth, and expansion of flavors through the mouth. These betoken relations that exist among the physical descriptive properties, and as such they require examining such interrelations. They have less clear criteria for application.

Finally, we come down to the drinker's purposes. For example, I often say that I love strongly hoppy IPAs (India Pale Ale-style beers). Although this is true, after the first two or three, I cannot drink anymore because the bitterness builds up, and having yet another becomes bitterly painful. It is then time to switch to a less bitter, cleaner, bubbly beer in order to scrub the tongue clean and give the palate a rest. Or, I like rich, dark malty beers on cold winter days, but I wouldn't relish one in the hot dog days of summer (though, of course, I might drink it if that was all there was). If I were drinking with bunch of blue-collar workers, in a dive bar, I might prefer, all things considered, to drink Coors Light to Pilsner Urquell. The Coors would be the more sociable option. Here we might say that much depends upon context. Context, however, is often a function of purpose. So we are back to purpose once more.

Before leaving the topics of description and evaluation, a word about rating scales is important. It is common today to find taste pundits who write or speak in the media proclaiming what is good and bad about beers, wines, movies, music or almost anything. They often have some symbolic rating system, such as a score from 1 to 100, or a system of 1 to 5 stars, or some such. The score is supposed to represent the quality of the object being scored. Now such quality scoring may provide a seeker of the good with some useful information, *if* one shares the tastes of the scorer. Such sharing can only be ascertained by your taste testing of their recommendations. But more importantly, the numbers themselves cannot do the whole job, for if beer sage gives 97 points to Chimay Grande Reserve Trappist Ale from Belgium, I still may not like Chimay-style beers because they are too sweet and fruity.

A beer may be the best of its kind, but I just don't like the kind. Perhaps an analogy will help. Some years back I became quite expert at judging cubist paintings, and could see immediately the differences between Georges Braques, Pablo Picasso and Juan Gris, and even date the painting fairly accurately. I also had some measures for who was a good cubist practitioner and who was not. But I did not then, nor do I today, particularly enjoy looking at cubist paintings.

More generally, evaluations work well when we judge a particular thing relative to others that are very much like it or of the same kind. Because we are familiar with the main properties that make or define the kind or class to which the object belongs, having those properties, or having them in greater degree, or in better balance, makes one instance of the kind better than another. The attempt with rating systems is to find a context-neutral setting, abstracting away from context-driven interests. But such abstraction is nigh impossible. Even in cases where it becomes fairly easy, with practice, to recognize what is better or worse of the kind, such a judgment leaves the worth of the kind or category completely untouched. Even being a professional judge, I need to keep in mind the context and purpose of the judging, and how the results are going to be used. Further, when the category or kind is very broad of scope, or the choice is between radically different kinds, such judgments of relative merit become more difficult, and in some cases truly silly. Is Bach really better than Rembrandt? Is Guinness really superior to Pilsner Urquell? Such questions are truly silly unless one is playing some weird game. The point is that judgments of quality, or evaluations, may be made and have some "objective" basis that may be supported by proper descriptions, and yet these evaluations may be irrelevant to what one enjoys (unless one is evaluating objects as to how one will enjoy them).

Moreover, a general rating will not help me choose wisely if the bottles of Chimay I find for sale in the Caribbean have been there for four years and are stale and tired. Once again, much depends on context. The five stars for Sam Adams Honey Porter will not mean much or be a good guide when sitting in the hot sun on a summer picnic. So be wary of rating systems.

The examples of evaluations given above very often were narrated in ways that included the reasons for the evaluation. In this sense an evaluation is a judgment of quality that needs to be justified if it is to be considered as more than mere expression of subjective preference. That is, as William Lycan and I put the point many years ago,[2] there is a difference between saying, "I like it" and "It is good." If the claim is about the goodness of an object, of a kind, this usually means that it is a good example of its kind, and such a claim needs support by describing what properties the object has that make it good, and by showing how another similar object lacks those properties or has them in a lesser or less important degree. If I say "I like it," I am reporting an autobiographical fact; usually about the pleasure I am having or have had.

If I say I Belhaven Scottish Ale is good because it has subtle flavors of malt and fruit that dance lightly on the tongue, I am giving reasons, which I offer to someone in order that they may confirm the description for themselves. Metaphorical descriptions are not always easy to identify or recognize. And sometimes, they really do just come down to expressions of liking something. I recall one beer tasting where a novice woman taster had her first Saint Pauli Girl, which was one of her first times tasting imported beer, and she exclaimed, "It's like an angel pissing on my tongue." Now it may be that my description using "dance" can be explicated in more non-metaphorical terms than the woman's micturation metaphor, but this is not the real point. The point is that apt descriptions allow one to identify properties of the beer which when experienced may be treated as a reason for affirming its goodness. If the description provided as a reason does not enable the hearer to identify the property, then for that hearer it is useless. This may be due a vague or inept description, to the lack of the ability of the hearer to discriminate what is referred to, or because the hearer believes that such properties are not good making. The person just does not like those properties in a beer.

If one looks back at the Beer Flavor Wheel, it can be noticed that most of the taste qualities on that wheel are metaphorical. There are no nuts in beer that make it nutty, nor leather that makes it leathery. Chemical descriptions may be literal in that they actually refer to a

---

2   W. Lycan and P. Machamer. A theory of critical reasons. In B. R. Tilghman, ed., *Language and Aesthetics*. Kansas State University Press, 1971, 87–112.

59

compound that is present in the constituents of the beer. Nevertheless most of our evaluation-justifying vocabulary does not refer in such literal ways, especially when we are dealing in the area of taste and flavor. Sometimes metaphors are all we have.[3]

Context and Purpose

I said above that descriptions and evaluations depend on the context in which they are given. Further I claimed context is a function of purpose. It should be obvious that people may drink beer for many purposes. Sometimes, some people just drink beer to chase away the cares of the day. Some young people (and some older ones too) sometimes just drink to get drunk, perhaps in order to show off in front of their friends. Sometimes you drink a beer to quench your thirst. I still recall one day, years back, at the Seventh Avenue Deli in New York City, the person with whom I was lunching ordered a Coke, remarking that she didn't want a beer because she was too thirsty. In good New York fashion the waitress gruffly said, "Drink a beer, it will quench your thirst better." And it did. Coke would have been too sweet for real quenching.

One way to approach the question of purpose and context is to think of all the different social settings in which you may find yourself drinking beer. Consider the following scenario: It's a Friday afternoon after work, at the end of a month, and you're out with good friends planning and practicing for the weekend's revelries. Since it's the end of the month, most, if not all, of you are somewhat broke. Obviously this financial constraint will have an effect on what beer you will drink and where you go to drink it. You will tend towards inexpensive beers and saloons that are not posh and pricey. Since it is Friday, it means you may have more time to drink more and longer than you would if it were a weekday evening. So quantity and duration also determine you to think cheap. The main purpose of getting together is to be with your friends to talk and have fun, which means that probably you will care less about what kind of beer you will be drinking. The Conviviality Factor is a most important aspect of beer drinking and of drinking in

---

3   Compare P. Machamer, The nature of metaphor and scientific descriptions. In F. Hallyn, ed., *Metaphor and Analogy in the Sciences*. Dordrecht: Kluwer, 2000, 35–52.

general. Beer, like all alcohol, functions as a relaxant and social lubricant. The relaxing part is why it is always good to have a sober designated driver or to take taxis after such occasions. The lubricant function offers chances for sharing and common pursuits that may not be present under other conditions. After all, you are gathered to have fun and enjoy each other's company. Drunkenness most often inhibits pleasant social intercourse. Inebriation has a devastating effect on moods, ego or performance (or all three).

There are many other kinds of social settings in which one drinks beer. You may attend beer tastings just to be able to find out about the range of kinds and flavors or to develop a pretentious vocabulary. You may drink just for the novelty of trying something new, or for the nostalgia of recognizing something old and familiar. You may choose a beer to sip because you like the look of the label, because a friend recommended it, because you're expected to order *something*, or because you want to steal the glass. These are all purposes some person might have. Purposes then, at least sometimes, help choose settings or contexts. When in Gent, I could not steal a Belgian Barbar beer glass, which is a really cool glass, unless I went to place that serves Barbar, and such a place is not easily found. So I must choose my beer bar carefully. Further, I am quite inept at stealing so I had to take along a young friend who was mildly larcenous and adroit in such matters. The lines along which purpose may determine context should be clear from these examples.

Yet sometimes, context determines purpose. If I find myself by accident with someone with whom I would like to become friends, I may order an erudite and rare beer in order to impress him. If I am with an impecunious fellow for whom I care, I may order something very inexpensive so as not to show off my relative wealth. If I am, at a bar, listening to my friend's troubles, and know that this will take a long time, I will order light, non-filling beer so that I can maintain some sobriety and a proper concern through the session. If I am in a bad bar, where it is too hot and the people around are all too surly, I may be able to find no purpose in staying or in drinking.

So far I have concentrated on social contexts and social purposes. We could think of these as external forces that constrain our behaviors. But there are also internal factors that often come into play and which affect purposes and contexts when describing, evaluating or enjoying. If someone is in a blue funk or in pain, then it may well be that nothing

61

will taste good, no description will seem apt, and they will be indifferent to all choices. Another person may believe that drinking beer will help them to get over a bad love affair. So set 'em up, Joe . . .

Pleasure and Taste

The brief discussion above about internal contexts and purposes brings us properly to a discussion of pleasure. Pleasure, as a desirable emotional state, is certainly a personal, context-dependent purpose that one may have. While it is sometimes true that a person will drink beer because it brings pleasure, some of the examples above make it clear that pleasure is not the only purpose one can have for such consuming occasions. Further, there is much interpersonal variation among what brings pleasure, for pleasure depends on past learning and training, and so reflects a person's autobiography. There is also intrapersonal variation. What is pleasing to a person in the bright morning light may not be at all like what pleases her in the darkness of evening.

Pleasures, even when social, are ego-centered, though they are not merely subjective. There are, if you will, objective features of objects, including beer, which bring people pleasure. For example, many very young children like beer because it has a bitterness to it that is otherwise not much present in their diet. But by the age of three or so, they will have developed their sweet preferences to a point where the bitterness will become unpleasant. It will then take some dozen years or so for them to regain a taste for beer, and some people never do.

As we noted earlier, the properties referred to by many of the descriptions of beers are objective. That is, they refer to and can be identified as belonging to the object. When such descriptions are proffered as reasons as to why an object is good, they function as criteria for testing whether the claim being made is true. So if I tell you that the Harpoon IPA is quite good because it has an excellent bitter, hoppy taste, you may try it and find out if my description is true. Of course, the accuracy of my description does not ensure that you would derive pleasure from such a taste on this occasion, or even that you would tolerate it.

Yet if I tell you that it is good, I am thereby encouraging you evaluate it and, probably, to enjoy it as I do. Immanuel Kant (*Critique of*

Judgment, bk. I, pt. I, 6)[4] erred seriously when he claimed that judgments of taste were meant to be universal. If I want another person (or group) to enjoy what I enjoy, this is not universal. I don't really ever care (and I don't believe anyone ever does) if everyone – all the people in the world – enjoys this beer. Moreover, if universal is meant to range over all time and space, then such a desire is impossible to frame. I am saying, however, that I want this person to share my enjoyment, particularly if she is a friend. Friends and lovers are the people with whom we all enjoy sharing things. Such commonality of shared interests and tastes is one reason why we're friends. Yet I do not demand that my friend shares my taste and conforms to my judgment. I also value her as a friend because she is independent and different from me. She may not even like beer at all. With beer, as with all objects that we judge aesthetically, there is no necessity attached. There is no reason, universal or otherwise, why one *ought* to like to drink beer, or listen to Puccini, or go skydiving. As said, among friends some shared likes are good, though no one or even two are necessary.

Here's one last example. Some years back I ran a beer tasting for a newspaper. The tasting was held in Chiodo's Tavern, a steel workers' bar. The owner invited a truly amazing young man from the Homestead mill to participate. He could name every domestic beer we tasted, but when it can to the imports, he'd say, "That's foreign. I don't drink that stuff." Blatz, Rolling Rock, Budweiser, Miller, Iron City, he could identify them all correctly. I even tried him on triad tests where two beers were the same, one different. But when it came to foreign beers, he just didn't care. He had one of the best palates I have ever met, and no one could convince him to drink imported beer. His overall belief system prevented him from liking or even trying foreign beers. No reasons given about a beer's quality could break through that belief network. Maybe it was a patriotic stance; steel workers then didn't much drive foreign cars either. Of course at that time you could tell where a car was made.

In offering you my evaluation and the reasons for it, I am trying to persuade you (with reason) to experience what I experience because for me it is valuable. The value attaches to the purpose of the activity. The value may be just pleasure. The reasons are meant to focus your

---

4   Immanuel Kant, *The Critique of the Power of Judgment*. Translated by E. Matthews. Cambridge: Cambridge University Press, 2001. First published 1790.

attention on certain aspects of the experience. I am saying to you that I find these properties important aspects of what makes the beer enjoyable (or disagreeable.) Some of these aspects are referred to objective properties of the experienced object. Some are a function of context. Some are a function of purpose. These are not distinct or exclusive classes. When I give you my reasons I am trying to teach you how to attend to this kind of object. You, of course, already may know all about such objects and already may have discovered that you do not value them or even enjoy them. We all like to play Pygmalion. We just have to learn when to stop.

5

Quality, Schmality
Talking Naturally about the Aesthetics of Beer; or Why is American Beer So Lousy?

Martin Stack and George Gale

People make all sorts of remarks about beer: "This is nice and cold." "Where are the bubbles?" "I'd prefer a Bud, thanks." "Where does this Czechvar beer come from?" But none of these comments is of obvious philosophical interest, even when uttered most earnestly by the most earnest of philosophers. Yet, let someone say, simply, "This is an excellent beer," and the philosopher's ears (and interest) perk up. We have here an unequivocally aesthetic judgment, an evaluation of the quality of an artisanal production, a statement primordially germane to a philosopher's analysis. But beer is quite unlike the usual targets of aesthetic analysis; a good quaff seems quite distinct from a fine painting or a great piece of music. How might we even begin to aesthestically evaluate beer?

A good beginning might very well take some guidance from efforts to analyze wine. Beer and wine have many relevant similarities, significant ones; relying upon these similarities might prove helpful in the analysis.[1] Beer, like wine, is an artisanal product, designed for human consumption, a simple feature that provides strong constraints regarding the product's flavor and taste attributes. Moreover, there are long

---

[1]   G. Gale, Are some aesthetic judgments empirically true? *American Philosophical Quarterly*, 1974, 12 (4): 341–8.

historical traditions which dictate precisely how certain styles and varieties of wine and beers must taste. Thus, in order to carry out any aesthetic analysis of beer, account must be taken of these factors, paying particular attention to the ingredients of the product, the processes involved in production, the relation between product and human observation, and, finally, the situating of the product in its historical tradition based on style.

Our aim is to be able, in the end, to understand some of the ingredients of aesthetic evaluation of beer, to be able to point to some factors which allow us to say, "That's an excellent (or bad) beer." A parallel question is of personal interest to us, and perhaps to many of our readers. It concerns American mass-market beers such as Budweiser, Coors and Miller, and quality. It can safely be said that the universal, worldwide estimation of these beers is that they are of poor quality. One can hardly avoid hearing such jeers as "horse piss," "fizzy horse piss," "really pale fizzy horse piss" in pubs in England, Bierstuben in Germany, bars in Sydney, even bistros in France – indeed, everywhere in the beer-appreciating universe. Can our general analysis of beer quality in terms of ingredients, processes, historical tradition, reveal anything interesting about this universal negativity about American popular beers? Nicely enough, we believe we can. To this end, we situate our discussion in the context of American beer, and its quality . . . or lack of same.

In what follows we talk first about the *intrinsic* features of beer: the ingredients and how they are put together. Our next discussion section provides a detailed analysis of how the use of raw materials in American beers have evolved over the last hundred years: this section concludes with a claim made obvious by the data: American beers are evaluated as "low quality" because they don't have much in them – there's not much "there" there in your typical American popular beer.

Our final discussion section looks at beer quality from a novel standpoint: an analysis of one single *extrinsic* factor – how beers are marketed – shows a marvelously ordered set of clusters, clusters which correlate very highly with the preceding quality analysis based on intrinsic factors.

We conclude with some final words about beer quality and how it can be used to fruitfully explain recent developments in the beer market.

66

Intrinsic Factors: Human Limitations

Beer and wine – like all other beverages – must ultimately prove fit for human consumption. While there are a number of flavor, taste, and biochemical dimensions that potable drinks must satisfy, two particularly important ones are acidity and bitterness.

Acidity, perceived tartness, is measured by the pH scale: low values on the scale indicate high acidity, high values indicate high alkalinity. No human beverage can have a pH value = 1. This is battery acid. Correspondingly, none can have pH = 14. This is Drano, drain cleaner. As a matter of fact, wines generally exhibit pH values centered on 3.5, while beers typically exhibit values in the low 5s. Within these ranges, humans perceive generally pleasant sensations ranging from "tart" to "mild." Clearly, the limitations of the human mouth set the constraints on what is possible within the beverage, whether it be beer, wine, or soda pop.

Bitterness, a major consideration in beer appreciation, behaves similarly. A good example of this constraint is illustrated by two fruits native to America. Most extreme is the aptly named chokecherry. While the chokecherry fruit is non-poisonous, even the tiniest sample induces an extreme reaction from the taster: choking on the bitterness. Persimmons, while not so extreme, produce a similar but lesser reaction: a single bite produces severe puckering, jaw-clenching, teeth-slaking, and an instant attempt to spit out the offending morsel. On the other end of the scale would be water: no bitterness at all. Whatever bitterness beer exhibits, it must be within limits defined by these extremes.

A clear conclusion from these considerations is that beverages such as beer and wine must provide experiences within the limitations dictated by the human body and its perceptual apparatus. Moreover, and perhaps more important, aesthetic evaluation of beer and wine can operate only within their relevant boundaries. To that significant extent, since the ingredients of these beverages play a very significant role for the end product of evaluation, these ingredients provide essential and necessary conditions for any evaluation of quality.

Other constraints are set by tradition and the necessities of the artisanal processes that create the beverage. A brief look at traditions will set the stage for a more detailed analysis of how the variables of beer production end up setting the grounds for quality and its evaluation.

Two rough and ready traditions determine style in beer. Ales dominate England, Ireland, the microbrewery movement in the US, and small regions of Belgium, France (around Lille), and the Rhine region – principally around Cologne – in Germany. Using distinct yeasts, these beers are produced at higher temperatures, more quickly, and with higher bitterness levels than lagers, which are the dominant beers produced throughout the rest of Europe, America, and Australasia. Lagers take more time to produce, and are, generally speaking, less bitter with more subdued flavors than ales.

Ales, due to their shorter production cycle and wide array of yeasts, have a different flavor spectrum than lagers, although this difference is at times quite subtle. Yet, even with these differences, in the end, the aesthetics of both categories depend primarily upon the chief ingredients that go into the brew. In order to fully appreciate the vital role raw materials play, it is necessary to investigate the brewing process itself.

Beer, and How to Make It

As decreed by tradition and law,[2] beer is a beverage fermented from grain. But therein lies a problem which is key to understanding beer quality. Unlike grapes, which contain up to 25% sugar in their juice, grains contain no sugars, only starches. But fermentation works only on sugars, not starches. Somehow, the brewer must contrive to transform the grain's starches into sugars. Luckily enough, the grain itself contains the seeds of this transformation: when the grain gets wet and begins to germinate – sprout – it produces on its own the chemical transformative agents, enzymes, that can carry out the conversion of starches to sugars. Yet most grains germinate badly as far as the brewer is concerned: their sprouts are too delicate, or they are covered by an impenetrable husk, or they are difficult to germinate en masse. One grain, however, satisfies all the needs of the brewer in its sprouting and production of the requisite enzymes: barley. Hence, from time immemorial, barley has been the choice of brewers as the fundamental stuff of the brew. Barley is the *sine qua non* of beer production, and, thereby, the foundation of beer quality. That's where the process begins.

---

2   Code of Federal Regulation, 27 CFR Part 7.

An overview of the process

We begin with a brief overview of the brewing process, and then examine in more detail the key raw materials used in brewing. The first step is to prepare the basic grains, the most important being barley. The barley is *malted* – germinated and roasted – in a procedure that produces enzymes that convert the starches in grain to sugars. The malt is then ground into a fine grist that is added to water, heated, and steeped over several hours. During this process, known as *mashing*, the enzymes work to convert the starches in the malt into sugar. At this time brewers may add in other cereal *adjuncts* such as rice or corn. These adjuncts lack enzymes, so it is up to the malt enzymes to convert the starches in the adjuncts into sugar as well. Adjuncts are controversial. Most traditional European breweries and many US microbreweries refuse to use them. Indeed, a long-standing German beer purity law – the *Reinheitsgebot* – forbids their use. Since they add no flavor, and are low cost, adjuncts – especially rice – provide a cheap source of alcohol and nothing else.[3]

The enzymes that convert the starches to sugars are biological catalysts. The most important ones in brewing are alpha-amylase and beta-amylase. Alpha-amylase produces both maltose and dextrose, while beta-amylase yields only maltose. Maltose is highly fermentable and it helps give beer its body. As the sugars dissolve into the water, the sweet liquid that emerges is called the *wort*. After mashing, the hot, sweet wort is transferred over a period of several hours from the mash tun into the brewing coppers or kettles, where it is boiled. As the wort is boiled in these kettles, the brewer adds in hops. Hops play several important roles in the brewing process. At this point, they help kill bacteria in the wort and destroy the starch-converting enzymes. Later, of course, they provide the bitterness essential to the taste of beer.

Before *fermentation* can begin, the temperature of the wort must be lowered. Once it reaches the appropriate level, the cooled wort is pumped into fermenting vessels and yeast is added. Enzymes in the yeast convert the sugar into alcohol and carbon dioxide. Fermentation raises the temperature of the wort by about 20 degrees Fahrenheit. The length of the fermentation process depends on the style of beer

---

[3] J. S. Hough, D. E. Briggs, and R. Stevens, *Malting and Brewing Science*. London: Chapman and Hall, 1971.

being brewed: ales ferment in about seven to twelve days at moderate temperatures (about 60 degrees Fahrenheit), while lagers require two to three weeks at quite lower temperatures. After fermentation is finished, the beer must be *conditioned* before it is ready to drink. The amount of time required for conditioning varies, with lagers, in general, taking longer. Today, most American beers at this stage will be filtered and pasteurized. *Pasteurization*, a process developed by Louis Pasteur in the 1870s to sterilize beer, has gained wide currency in mass-production brewing, but it necessitates a series of trade-offs. It entails heating beer to a very high temperature in order to kill any residual yeasts or bacteria. While pasteurization makes beer more stable, and allows it to be shipped longer distances and stored without refrigeration for extended periods of time, it significantly changes the flavor and nature of the beer.

The ingredients of beer, good and bad

Having outlined the basic steps involved in brewing beer, let us next review in more detail the different raw materials that are used, since the eventual quality of the beer depends directly upon its ingredients. *Barley* is the source of beer's most fundamental ingredient, *malt*. There are six steps involved in converting barley to malt: (1) *select* the appropriate barley; (2) *clean* the barley; (3) *steep* the barley in water, a process that eliminates light-weight kernels, and prepares the barley germ for activity; (4) *germinate* the barley, a step that causes the kernels to grow under very controlled conditions of temperature and humidity; (5) *kiln* – roast – the barley, a procedure that produces the malt's flavor, color, and aroma; and (6) *clean* and store the malt.[4]

There are two varieties of barley, two-row and six-row. European brewers have historically preferred two-row barley, and many brewing experts argue that because its kernels are better developed and its husks thinner, it is more suitable for malting and brewing.[5] Moreover, many experts believe that two-row barley produces a smoother, mellower beer.[6]

4   E. Vogel, F. Schwaiger, H. Leonhardt, and J. A. Merten, *The Practical Brewer: A Manual for the Brewing Industry*. St. Louis, MO: Master Brewers Association of America, 1946.
5   *One Hundred Years of Brewing*. Chicago and New York, 1903; Arno Press Reprint, 1974.
6   J. DeClerck, Barley. In *A Textbook of Brewing*, vol. 1. London: Chapman and Hall, 1957, 7–49.

Compared to two-row barley, the six-row variety has much higher levels of nitrogen, a property that can lead to problems in head retention in finished beers. However, the higher nitrogen levels provide sustenance to the yeasts during adjunct fermentation, something unavailable from two-row barleys. Thus, since mass-market American beers typically require adjuncts, six-row barleys dominate American brewing.[7]

The question of the relation between barleys and adjunct-brewing in American beers deserves a few remarks. Though turn-of-the-century American farmers successfully grew two-row barleys such as Chevalier, two-row barleys were not widely adapted to American growing conditions. Six-row barleys, however, were widely adapted, and came to dominate American agriculture. Yet, for a variety of reasons, not the least of which was cost, many domestic brewers came to prefer brewing adjunct rather than all-malt beers, which is more difficult to brew with low-protein two-row barleys. The move to an adjunct-supplemented, six-row-barley-based beer led to a very different product, since brewing with rice or corn typically yields a lighter colored, less flavorful, more homogeneous beer. As we will show in the next section, this development marked the beginning of a distinctive American style of beer.[8]

Hops, the second major ingredient in beer, perform several functions. They act as a preservative, helping to stabilize the beer by preventing bacterial infection, and they add aroma and bitterness, important counterparts to the sweetness of malt. Because bittering was and continues to be an essential contribution of hops, it is important to be able to evaluate the bitterness of different beers. There is an internationally accepted scale to measure bitterness, International Bittering Units (IBUs). The number of IBUs in a beer measures the quantity of hops used and the level of the hops' acids.[9]

Prior to Prohibition, brewers principally used either whole (loose leaf) hops or hops extract. While whole hops provided fuller flavor, they were more expensive and fussy to use; increasingly, mass-market brewers began to substitute hop extract. Since the late nineteenth century, American beers have used fewer and fewer hops, either leaf or

[7]   P. B. Schwarz and R. D. Horsley, Malt quality improvement in North American six-rowed barley cultivars since 1910. *Journal of the American Society of Brewing Chemists*, 1995, 53 (1), 14–18.

[8]   D. Choi and M. Stack, The all-American beer: A case of inferior standard (taste) prevailing? *Business Horizons*, 2005, 48: 79–86.

[9]   R. Protz, *The Ultimate Encyclopedia of Beer*. London: Carleton Books, 1995.

71

extract, a trend that, along with the increasing use of adjuncts, has contributed to a less bitter and flavored beer.

A final point to consider is the color of beer. Three principal factors greatly affect beer color: the types of grains that are used (all-malt or malt plus adjuncts), the roast of the malt, and the quantity of malt and adjuncts per barrel of beer. All-malt beer is usually darker in color, as adjuncts typically lighten a beer's hue. The style in which the barley malt is roasted also affects beer color. There are scales in America (degrees Lovibond) and Europe (European Brewing Convention) to assay a malt's roast.[10] The process of roasting malt is similar to the roasting of coffee beans, and the end result is similar as well: the darker the roast, the darker and more flavorful the drink. It is partly the use of darker malts that distinguishes porters and stouts from lighter colored ales, and dark lagers such as *dunkels* from lighter lagers such as *helles*. Finally, the ratio of malt and adjuncts per barrel of beer also helps determine the color of a beer: in general, the greater the ratio of malt, the darker the color.

Taken together, then, these are the elements and processes which shape the final product.

The Making of Quality

The next step, then, is to explore in more detail this relationship between how beer is brewed and beer quality. That is, we address the question of how we might make empirical observations and measurements that have direct bearing upon aesthetic evaluations. Our method, although indirect, most clearly has some traction. We begin from a point noted earlier: American mass-market beer is almost universally admitted to not be very high quality, while many European and American craft beers are almost universally admitted to be of very high quality. Given our analysis of the beer-making process, can we point to empirical observations which would be necessary (though perhaps not sufficient) elements in explaining the different aesthetic outcomes of American vs European beers? We most certainly think we can.

---

[10]   F. Eckhardt, *The Essentials of Beer Style*. Portland, OR: Fred Eckhardt Communications, 1995.

Table 5.1   Raw material usage per barrel of beer 1915–90

Year	Malt (lbs/bl)	Corn (lbs/bl)	Total Fermentables [Malt, Rice & Corn] (lbs/bl)	Hops (lbs/bl)
1915	35.8	10.1	48.7	0.65
1920–33: Prohibition				
1935	38.2	7.5	48.8	0.70
1940	35.7	8.0	47.1	0.58
1950	30.5	9.6	43.7	0.43
1960	28.5	11.2	43.4	0.33
1970	27.6	10.8	42.2	0.23
1980	26.7	8.0	39.0	0.21
1990	24.3	5.4	35.3	0.22

Source: Choi and Stack (2005).[11]

One way to explain how mass market American beers differ from many craft beers is to examine how these beers differ in terms of their ingredients. Table 5.1 shows how the industry overall has used progressively fewer and fewer raw materials per barrel of beer.

By steadily decreasing the amount of raw materials per barrel of beer, American breweries began to produce a steadily lighter and less flavorful product. Yet, these data are for the overall industry: while it is true that the average beer was becoming lighter and lighter, there were (and are today) some beers that are much more distinctive.

To help capture the differences between specific beer brands and beer styles we develop in Figure 5.1 a product map which organizes beer brands by their color and their level of hops. There are four principal groupings: (1) lighter color, low hops; (2) lighter color, high hops; (3) darker color, low hops; and (4) darker color, high hops. The beers that have dominated the US market since the repeal of Prohibition fall in the "lighter color, low hops" category. It is this combination that F. M. Scherer is referring to when he asserts that "the leading US

[11]   Choi and Stack, The all-American beer.

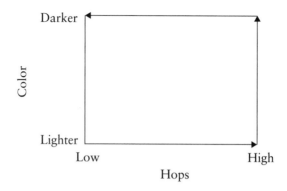

Figure 5.1   Product map by color and level of hops

premium brewers have deliberately chosen formulas sufficiently bland to win a mass following among relatively inexperienced consumers and (through repeat purchase) consumers acculturated to bland beers."[12] Beer analysis data show that the primary offerings from Anheuser-Busch, Molson-Coors, and SAB-Miller fall into this category.

In contrast, most microbreweries, and many (though not all) imports seek to differentiate their beers through higher levels of hops or darker color or both. When beer writers such as Jackson and Protz complain about the bland taste of America's homogeneous national offerings, they are talking about very pale, low malt, low hop beers; when these same writers extol some craft and import beers, it is typically because these beers are differentiated through measurable variables such as hops or color.

Tables 5.2 and 5.3 provide hop and color data on 25 domestic and import beers.[13] Table 5.2 ranks these beers according to their hop levels: increasing IBUs reflect a more assertive hop flavor, generally associated with a higher degree of bitterness. Table 5.3 presents these beers in terms of the color variable developed by Eckhardt. Together, these tables present a series of flavor–color combinations that illustrate how objective data can be used to effectively segment and group beers.

---

12   F. M. Scherer, *Industry Structure, Strategy, and Public Policy*. New York: HarperCollins, 1996.

13   These beers were chosen to illustrate the various hop and color combination of the most well-known US beers along with a representative sample of US regional and craft beers along with a sample of imported beers.

Table 5.2   How do beers differ? (sorted by Hop IBU level)

Beer Brand	Hops (IBU)	Color
Coors Light	9.0	1.5
Heilemans Old Style	9.3	2.5
Budweiser	10.5	2.0
Stroh	10.5	2.0
Schlitz	11.0	2.5
Michelob	14.0	2.5
Coors	14.5	2.5
Miller	15.5	2.5
Heineken	18.0	2.5
Bass Pale Ale	19.0	6.0
Miller Lite	19.5	2.5
Dos Equis	22.0	6.0
EKU 28	26.0	6.0
Ayinger	29.0	3.5
Sierra Nevada Pale Ale	32.0	6.0
Sierra Nevada Porter	34.0	9.0
Sam Adams Boston Lager	35.0	3.0
Anchor Steam	40.0	5.0
Pyramid Pale Ale	40.0	6.5
Pilsner Urquell	43.0	3.0
Sierra Nevada Stout	44.0	9.5
Anchor Liberty Ale	45.0	5.5
Guinness Extra Stout	50.0	9.0
Grant IPA	55.0	4.5
Thomas Hardy Ale	100.0	7.0

Source: Data compiled from Eckhardt (1995).[14]

The data speak for themselves: American beers, with the exception of Miller Lite,[15] occupy the ranks of the least hoppy – therefore least bitter-tasting – of all the beers on the chart. If hops are an essential part of beer, then there's not much of this essence in mass-marketed beers.

[14]   Eckhardt, *The Essentials of Beer Style*.
[15]   Miller Lite is an interesting anomaly. It appears to have more color and bitterness than two imports, Heineken and Bass Ale. Two possible explanations offer themselves. First, since Miller Lite is lower in alcohol, which means lower mouthfeel, it makes up this lack with bitterness and good visuals. Secondly, in both their native countries, Heineken and Bass are considered mass-market beers.

Our second comparison orders the dataset by color. Color, as we have seen earlier, is an empirical property that reflects the type of ingredients (more malt, more color; more adjuncts, less color), the roast (darker, more flavorful roast gives more color), and, finally, the density of ingredients (more ingredients per volume gives more color). The results of the data analysis will surprise no one.

Table 5.3   How do beers differ? (sorted by color)

Beer Brand	Hops (IBU)	Color
Coors Light	9.0	1.5
Budweiser	10.5	2.0
Stroh	10.5	2.0
Heileman's Old Style	9.3	2.5
Schlitz	11.0	2.5
Michelob	14.0	2.5
Coors	14.5	2.5
Miller	15.5	2.5
Heineken	18.0	2.5
Miller Lite	19.5	2.5
Sam Adams Boston Lager	35.0	3.0
Pilsner Urquell	43.0	3.0
Ayinger	29.0	3.5
Grant IPA	55.0	4.5
Anchor Steam	40.0	5.0
Anchor Liberty Ale	45.0	5.5
Bass Pale Ale	19.0	6.0
Dos Equis	22.0	6.0
EKU 28	26.0	6.0
Sierra Nevada Pale Ale	32.0	6.0
Pyramid Pale Ale	40.0	6.5
Thomas Hardy Ale	100.0	7.0
Sierra Nevada Porter	34.0	9.0
Guinness Extra Stout	50.0	9.0
Sierra Nevada Stout	44.0	9.5

Source: Data compiled from Eckhardt (1995).[16]

[16]   Eckhardt, *The Essentials of Beer Style*.

Integrating data from Tables 5.2 and 5.3 with the historical record presented in Table 5.1 yields a straightforward grouping of beers into two distinct categories. One grouping consists of the best known national and many regional beer brands: Budweiser, Coors, Miller, Heilemans, Strohs, Schlitz. These beers all use very small amounts of hops and they all are very pale. That is, these beers are not readily distinguishable by taste, flavor or appearance. Bill Coors, the Chairman and CEO of Adolph Coors, admitted as much (and more) when he asserted that "you could make Coors from swamp water and it would be exactly the same."[17] As Table 5.1 reveals, this trend began towards the end of the nineteenth century, but it gained momentum in the years following the repeal of Prohibition in 1933. In 1959, an article in the trade journal *American Brewer* lamented that "the trend toward a single type of American lager beer" was "fairly well established."[18] This is not to suggest that the brewers themselves approved of this slow but steady homogenization of the product. The authors of another trade journal article from the 1940s asked "why should we not now prepare to offer our public different beers on different occasions to quench different varieties and kinds of thirst."[19] Yet, despite such laments, the evidence is quite clear that from Prohibition to the present, the US's leading national and regional breweries moved inexorably towards an increasingly homogeneous bland style of beer.[20]

Yet, as Tables 5.2 and 5.3 also show, there is also a second grouping comprising many breweries from Europe which have long brewed quite distinctive beers, along with a growing number of craft and regional breweries in the US which have grown steadily more popular since the microbrewery revolution of the mid-1970s. This grouping produces a wide range of styles which differ from each other as much as they differ from the homogeneous mainstream beers. This grouping's more distinctive beers can be roughly divided into three categories: (1) import and domestic *lagers* that differ from the mainstream beers above through

---

[17] G. Pankaj, Adolph Coors in the Brewing Industry. *Harvard Business Review Case #* 9-388-014 (1987): 10.

[18] E. Stewart, Trends in materials and products. *American Brewer*, 1959 (December): 28–35, 54.

[19] R. Schwartz and S. Laufer, Composition and character of American beers before, during and after World War II. *American Brewer*, 1947 (November): 21–3, 43–4, 52–4.

[20] Choi and Stack, The all-American beer.

77

their darker color and higher hop levels: typical of these beers are Dos Equis, Samuel Adams, Pilsner Urquell, and Ayinger; (2) import and domestic *pale ales* that also have higher hop levels and darker colors; and (3) import and domestic *porters* and *stouts* that manifest the darkest colors and often very high levels of hops. Any beer from any of these three categories is considerably more flavorful than any American mass-market beer.

Self-Analysis and the Market

In the previous section, we showed how data on ingredients and beer attributes can be used to group beers into two broad categories. Our last step is to introduce a novel analytical tool – the *strategic map* – to tie all the preceding elements together into a compelling narrative. All businesses strive to articulate clear ideas about who they are and what they are about. For breweries, the goal of this self-analysis is twofold: to identify their proper markets, and the most effective ways to compete in these markets. As we shall see, breweries' own self-concepts – as revealed by their marketing strategies – map surprisingly well onto the groupings presented above which reflect different brewing styles and uses of raw materials.

We use the concept of a strategic map to show that the product differences noted above are integral to the varying strategies employed by breweries in the US market. Economists and business strategists use strategic maps to convey the nuances of how firms in a broadly defined market actually position themselves. For example, Anheuser-Busch, Genesee, Sierra Nevada, and Boulevard Brewing all compete in the American beer market, but in reality each of these breweries competes in quite distinct strategic groups within the broadly defined US market for beer. Anheuser-Busch, for example, competes most intensively with the other two large mass market national brewers in the US, SAB-Miller and Molson-Coors. Genesee, a regional brewer based in New York, competes most intensively not with the big three mass-market breweries but with other regional breweries that compete primarily on price. Sierra Nevada from Chico, California and Boulevard Brewery from Kansas City, Missouri are both craft breweries, though the first is distributed nationally while the second has a local/regional orientation.

Craft beer often costs more than beers in the other two categories, electing to compete more on its product attributes than on price or through extensive marketing campaigns.

To be most useful, a strategic map must pick the most meaningful variables by which various firms in a market can be grouped and differentiated. Strategic group analysis argues that competition is typically much more intense *within* rather than *among* strategic groups and that the further away specific groups are from one another on a strategic dimension, the less these constituent firms view themselves as direct competitors. A number of strategic maps can be developed for the US brewing industry, but our goal is to develop a map that links directly back to the preceding discussion on ingredient and production quality. The map we have developed in Figure 5.2 integrates advertising intensity (how heavily do breweries advertise and market their beers) and retailing pricing (the price which breweries charge for a typical six-pack).

For simplicity, we have divided this strategic map into four strategic groups. Group 1 consists of Anheuser-Busch, SAB-Miller, and Molson-Coors. These firms engage in very high national advertising campaigns and they price their products at a mainstream level: less than most imports and craft beers but more than the low-end beers of Group 2. Group 2 consists primarily of regional breweries that compete almost exclusively on price: they do not engage in extensive marketing and their beer is priced well below the well-known national beers from

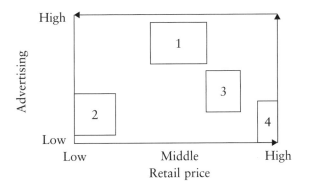

Figure 5.2   Strategic map of the US brewing industry

Group 1. Group 3 features the most well-known import beers such as Heineken, Corona, and Carlsberg. They are typically priced a bit higher than Group 1 but are not advertised nearly as intensively in the US market. Group 4 combines both lesser known imports and US craft beers: typically, these beers are not advertised extensively, though there are differences between some of the better known imports and craft beers (e.g. Guinness, Samuel Adams) and lesser known imports and regional craft beers (e.g. Chimay and Boulevard Brewery), and they are usually a bit more expensive than the Group 3 products.

So now, the question is, how can we relate this discussion that groups beers in America according to their advertising intensity and retail price with the earlier examination from Figure 5.1 regarding beer attributes? What we find is that the beers in Strategic Groups 1 and 2 typically have a very light color, relatively small amounts of hops, and are generally less flavorful and differentiable than are the beers in Strategic Groups 3 and 4. Scherer[21] echoes this point when he argues that "carefully structured double-blind studies . . . have revealed repeatedly that consumers, or at least 90 percent of all consumers, cannot tell one conventional lager beer from another." Under these circumstances, the question becomes, how do these breweries seek to compete? According to our strategic map (Figure 5.2), they have answered this dilemma in two ways: either through aggressive pricing or through aggressive advertising. For people who are very price-conscious, product characteristics and quality may not matter as much, though the attributes of the beer they drink are still a function of how beer styles have evolved in their country. As Tables 5.2 and 5.3 illustrate, the beers in Strategic Groups 1 and 2 are very similar, and it is quite possible that many beer drinkers in these two categories will not be able to differentiate specific beer brands in blind taste tests. The primary differentiators will be brand loyalty (a function of advertising and personal consumption history) and price. In contrast, breweries in Strategic Groups 3 and 4 do not have to rely on advertising or aggressive pricing to differentiate their beers. Typically, these beers will be more expensive than Group 1 beers but they will not have anywhere near the same brand advertising; rather, these breweries seek to distinguish themselves through their products' intrinsic

---

[21] Scherer, *Industry Structure, Strategy, and Public Policy.*

differences through high malt and hop levels, darker colors, and more interesting flavors.

Conclusion

This essay has tried to address an oft-heard complaint that talking about quality in a product like beer is nearly impossible since "beauty is in the eye of the beholder." But, in this case, beauty is not only in the eye, it is in the palate and nose of the beholder: beer is something which we bring into our bodies and literally consume, completely unlike our mode of appreciation of music or visual art. And this makes beer a special aesthetic case: good taste involves tasting good. As we have shown in this paper, just as we can discuss the aesthetics of art and music, so too can we have conversations about the meaning of quality in food and drink. Of principal and primary importance is the simple point that there are in fact several dimensions which influence the final taste, appearance, and quality of a beer. Thus, any discussion of beer aesthetics must begin – as we do – with the essential ingredients and processes which directly determine the ultimate quality of the evaluated brew. From this beginning it is a natural step, a step which we take, to link variations in ingredients and processes to variations in quality. While this essay has focused on showing how and why mass-market American beers vary from many European beers and even craft American beers in terms of ingredients, processes and final quality, this type of aesthetic evaluation of the properties of the product can be fruitfully extended to a range of other foods and drinks. In fact, there are distinct parallels between the rise of homogeneous beer in America, and the emergence of bland, white bread and insipid tasting coffee. What is of great interest is how during the last 20 years or so, craft bakeries and artisanal coffee roasters have emerged, offering products as different from mass-market bread and coffee as are the beers from craft breweries such as Anchor Steam, Sierra Nevada, Boulevard Brewing, and Bell's Brewing. Food history and philosophy is a rapidly growing field, and a great part of it deals with aesthetic issues such as why high-quality, flavorful breads and beers gave way to homogeneous, marketed national brands.

In addition, this essay has also tried to show how the emergence of these specific beer styles in the US reflects conscious decisions by

81

breweries regarding how they want to compete in the overall market for beer. As we showed in the last section, the aesthetics of beer is closely related to firm strategy and industry structure: some breweries in the US purposely choose to compete using bland, thin beers, while the newer generation of craft brewers, along with many traditional breweries in Europe, choose to emphasize their unique beer's specific attributes. In the end, "quality out" depends on "quality in," both materially and intentionally.

6

Extreme Brewing in America

Sam Calagione

The term "extreme brewing" first entered the lexicon of mainstream media in 2003 in a front page *Wall Street Journal* article written by Ken Wells.[1] Ken went on to write a great book about the place of beer in modern America called *Travels with Barley* which includes a whole chapter on extreme brewing centered around my company, Dogfish Head.[2] Since we opened in 1995, it has been our goal to brew beers that were very different from those being drunk by most Americans at that time. Our motto has always been: "Off-centered ales for off-centered people." Thankfully there are a lot more off-centered beer drinkers today than there were when we opened over a decade ago.

Some of the first beers we produced included Raison D'Etre, which is brewed with raisins and beet sugars, and Immort ale, which is brewed with maple syrup and vanilla beans and aged on French Chardonnay Oak. While we were one of the earliest practitioners of extreme brewing in the American craft-brewing renaissance, we certainly didn't invent the idea. Like many great ideas the evolution of extreme brewing has centered around the cumulative development of numerous similar ideas. Ideas like: (1) there is more to beer than the slight variations of domestic light lager being made by three giant breweries and (2) the definition of beer is expansive and iterative and a small American craft

---

[1]   K. Wells and C. Lawton, "It Ages Well, Goes With a Good Cigar and is Kept in Cellars – It's Called Extreme Beer – For Price, Alcohol Content; Seeking the Cognac Crowd." *The Wall Street Journal*, April 29, 2003, A.1.

[2]   K. Wells, *Travels with Barley: A Journey through Beer Culture in America*. New York: The Free Press, 2004.

brewery is as capable as any multinational brewing conglomerate of enhancing the world of beer. Extreme beers are becoming a significant part of this world. If not yet in volume then at least in excitement and influence.

Extreme beers are either beers that are brewed with greater-than-usual quantities of traditional ingredients or beers that are made with non-traditional ingredients. The average mass-produced lager is slightly less than 5% abv (alcohol by volume) and less than 10 IBUs (international bittering units). The average double or Imperial India Pale Ale, probably the fastest-growing style within the extreme brewing niche, weighs in around 10% alcohol by volume and 80 IBUs. Some of the more popular non-traditional ingredients being used by innovative brewers today include fruits, spices, vegetables and herbs. Traditional brewing ingredients, as defined by the regulatory arm of our own federal government, are barley, hops, yeast, and water. The government also accepts corn and rice as ingredients within this definition to appease the gigantic breweries who are fond of using these cheaper-than-barley adjunct grains because they keep the production cost (and taste profile) of their beers very low. A partial list of the unusual ingredients we brew with every year at Dogfish Head includes maple syrup, beet sugar, crystallized ginger, vanilla beans, juniper berries, basmati rice, hawthorn fruit, thyme honey, allspice, chicory, apricots, peaches, pumpkins, cinnamon, coffee, figs, dates, grapes, raisins, orange peels, blackberries, and nutmeg.

Before Dogfish Head even opened, breweries like Sierra Nevada and Anchor were brewing gigantic, hoppy, barleywines. Even further back in the fifties and sixties, before the craft-brewing renaissance truly began, Balantine Brewery was making a strong beer that was aged on hops in wooden casks for months called Burton Ale – the precursor to modern Imperial IPAs. But today's extreme brewing movement's true roots are in the old world – more specifically Belgium. Belgian breweries have been incorporating what we could call non-traditional ingredients (fruits, spices) and non-traditional methods (spontaneous fermentation, aging on wood) for centuries.

It does, however, seem that extreme brewing is enjoying a heightened level of appreciation today as both the consumer and many craft brewers have embraced these more exotic beers in record numbers. The mainstream is hot on the heels of the avant-garde as mass-media publications as diverse as *Men's Journal, Details, Real Simple, The*

New York Times, *Penthouse*, and *Forbes* sing the praises of extreme beers. The online beer community has also been a great meeting place, sounding board and feeding ground where beer enthusiasts come together and grass-roots demand for niche beers percolate. Immediacy, customization, interactivity, community – these are words that can be used to describe both the phenomena of the World Wide Web and the explosion of boutique beers across the country.

There are dozens of traditional beer styles in existence, hundreds of unique extreme beers out there, and well over a thousand breweries in America. Yet only three breweries make over 80% of the beer we drink. This has happened in a country that supposedly champions individuality and freedom of choice. The good news is that a larger and larger fraction of the beer-buying public is realizing that this sad fact is unacceptable and doing something about it. They are seeking out and buying alternatives. While the sales of these giant breweries have been flat, craft beer sales have grown 7% in 2004 and 9% in 2005 – representing higher percentage growth than big-brewery beer, wine or spirits in the United States. The excitement around the craft segment and more extreme beers has even prompted the big breweries to covertly wade into the water in an attempt to capitalize on our segment's growth. Coors makes and sells a Belgian-style wheat beer under the name Blue Moon with very little reference given in labeling and promotional materials to its Coors genealogy. Anheuser-Busch recently launched its own quasi-craft products with names like Devils Hop Yard India Pale Ale. I call them quasi-craft products because while they are made with similar ingredients to true craft beers they are not made from a similar craft-centric philosophy. In other words – a company that focuses 99.9% of their energies on selling a light, rice-brewed lager will never be a craft brewery. I am hopeful that the marketplace will bear this out and that enlightened craft beer enthusiasts and consumers will vote with their dollars and choose true craft beers made by true craft breweries – not opportunist, speculating multinational brewing conglomerates capitalizing on a trend. If someday one of the big-three breweries finds itself making 50.1% of their beer from all-malt with no rice or corn then I would say, welcome to the community of craft brewers.

The craft-brewing philosophy in general and, more specifically, the extreme brewing philosophy is one centered on outsider art. Small breweries are artisanal and experimental by nature. Big breweries are industrial and seek to homogenize and commodify in an effort to be all things to all consumers. Big breweries make a product, small breweries make consumable art. This fact is obvious when you look at the kinds of beers, brewers, and breweries that are seeing incredible growth in the craft segment. Experimental, ambitious beers like those from Dogfish Head, New Belgium, Avery, Alesmith, Russian River, Bells, Port Brewing Company, Allagash, Stone and Rogue are continually widening the definition of what great beer can be.

These independent, small, adventurous breweries and hundreds like them have forged a new identity for American beer. They have returned a vibrancy to the American beer landscape that now reflects the diversity, distinction, and determination of the American people as a whole. These brewers are locked arm-in-arm with beer enthusiasts, homebrewers, and enlightened consumers who are helping to spread the message that the world of beer has more to offer than generic light lager. As brewers, our beer is the public conversation that we share with the world but it's also part of a greater communication of independence that, as a country, we cherish.

In a commencement speech at West Point in 1969 the African-American writer Ralph Ellison described the impetus for his novel *Invisible Man*[3] in this way: "I wanted to tell a story. I felt there was a great deal about the nature of the American experience that was not understood by most Americans." The central theme in his speech that day was that American diversity carried the key to the American experience, because, as he said, "Much that appeared unrelated was actually most intimately intertwined." It's my goal in this essay to point out the obvious – how deeply intertwined the American craft-brewing renaissance is with the quintessential American experience.

The first people who immigrated to this country were motivated by the belief that they could create an alternative to what they had known. They fled class-ridden conformity, outright tyranny and rigid systems of the status quo. I'm sure many were told that the odds of making it were against them but, like modern entrepreneurs, they didn't believe it because they believed in themselves. They longed to make the alluring promise of America a reality. They were trailblazers who cleared forests, built railroads, erected cities, and set the pace of an industrial revolution. They did it for themselves but they didn't do

---

[3] R. Ellison, *Invisible Man*. New York: Random House, 1952.

it by themselves – they did it communally. They came over on crowded boats maybe armed with little more than a couple of loaves of bread and a holey blanket. But what really sustained them was this belief in themselves – a belief that they deserved the right to put their own thumbprint on the world. So they turned their backs on societies where despotic governments and monarchs ruled with iron fists to make a new world where the real hero was the working man. As Walt Whitman wrote, "It is not consistent with the reality of the soul to admit that there is anything in the known universe that is more divine than men and women . . . No one government, no one race, no one brewery is anymore important than any single individual . . ."[4] Well, OK, I added the brewery part myself. So we have this amazing entrepreneurial, freedom-loving lifeblood flowing through our communal DNA. This lifeblood pumps harder when our society stops reflecting the individual people of which it is comprised – when the DIY work ethic that this country was built upon gets marginalized by the return-on-investment obsession that we sometimes get mired in.

A great example of this phenomenon exists in the world of music – another industry dominated by a very few suppliers – in this case major record labels. The American Folk Music tradition was reinvigorated in the sixties when musicologists like Alan Lomax hit the road in search of original sources like Robert Johnson, Odetta, and Howlin' Wolf. As it evolved into a mainstream industry, divisions came into play – had American folk music lost its ability to represent the diversity and distinction of so many different American folks? Had it become a milquetoast, a homogenized shadow of its former self? There was a pivotal moment in 1965 when Bob Dylan and his Band plugged into amplifiers and rocked the Newport Folk Festival amid cries of "Judas" and insults from the offended old guard. But make no mistake – also present were a small group of passionate individuals who were revitalized by Dylan's audacity to color outside the lines.

The bands that took the stage that weekend in Newport included the Kingston Trio and Peter, Paul, and Mary – who presented a very polished, very innocuous, and very popular form of folk music, the easy-listening equivalent of easy drinking. Just because this music was popular with some people didn't mean it was loved by all. There were

[4] W. Whitman, *Leaves of Grass*, 1855. Modern edition by Pocket Books, 2006; passage from Preface.

a growing number of listeners who wanted more from their music than something to tap their toes to – they wanted music and lyrics that represented the challenging, vibrant, sometimes incongruous time they were living in. They were leading exciting lives but there was no music that honestly reflected their excitement. Dylan had the courage to stand up there and change music, to invent, innovate, experiment and follow his own muse. Maybe he knew the reception he would get from the carriers of the status-quo torch who invited him to play. Maybe he knew and didn't care. A risk-taking artistic entrepreneur if there ever was one. Here is what he had to say about the reaction he got:

> There were a lot of old people there too. Lots of whole families had driven down from Vermont, lots of nurses with their patients, and, well, like they just came to hear something relaxing – hoedowns, you know an Indian polka or two, and just when everything is going alright, here I come on, and the whole place turns into a beer factory. (Quoted in Hajdu, 2002)[5]

. . . A beer factory indeed. Instead of staying in their comfort zones, with light, unthreatening music, the old-guard folkies were confronted with a Dionysian revel: intoxicating, heady, dangerous. Dylan's critics, fearing diversity and change, wanted to define for everyone what folk music meant – whereas Dylan was calling out to the individual listener and saying: you have ears, you have a mind, you are more capable of defining what folk music means to you than anyone else is. Screw the establishment. Create your own establishment. What is more punk rock than saying: how does it feel – to be on your own? It feels pretty exhilarating.

Dylan is a one-man vortex of folk, country, blues, and psychedelia – he contains multitudes (to quote Whitman again). With music as with craft brewing – it's the archaic artist who howls into the zeitgeist and alters it, and if he has hit his mark the zeitgeist begins to howl back.

Like a rolling stone is punk rock – just as much as DJ Herc, The Pixies, and Black Flag were 20 years ago and Cat Power, The Roots and Green Day are today. I'm talking about punk rock as a subversive ideal not the three-cords and a mosh-pit definition. The punk rock

---

[5] In D. Hajdu, *Positively 4th Street: The Lives and Times of Joan Baez, Bob Dylan, Mimi Baez Farina and Richard Farina*. New York: North Point Press, 2002, 261.

aesthetic mirrors the extreme brewing aesthetic – both are vehicles for the counter-cultural attitudes that provoke social upheaval against the status quo. A country that is drinking 85% of its beer as light lagers made from one of three breweries is in need of a little upheaval.

So flash forward a couple decades or so after Dylan took the stage in Newport. A certain fraction of us beer lovers were experiencing a bad case of déjà vu from living in a world that didn't represent us very well. Like our immigrant ancestors there was a longing for an alternative. There was a feeling that we deserved more. Not more quantity but more quality and more diversity. There's more to America than glamorized Hollywood freaks and fetishized weapons of mass destruction – more than McDonald's, shopping malls, volume, delirium, and mediated hype. There were millions of different people with millions of different tastes and their tastes weren't being reflected by the choices they had in the kinds of beer that were readily available.

So another generation of entrepreneurs rose to the challenge. They created the American craft-brewing renaissance by the seats of their pants and consumers saw what they were doing and supported it. Because they recognized their own struggle for integrity and independence in the struggle that these brewers were facing. These brewers were telling their fellow Americans to wake up – you have taste buds – you have a mind – you know what you want to drink more than your television or a billboard does.

They experimented with ingredients and processes, taking old techniques and marrying them to new innovations. It was time to recreate a tradition that reflected the greater American tradition – because tradition is nothing more than a series of experiments that have proven to work. And, as Americans, experimenting is what we do best.

It started to work. The craft-brewing pioneers banded together and established a beachhead. They grew a cottage industry from the roots of their own labor and passion. They succeeded until we almost got swallowed up by our own success. In the mid-nineties the craft beer segment grew by 40% a year. The photographs in the local paper's stories on craft brewing morphed from the image of a proud brewer, wiping the sweat from her brow, standing next to her mash tun, to images of bar graphs and intricate calculations. Craft brewing was hot. The beer rush was on, like the gold rush of the 1800s, and suddenly you had a group of disingenuous opportunists hooking their wagons to the craft beer horse. A bunch of suits who cared more about making money than they did about making beer were suddenly in the news. "You mean I'll make a million dollars and party on the clock – sign me up!"

It reached a tipping point in 1998 when suddenly supply overtook demand. The consumer became overwhelmed by the glut of choices on the shelf. The big beer distributors freaked out as they had fought alongside the major breweries for many decades to reduce and not increase options in the marketplace. There was infighting, discounting, stale half-empty bottles of Bad Toad Lager and Naked Chick Light being tossed into garbage cans by consumers who thought they recognized themselves in the reflections off these new beers they found in their local store. And overnight the perception of the craft-brewing industry seemed to go from fresh and original to clichéd, derivative and played out. My own brewery, Dogfish Head, was nearly pushed into bankruptcy during those years – but we didn't dumb down or discount our beers; we stuck to what we believed in and struggled forward. Nevertheless, collectively, as an industry, we got rear-ended at the corner of Wall Street and Madison Avenue. It was a hit-and-run. Then they peeled out to chase the new new thing, the dot-com phenomenon – "You mean I can make a million dollars while surfing porn in my pajamas? Sign me up!" . . . But as the dust settled on the crash site that brewer was still standing there, smiling, as she dug out her mash tun. And the true believers stayed on and supported her efforts. Economic Darwinism took hold and the consumer decided who deserved to exist and thrive and whose equipment got gobbled up in the latest bank foreclosure. Because it wasn't about growth, or going public, or selling out. It was about the beer. More importantly it was about the people who made and sold the beer and the people who bought and enjoyed the beer.

And here we are today – the craft breweries who stuck to their guns, survived and thrived. The people who refused to let the tail of money wag the dog of inspiration. We learned the hard way to abandon the expectations of others and live up to our expectations of ourselves. We got wicked good at making beer, running pubs, and educating the world on what we were really all about. In the mid-nineties we almost allowed the powers that be to distort the image of our industry from a beautiful organic thing that we created to a fad they would nearly destroy. As craft brewers we are not in the business of growth – we are in the business of making world-class beer. Growth is just a by-product of our business. Money is a means to our end and not an end in itself. The reason we got into trouble eight years ago is that some people started to think that growth was what we were all about. Now that we have come through those dark times we need to make sure we've learned our lesson and keep moving forward to educate people on the diversity and distinction of American beer. We can learn a lot from our peers in the high-end wine industry who have, up until recently, done a better job than small breweries at explaining to the world why an amazing bottle of Pinot Noir can justifiably cost three times as much as a mediocre bottle of Pinot Noir. Extreme beers are slowly breaking down the pricing ceiling and blue-collar perception that beer in general suffers from. There is as much diversity in styles, and even more use of experimental ingredients and process in the craft beer world than there are in the wine world. We just need to work harder within our community at getting the word out.

On May 24, 1976 there was a wine tasting in Paris that changed the course of history. A group of French vintners, critics, and vineyard owners gathered to blind-taste and judge some world-famous French wines against a group of American wines. When it was over, much to the Francophiles' dismay, the American wines won both the red and white categories. A single journalist from America's *Time* magazine was present. His story was soon picked up by other major publications around the world. The epicenter of the international wine community shifted away from Western Europe and toward Napa Valley literally overnight. The vineyards that beat the French quickly succeeded in raising the prices and the reputation of the burgeoning American fine-winemaking community. Our craft-brewing community has not benefited from a singular epiphany of this magnitude.

Today wine is made all over the world but the magic and mystery of quality wine always seems to come down to place. The experts are always claiming that great wine can only be produced in exclusive places and in tiny quantities. They each preach the gospel of terroir. Holy land. Today there are almost 500 appellations, or micro-growing regions, in France alone. And there are numerous distinct terroirs within each of these appellations. It sounds confusing because it is. Divide and conquer. If you can't blind them with science, blind them with geography. Je parle français en peu and I'm pretty sure the translated definition of *terroir* is dirt. The wine world has wrapped this one word with mighty voodoo powers and created a cult of exclusivity around it but it is not exclusively their own.

91

Breweries have terroir as well. Instead of revolving around a patch of land, our terroir is centered on a group of people. We operate our business on a human scale and with a human face. Today, between the constant media-blitz of advertising and marketing and the breakneck pace of production and distribution, it can be easy to overlook the passion of the person selling and that of the person buying. But it's this shared human passion that has always fueled commerce; this opportunity to create extraordinary circumstances for the production and procurement of something new, exciting and worthwhile.

Pick up a bottle of craft-brewed beer. Consider the logo – what does that company represent to you? In the world of craft brewing each logo communicates its own distinct and indelible terroir. But these terroirs are not based on the brick-and-mortar places where the breweries exist. They belong to the people behind the breweries: Tomme Arthure of Port Brewing Company adding sour cherries to beer fermenting in oak barrels. Garrett Oliver of Brooklyn Brewery hosting a beer and food pairing. Phil Markowski of Southhampton Brewing adding edible flowers to his wheat beers. Or Jack Joyce – and his band of merry pranksters – laying waste to every windmill they encounter on their quest to build a Rogue nation. Dick Cantwell and Dave Beuller of Elysian Brewing tapping a pumpkin ale from an actual pumpkin at their brewpub as they serve nearly a dozen other pumpkin ales along-side their own. None of these events has the singular power of that wine tasting in Paris. But, as craft brewers, collectively, communally, we are rolling the barrel forward. Every time we execute one of these events we are expanding this special place for ourselves in the beer industry and we are succeeding; we are finally in synch with our market, the world around us, and most importantly with each other. The soul, the greater terroir of the craft-brewing community, is resonating with a growing minority of American beer consumers because they recognize their own struggle in ours. So we have intrinsic, emotional, real connections that cannot be bought or sold but must be earned. The logos of the above-named craft breweries only resonate because the people behind the logos have brought them to life – they are not status symbols so much as they are symbols of independence from our status-obsessed culture. Every time a consumer chooses an extreme beer that has earned its place on a line of taps at a bar or on the shelf at the store, because it was unique, made with the highest-quality ingredients and flat-out tasted great, instead of choosing the least flavorful beer with the most ubiquitous advertising campaign, they are acting out their own declaration of independence one six-pack or pint at a time.

I recently got to go on an amazing trip through Belgium with four other experimental American craft brewers to do events and research for my book, *Extreme Brewing*. We wanted to pay tribute to a brewing culture that inspired us at the same time that we shared our own beers with the Belgian brewing community. Our beers were really well received and each of us was as proud to pour and describe one another's beers as we were our own. We knew we weren't just representing the five breweries present but all 1,400 American craft breweries as we turned more and more people on to the amazing beers being made all across this country. Each craft brewery has its own terroir in differing stages of development and each one represents the colorful diversity of our industry.

I love it every time an extreme brewer busts out like a modern-day Charlie Parker or Hendrix and surpasses the perceived limitations of his instrument – Dale's putting great barleywine in a can, or New Glarus selling boatloads of Belgian-style fruit beers in Wisconsin. For those of you who are just settling into the world of craft-brewed beer I welcome you into one of the most respectful, creative, communal industries in existence. So many of my business heroes, the people who inspired me to actually pursue my dream and open a brewery, are still running the breweries they founded today. People like Jim Koch at Boston Beer and Ken Grossman from Sierra Nevada are not just working to growth their own companies, they are working to promote all the little guys who are up against the challenges of a big-brewery dominated marketplace. They do so in part by continuing to promote and distribute extreme beers like Bigfoot, Celebration, and Utopias alongside their pale ale and lager.

As craft brewers each of us is working to illustrate the evolution of our own unique, authentic howl – our terroir. And the sum-total power of our collective terroir resonates more deeply than any one of them alone.

We have hand-made and hand-sold our beers with our hearts on our sleeves and we have worked to indoctrinate our consumers, who are so much better educated and more self-aware now than they were eight years ago when supply temporarily overpowered demand. There is no doubt in my mind that these beer enthusiasts can now recognize the difference between the breweries that developed organically, out of service to their art, and the big-brewery culture vultures who will try to take advantage of our momentum.

Americans will always vehemently protect their right to create an alternative; not just an alternative to giant breweries, which is what we craft brewers represent, but to the increasing homogenization of American culture. Extreme beers are the most poignant examples of our protest. It's not outlandish to recognize our boil kettles as modern-day melting pots – the sources of beers as diverse and colorful as the people who buy them. *Made* by people as diverse and colorful as the people who buy them. Ideologically, there is little difference between the immigrant on the boat with the holey blanket and crust of bread, and the sweat-soaked brewer with the grain shovel. The blanket and the shovel are just tools to be used to make something much more important – these *things* won't be responsible for the success or failure of these people. What really sustains them is a belief in themselves – a belief that they deserve the right to put their own, unique thumbprint on the world; their hard-earned opportunity to create an alternative to the status quo. Americans are at their best when they are creating. The creation of diverse and distinct beers is what we as experimental craft brewers do. Oftentimes, as brewers, when we do our jobs well and create something unique, exotic, and monumental, a new extreme beer is born and our community is expanded yet again. There has never been a better time to be a beer maker in America than this very moment, and there has never been a better time to be a beer *drinker* either. I invite all beer enthusiasts to take baby steps outside your comfort zones. Experience the creativity, quality, and hard work that your local, small, independent brewers have put inside their bottles and kegs. You won't be disappointed. Cheers.

Part II

The Ethics of Beer
Pleasures, Freedom, and Character

7

Mill v. Miller, or
Higher and Lower Pleasures

Steven D. Hales

You may be confronted, as I am, with a bewildering array of beers lining the shelves of your favorite store. Fuller's ESB? Franziskaner Hefeweizen? Brooklyn Black Chocolate Stout? Arrogant Bastard IPA? Rogue Dead Guy Ale? Miller Genuine Draft? Once you have decided the style of beer you are in the mood for (or goes best with dinner, or would be appreciated by friends), there are two things to consider in making the momentous decision: price and taste. Complicating matters is that for the same money you might buy more of a lesser beer or less of a finer beer. A very tough decision. So what should the hapless and thirsty shopper do?

When it comes to offering advice on what you should do, you can't beat a moral philosopher. The nineteenth-century polymath John Stuart Mill considered thorny issues of just this sort, ultimately arguing that we should buy the better brew. He thought a better life was one spent enjoying a few pints of excellent ale, not one chugging kegs of fraternity-grade lager. I will argue that while defensible against the standard objections, Mill's views on quality are far-reaching and controversial, even for aficionados of quality. To see these things, though, we must first look a bit into Mill's general moral thinking.

Mill was a hedonistic utilitarian, meaning that he considered the highest good to be pleasure and that the consequences of our actions – to be measured in terms of the production of pleasure or pain – were all that morally matters. At any moment we are faced with all sorts of actions we might perform. Mill's view was that our moral duty is always to perform the action that has the best consequences of any of the actions available to us. Our duty, in short, is to increase the total

97

amount of pleasure in the world as best we can. It is evil to bring unnecessary suffering and good to minimize it.

Utilitarianism is a beautiful and elegant theory. Armed with it we can determine what our moral duties are in every possible scenario. Should I rob a liquor store? Should I be a vegetarian? Should I double-park? Should I send my platoon to storm that hill? Should I finish writing this essay? Should I drink another beer? In every case I simply weigh out the pros and cons – the future pleasures and pains – of each possible action, and do the thing that will make the world a better, happier, place.

Sounds great, right? Well, really living the utilitarian life is not that easy. Just ask Peter Singer, the well-known utilitarian and public scold at Princeton, who thinks it requires that we make major changes in how we treat non-human animals and the poor. Singer argues on utilitarian grounds that it is wrong to use animals for food or experimentation, and that wealthy persons and nations have considerable duties of aid to the impoverished. There are various other concerns with utilitarianism, which legions of hard-working and contrarian philosophers have been all too enthusiastic to present in voluminous detail. Mill himself worried about the objection that utilitarianism is a moral philosophy fit only for pigs. He writes:

> Now, such a theory of life excites in many minds, and among them in some of the most estimable in feeling and purpose, inveterate dislike. To suppose that life has (as they express it) no higher end than pleasure – no better and nobler object of desire and pursuit – they designate as utterly mean and grovelling; as a doctrine worthy only of swine, to whom the followers of Epicurus were, at a very early period, contemptuously likened; and modern holders of the doctrine are occasionally made the subject of equally polite comparisons by its German, French, and English assailants. (*Utilitarianism*, ch. 2)[1]

Mill's response to the pig objection is obvious; "The Epicureans have always answered, that it is not they, but their accusers, who represent human nature in a degrading light; since the accusation supposes human beings to be capable of no pleasures except those of which swine are capable." Clearly human beings enjoy many pleasures that

---

[1] John Stuart Mill, *Utilitarianism*. Indianapolis: Hackett Publishing, 1979. First published 1863.

pigs do not, like the pleasures of literature, sports, films, music, and bottle-conditioned Belgian saison ales. So why would the comparison with swine be seen as degrading, as a real objection to utilitarianism? No doubt because the animal pleasures available to pigs are viewed as somehow inferior to the more elevated and refined pleasures of human beings. Human pleasures are better pleasures, and to think otherwise is to lower human beings to the status of pigs, rutting, slopping, and rolling in the muck.

Not everyone fears this fate, however. Mill's predecessor Jeremy Bentham famously denied that there were such differences in the quality of pleasures, and held that pig pleasures were every bit as worthy and admirable as human ones. Bentham's often misquoted line is that "Prejudice apart, the game of push-pin is of equal value with the arts and sciences of music and poetry. If the game of push-pin furnish more pleasure, it is more valuable than either" (*The Rationale of Reward*, bk. III, ch. 1).[2] Push-pin was a child's game much like tiddlywinks. In essence, Bentham is saying that there is no qualitative difference between beer pong and a Shakespearean sonnet, no qualitative difference between a Saturday night with a warm six-pack and NASCAR and an evening waltzing to Strauss. All that matters is the quantity of pleasure produced. Bentham embraced his inner swine. Mill, however, did not. Mill claimed that there are distinctions of quality among pleasures, and that pleasures might be better or worse in some way besides mere amount.

So how exactly can we determine which pleasures are the higher-quality ones and which are the lower-quality ones? Mill gives a test: take any two pleasures of equal quantity and poll people who have experienced both of them. The one that most people would prefer, irrespective of any feeling of moral obligation to prefer it, is the higher-quality pleasure. In other words, the quality of pleasures is to be democratically determined by vote. Mill even claims that people would prefer a higher-quality pleasure to a lower-quality one, "even though knowing it [the higher-quality pleasure] to be attended with a greater amount of discontent, [he or she] would not resign it for any quantity of the other pleasure which their nature is capable of " (*Utilitarianism*, ch. 2). In other words, no amount of a low-quality pleasure can trump

2 Jeremy Bentham, *The Rationale of Reward*. London: J. and H. L. Hunt, 1825.

even a tiny amount of a high-quality pleasure, and no one would choose it.

Objection One: Lowbrow (or Löwenbrau) Preferences

The problem is that people often choose what seem to be lower-quality pleasures, even when higher-quality pleasures are available to them. For instance, beer aficionados are all familiar with untutored friends who would prefer to have a can of Budweiser than, say, a snifter of Ommegang's Three Philosophers quadrupel, even if both are available. What can possibly explain such behavior? Mill seems to think that everyone would choose a mere sip of Three Philosophers over a whole case of Bud. Yet he is obviously wrong – people often choose the lower quality.

Mill is perfectly aware that people make such irrational choices, and he has two explanations. The first is the *Competent Judges* reply. Anyone who would rather have a Coors Lite instead of a La Fin du Monde by Unibroue is an incompetent judge of beer – he is not someone who has *really* tried both. A single sip does not turn one into a beer authority; one must spend some time and effort to acquire a discriminating palate. Likewise a stroll through the Louvre does not make one an art critic, nor does attendance at a Boston Pops concert make one a musicologist. If one is not a competent judge, Mill argues, then one is not eligible to vote on the quality of a particular pleasure. This makes good sense. If one is planning to buy a new bicycle, pick a new novel to read, get a copy of Mahler's Second Symphony, or just about anything else, one wants the advice of knowledgeable cyclists, readers, and classical music buffs. Why poll the ignorant?

Mill's second rejoinder is the *Weakness of Will* response. Even if one is a competent judge and has full knowledge of the superior pleasure, one might still pick the lower-quality one. Mill notes that sometimes the lower-quality pleasure is just *easier* to achieve, and one might not feel like making the effort to attain the higher-quality pleasure. Mill aridly comments that "men often, from infirmity of character, make their election for the nearer good, even though they know it to be the less valuable . . . they pursue sensual indulgences to the injury of health, although perfectly aware that health is the greater good"

100

(*Utilitarianism*, ch. 2). If I am perusing my bookshelf, looking for a read, I might pick a Robert B. Parker mystery rather than the latest by Richard Powers. Sure, Parker is a bag of buttered popcorn and Powers is a five-course meal at the Ritz, but the pleasure of Parker is easily accessible, quick, and effortless. Mill is probably right; to knowingly choose the lower pleasure is a character deficiency.

Objection Two: Elitism

Even if Mill can explain away lowbrow preferences, one can't help but wonder if there is a bit of superciliousness involved. After all, Mill was a guy who began his formal education at age two, read Greek at three, knew Latin by the time he was four, and had a substantial knowledge of classical and historical literature by the time he was eight. Mill's idea of a party night out was probably attending a performance of Mozart's *Così fan Tutte* followed by claret at the club and a couple of chapters of Plato's πογιτεία. Indeed, Mill offers "pleasures of the intellect, of the feelings and imagination, and of the moral sentiments" as examples of the higher quality. It is hard to picture Mill at the bar of his local pub, quaffing a few pints of bitter and throwing darts with his mates. Indeed, Mill expert Alan Ryan of Oxford comments, "Mill is not known to have entered a pub ever in his life."[3] In other words, one suspects that behind talk of "higher pleasures" there lurks an upper-class Victorian snobbery that looks down its aquiline nose at the baser pleasures of the proletariat. A beer-drinking workingman might be well moved to dismiss Mill as Little Lord Hoity-Toity, telling the masses how to live. Perhaps it is best to side with Bentham – the amount of pleasure is all that matters, no matter what its source.

Mill does not consider this objection, and so I offer a response on his behalf. Elitism is a danger only if Mill enumerates those pleasures or kinds of pleasures that are "higher" ones and those that are "lower." Although he is clearly tempted to do so, Mill need not start giving lists that would be immediately subject to criticism from the egalitarians. Instead, the right response to the elitism objection is to insist that *any sort* of pleasure can be assessed in terms of quality. Both Plato and porter can be evaluated in terms of quality – *Symposium* is a higher-quality

---

[3] Personal correspondence.

Platonic dialogue than *Philebus* (which is unfortunately didactic and humorless) and Stone Smoked Porter is of higher quality than Saranac Caramel Porter (which is regrettably thin and watery). There is no reason that Mill must insist that Plato, *tout court*, is better than porter, *tout court*, no matter how tempting it is for the snobs. Evaluation of the quality of pleasures is within a kind, not across kinds.

There is a bit of a residual problem about generality, though. I have recommended that we rank-order all pleasure within a type, so that a beer may be better or worse than another beer, but it is senseless to insist that beer is qualitatively better than wine, Platonic dialogues, country living, ballet, or the current President. Yet how fine-grained shall we make our comparisons? Is it legitimate to order by quality Sam Adams Lager, Guinness, Ayinger Celebrator Dopplebock, and Hoegaarden? Or is it only fair to compare a stout to a stout, a pilsener to a pilsener, and so on? And if we must compare a stout to a stout, what about even finer grained divisions – should we only compare Samuel Smith's Oatmeal Stout to another oatmeal stout or may we judge it against dry stouts, imperial stouts, milk stouts, and chocolate stouts? These are not easy questions. Problems of generality, vagueness, line-drawing, and whether nature can be carved at the joints range across the whole of philosophy, and cannot be solved here. Nevertheless, even if not all the details are ironed out, the solution to the elitism objection is to equitably maintain that for each kind or type of pleasure, there are pleasures of higher and lower quality.

Objection Three: Equivocation

Even if Mill's ideas about quality are not necessarily elitist, many think that his method of determining the quality of pleasures – namely by asking people who are knowledgeable about the pleasures under consideration which ones they prefer – is a hopeless logical bungle. Mill writes, "the sole evidence it is possible to produce that anything is desirable is that people do actually desire it" (*Utilitarianism*, ch. 4). This treatment of quality has been savaged by logicians who claim that Mill has made an elementary error: that of equivocating between the desired and the desirable. Polling people to see which pleasures they prefer will tell you only what is in fact desired. It will not tell you which pleasures are *desirable*.

The charge of equivocation is not the knockdown objection that Mill's detractors maintain. Polling the competent judges *is* a reliable way of finding out about the relative quality of things (objects, events, activities, etc.). The competent judges are not always right, but one is still likelier to discover some fine beers to sample by reading the books written by Michael Jackson, Garrett Oliver, and Bob Klein than by asking Cletus the slack-jawed yokel. At this point we may ask a question analogous to one that Plato posed in *Euthyphro*: are pleasures desirable because the competent judges desire them, or do the competent judges desire them because they are desirable?

Suppose it is the former: pleasures are desirable because the competent judges desire them. This means that their desire actually *makes* something desirable, a view that does seem to erase any distinction between the desired and the desirable. However, there are at least three difficulties with this view. The first is the very nature of desire. We desire, love, and wish for things because of their desirable properties. Those things are antecedently desirable, which explains why we desire them. It is seriously strange to suppose that something gains its desirable qualities after we begin to desire it. The second difficulty is that if pleasures are desirable because the competent judges desire them, then there literally is *no reason* for the competent judges to prefer one thing over another. If it is Michael Jackson's love of Chimay abbey-style ale that makes that beer desirable, or Bob Klein's love of Rogue Shakespeare Stout that makes it desirable, then their love of those beers is fundamentally *arbitrary*. In other words, if certain beers are not desirable due to their objective properties, then desiring them is groundless and random. The third difficulty is that the competent judges could change their mind at any minute and decide that Schlitz Malt Liquor is the finest beer ever made. If they were to do so, Schlitz Malt Liquor would immediately *become* the best beer in the world. If you want to insist that such a thing could never happen, or that anyone who so judged would no longer be a competent judge, then you are implicitly assuming that there are objective facts about beer quality to which any competent judge must be sensitive.

In short, it is a mistake to hold that pleasures are desirable because the competent judges desire them. Far more reasonable is the view that competent judges desire certain pleasures because those pleasures are antecedently desirable, and the judges, informed and educated about that kind of pleasure, are able to reliably detect the qualities that make those pleasures desirable ones. Audiophiles have trained themselves to hear amplifier distortion, speaker boxiness or coloration, listen for low-end rolloff in the audible range, and other factors that determine the desirableness and relative quality of a stereo system. Beer aficionados have learned to distinguish various flavor components in beer along with their balance, proportion, and intensity, and are sensitive to the role that density, carbonation, and temperature play in mouthfeel and taste. Philosophy journal referees have learned to detect clever or fallacious argumentation, tight writing, originality, timeliness and other attributes that determine the quality of an article submitted for publication. These are all objective factors that serve to determine the quality of beer, stereo systems, philosophy articles or any other pleasure. Far from naïvely equivocating, Mill accurately points out that when experts uniformly desire something, this is an excellent and trustworthy indicator that the object of their desire is in fact desirable.

Objection Four: Inconsistency

The fundamental utilitarian tenet is to produce as much pleasure in the world as we possibly can. Our moral duty is to do so. But now Mill is telling us that quality is important too. How can we possibly promote as much pleasure as possible, and also as much high-quality pleasure as possible? It's like telling someone to read as many books as possible, but also read as many good books as possible. Well, which is it? Reading Proust's epic *In Search of Lost Time* may satisfy the latter injunction but not the former. Reading a dozen romance novels over the same amount of time would satisfy the former injunction but not the latter. So should I read as many books as possible (the romances) or as many good books as possible (Proust)?

I can only partially save Mill from the inconsistency objection. Mill seems to suggest that it is better to have a small quantity of a high-quality pleasure than a large quantity of a low-quality pleasure. "Better to be a human being dissatisfied than a pig satisfied; better to be Socrates dissatisfied than a fool satisfied," he writes (*Utilitarianism*, ch. 2). Mill is just wrong about this, and it cannot be defended. Nevertheless, even if we defend the position of hedonistic utilitarianism that our moral duty is to produce as much pleasure in the world as is possible by our actions, there is still room for promoting quality as well.

Suppose that you could perform either an action X or an action Y, and both are superior to any other action you might do, but are tied with each other. Commonly, utilitarians say that it is then morally indifferent which you do; as long as you do either X or Y, just pick one. I recommend on Mill's behalf that instead when there is a tie in quantity of pleasure produced, we ought to choose the action that produces the higher-quality pleasure. Under this interpretation – when there is a tie in quantity of pleasure, go for quality – Mill's promotion of quality is far from innocuous. In fact, I believe that Mill's view is a substantive and radical proposal about how we ought to live. To make this clear, we will have to develop a more explicit positive theory of quality, one that shows precisely how the quality of pleasures is related to their quantity and explains the sort of life Mill advocates when he recommends the promotion of high-quality pleasures.

The Density of Pleasure

In a slogan, this is the notion of quality that I will defend: *quality is the density of pleasure.* Consider two fishing trips. On fishing trip A you fish all day, pulling up one modest fish after the next. There is always something on the line, so you never get bored and there is always a little thrill. But at the same time you don't really catch anything particularly noteworthy. On fishing trip B you fish all day and only catch one fish – but it is a monster. It takes all your skill and cunning to boat the giant lunker, but you eventually do. It does not take much imagination to suppose that the total amount of pleasure attached to both fishing trips is the same; we can even suppose that the total weight of edible meat is identical. The quantity of pleasure associated with the string of fish from trip A is identical with the quantity of pleasure represented by the string of fish from trip B; it is just that there is only one fish on the string in the latter case. Other things being equal, A and B are equally good choices as far as the quantity of pleasure is concerned.

Trip B has one key thing going for it: the giant lunker. This is a higher-quality fish than any of the ones caught on trip A, in fact that single fish is as good as the entire string from trip A. How should we understand this higher quality? Precisely as the density of pleasure: there is more pleasure concentrated in the lunker than in any of the other fish. Mill's recommendation that when quantity of pleasure is tied we should pursue high-quality pleasures, means in this instance that we ought to prefer fishing trip B to trip A. Given a choice between the two fishing outings, we ought to choose B.

This interpretation of quality well accords with our ordinary intuitions and I believe once we start thinking about quality in this way, we can see that it is ubiquitous. However, the pursuit of high-quality pleasures has its risks. Suppose that Jane has $30 to spend on a case of beer. (In Pennsylvania, where I live, state law requires that the minimum beer purchase is a case. We also have the most moronic, oppressive, and ill-considered liquor laws in the United States.) Jane is debating whether to spend her $30 on two cases of Coors Extra Gold pilsener or one case of Pilsener Urquell.

According to Bob Klein's *The Beer Lover's Rating Guide*,[4] Coors Extra Gold is "sharp, light, and tasteless . . . it quickly subsides into a typical pedestrian brew, even on a summer picnic with cold cuts and salads. Touted as a 'full-bodied beer' – yes, in comparison to Coors' regular pilsener." On a scale of 0 to 5, Klein rates Coors Extra Gold 1.8, which means it is below average and suitable only for the extremely thirsty. Pilsener Urquell, on the other hand, is the ur-beer for the pilsener style, and has been brewed in Pilsen, Czech Republic, for over 160 years. According to Klein, it is "crisp, fresh, and mustily hoppy pleasant, understated aroma; intensely carbonated; floral mouthfeel contains some bitterness, but it is subtle and well-calibrated; admirable textural strength; slides into tempered sweetness with spicy foods; a first-class beer to be enjoyed in multiples." Klein rates it 3.5, which is the middle of the above average range. If we assume that taste is objective, Klein is a competent judge of beer, and that Klein's rating system is linear, then Pilsener Urquell is about twice as good as Coors Extra Gold. Under these assumptions, Jane's choice is to buy two cases of Coors or half as much Pilsener Urquell, which tastes twice as good. The cost is the same, and the total quantity of pleasure to be produced is the same. How is Pilsener Urquell a higher-quality beer than Coors? There is twice as much pleasure per bottle.

If Jane follows Mill's recommendation that one ought to pursue higher-quality pleasures, then she will spend her $30 on Pilsener Urquell.

---

4   R. Klein, *The Beer Lover's Rating Guide*. New York: Workman Publishing, 2000, 2nd ed.

Complicating matters is the fact that beer neophytes are unable to appreciate the subtle nuances of fine craft beers to the same extent as the connoisseurs. The neophytes are sensitive to the fact that some beers taste better than others, but cannot understand the magnitude of differences, or the presence of the truly excellent as opposed to the merely superior. Conversely, a casual beer drinker will be more willing to knock back a corporate brew, and more likely to get a little pleasure out of it, than someone who consumes only cask-conditioned ales pulled from an English beer engine. Analogous things are true of other sorts of pleasures, whether it is food, antiques, literature, tennis racquets, movies, travel, romantic trysts, jazz, or Platonic dialogues. As one becomes more informed and more expert, one gains a finer appreciation for the high end while losing the ability to be satisfied with the low end. The recognition of quality comes at a cost.

Suppose that Jane Pivo, a beer enthusiast, and Joe Sixpack, who is just enthusiastic, decide to drink beer together every night for a month. Their financial resources are limited, so they cannot afford artisanal craft beer every night. Most nights they will be forced to drink mass-produced beer, but once in a while they splurge and drink the top-shelf stuff. Jane gets very little pleasure on the nights when they drink Pabst Blue Ribbon and very great pleasure the evenings they share an Allagash Curieux ale aged in bourbon barrels. Joe likes Pabst just fine, although he is not a complete idiot and enjoys the Allagash a bit more. On an average night, Joe is having a better time than Jane as they have a Busch, Miller, Coors, Schlitz, or Keystone Lite. But on the splurge nights, when they sample a Dogfish Head 120 Minute IPA, Aventinus Weizenbock, or Delirium Nocturnum, Jane gets far, far more out of it than poor Joe. Their month of tasting can be presented graphically (Figure 7.1).

For the month, Jane totaled 300 units of pleasure and so did Joe. Thus, from a purely quantitative standpoint, it is no better to be informed and knowledgeable about beer than not. Jane received no more pleasure than did Joe over the course of the month. Joe's pleasure was more frequent and more evenly spread out, whereas Jane's beer-induced pleasure was rarer and more concentrated. Obviously, this example and diagram is an idealization, but no more than any utilitarian calculation. The virtue of this way of presenting matters is that it brings out clearly the sort of life that Mill thinks is the morally optimal one.

Mill's view on quality is that we should live our lives like Jane Pivo – we should become knowledgeable about various pleasures, pursuing

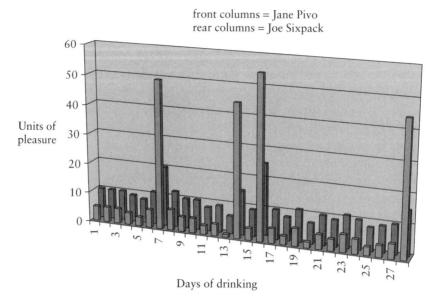

front columns = Jane Pivo
rear columns = Joe Sixpack

Figure 7.1 Jane and Joe's month of drinking

and promoting them. When confronted with two courses of action that produce the same quantity of pleasure, we ought to pursue the one with the higher-quality, concentrated pleasures, even knowing that it is at the expense of enjoying lower-quality ones.

Mill's recommendation here should be tremendously controversial; it is not some innocuous, modest view that every sensible person would obviously hold. Consider Jane. She might well wonder whether becoming a beer aficionado was worth it; after all she and Joe Sixpack drank all the same beers and on most nights Joe had a better time. Why isn't it perfectly reasonable for her to wish, as she sips an Old Milwaukee, that she could enjoy it as much as Joe?

One lesson here is that the appreciation of high-quality pleasures is certainly worthwhile when the cost of gaining those pleasures is low. If Jane and Joe both had unlimited resources and could afford to drink only the finest beers every night, then clearly Jane is better off. She will get more pleasure out of each beer, and since she will never drink a low-grade beer again, will end up with more total pleasure than Joe. Some pleasures are like this, even for the poor. Fine literature, for example, is in great abundance at public libraries and is available for low or no cost. There is no concomitant downside to learning to appreciate great literature, since it is free for the taking and in a supply greater than anyone could read in a lifetime. With the advent of digital music files that are easily shared, music is becoming like literature, where the abundance of inexpensive music is so considerable that we are well advised to seek out and grasp the higher quality. Music and literature are a vast *prix fixe* buffet – there is no point in loading up on the jello with mini-marshmallows when one could have the filet mignon instead. In these contexts, the pursuit of high-quality pleasures will lead to greater overall quantity, and the fundamental tenet of hedonistic utilitarianism is that we should perform those actions that produce as much pleasure as possible.

The controversy is in cases where either (1) the high-quality pleasures are in short supply, or (2) they are expensive or difficult to obtain. In such instances one might prefer to remain in ignorance and not become sensitive to and appreciative of the subtle nuances that make for fine art, desirable first editions, highland single malts, or super sports cars. I am certainly a competent enough judge to tell that the pleasure of owning and driving a Lamborghini is higher quality than my 10-year-old Saturn, but is it really in my self-interest to become too aware of the difference?

In the end, Mill's insight that there can be a quality to pleasure as well as quantity is, when interpreted as the density of pleasure, an entirely coherent and challenging proposal. Far from being elitist, his views are ones that beer lovers can embrace – as a relatively inexpensive pastime, it is far less costly to become a beer connoisseur like Jane Pivo than it is to become an oenophile who is dissatisfied with anything less than a $100 bottle of estate Bordeaux. Within our means, Mill is right – let us pursue high-quality pleasures. But we ought to be guarded about the appreciation of high-quality pleasures that are tantalizingly beyond our grasp, or only occasionally available to us. In these cases, perhaps ignorance is bliss.[5]

[5] Thanks to Richard Brook, Gary Hardcastle, Tim Johnson, Jason Kawall, Vanessa Klingensmith, Wendy Lee, and Lynn Medalie for helpful comments on earlier versions.

8

Beer and Autonomy

Alan McLeod

More than climate or genetics or anything else, drinking behaviour is governed by culture. And that culture is created by the laws that govern it.

Pete Brown, *Three Sheets to the Wind*

Being both a beer lover and a practicing Canadian lawyer, I am aware that beer is both a pervasive but highly regulated staple which has not only existed but been relied upon and enjoyed for as long as the English-speaking culture has been around as well as also a useful marker for a society's moral standards and taste for freedom.

Liberty is funny stuff. We Canucks have not always been as free under the law as our southern neighbors. Throughout the history of the English common law which Canada in large part has inherited, the right to liberty has been understood primarily related to the constitutional right to be free from physical restraint from the state, the right not to be jailed or arrested without good reason. That all changed in 1981 when Canadians gained our equivalent of the *Bill of Rights* of the United States called the *Charter of Rights and Freedoms*, which includes this key statement of the principles of freedom under section 7:

> Everyone has the right to life, liberty and security of the person and the right not to be deprived thereof except in accordance with the principles of fundamental justice.

In recent years challenges have been made to the older more limited view of freedom through the bringing and winning of claims against governments, demonstrating that the concept of "liberty" as set out in section 7 of the *Charter* also includes the right to privately make and act upon personal choices. These cases have proven that a government could not tell one of its workers where to live, how to raise his or her children and whom to pick as the person to live with in an adult relationship. The Supreme Court of Canada has endorsed the following statement on the nature of the right to autonomy that is included in the concept of liberty:

> The right to one's private life, which is considered one of the most fundamental of the personality rights . . . has still not been formally defined. It is possible, however, to identify the components of the right to respect for one's private life, which are fairly specific. What is involved is a right to anonymity and privacy, a right to autonomy in structuring one's personal and family life and a right to secrecy and confidentiality.

The right to liberty, then, includes the freedom to determine how to live as an individual and within one's family and, clearly, use of beer or in fact any consumable is something that can be understood as included in that structure of each of our personal and family lives. You would think these would be obvious sorts of basic liberties that would have long been understood to be part of the social fabric of the culture, that the question of where you lived and who you live with is no more anyone else's business than the simple and civilized act of having a beer.

The move to expand our liberty, however, was not a free-for-all as courts had to deal with claimants asking the court to use the new understanding to assist them in any number of sorts of cases. The courts have responded conservatively in many of these cases as in late 2003, when the Supreme Court ruled on a case in which possession of marijuana was involved. There, the Court determined that:

> this "privacy" aspect of s. 7 relates to "inherently private choices" of fundamental personal importance . . . What stands out from these references, we think, is that the liberty right within s. 7 is thought to touch the core of what it means to be an autonomous human being blessed with dignity and independence in "matters that can properly be characterized as fundamentally or inherently personal." With respect, there is nothing "inherently personal" or "inherently private" about smoking marihuana for recreation . . .

111

My immediate response to this ruling was great disappointment over the meaning of what it is to be free. That is because in many other areas of constitutional law, the right of an individual to define him or herself is a *subjective* if reasonable right, which means that a person's inner experience is taken into account and is often the deciding factor. But it looks like the subjective right to be, say, a genial slacker with a Pabst or even a rabid Belgian ale fan is simply not good enough for the law because we cannot be left to choose to do things that are "objectively" undignified even if that is our wish.

This raises hackles for me. If each Canadian is not granted his or her own choice for how we express ourselves through activities like homebrewing or experience pleasure in life through a great IPA, we are not then each so much uniquely individual but only as individual as is allowed according to a general measurement formed by an idealized standard of generic individuality. And while marijuana is subject to the criminal law, beer consumption is still socially frowned upon in a very similar way to recreational drug use. And this could bode very poorly for beer under the law as long as the powers that be can show that it is not dignified or personally private.

It is fair to say that beer is socially embraced by one part of the population and shunned by another, and that this division is framed by an immense deal of specific and varied regulation. These regulations are very important for our present purposes as they present a picture of the official or "objective" philosophy of beer, challenging the beer lover's personal or "subjective" views. They become the framework against which our hope of freedom is measured and as such shape the nature of that freedom. This chapter surveys the regulation of the following aspects of beer in Canadian society:

- homebrewing
- making beer commercially
- traveling with your beer
- packaging and advertising and the public experience
- wholesale and retail: taxes, fees and price.

Each of these aspects of the regulation of life and beer is reviewed in the paragraphs that follow from only a legal perspective without reference to most historical antecedents or social context. For a work of this length, there is no opportunity to be exhaustive, so it is hoped that the examples from throughout the regulatory framework will serve as illustration of contemporary Canadian jurisprudence and the philosophy of the law of beer in the Great White North.

Homebrewing

The production of beer is something that needs no involvement from either the state or commercial interests. The free production of beer by humans is a simple and traditional human activity. However, and as you might have guessed, despite the simplicity and dignity of making one's own beer supply, Canadian provinces all have liquor control legislation which includes limits on the right to brew for personal consumption and sharing.

In the eastern Canadian province of Nova Scotia, this legislation provides that "subject to this Act and the regulations, any person may engage in the process of beer or wine making for personal use . . ." and then goes on to impose strict limits on what a person can do. For example, it states that a person may only make beer "for personal use at the residential premises of the person." This may mean that taking home-brewed beer to a neighbor's house is illegal or that even inviting the neighbor over to have some beer you have made is out of the question as well. But more than sharing home brew is out of line, as Nova Scotia's law also states:

> No person shall for remuneration or other consideration assist or in any way participate in the process of beer or wine making by another person for personal use of the other person.

While the regulation does say that a person may be paid for information for making of beer, it also implies that the province could ban the right to sell information on beer making if it wanted. There are few other areas of law where sharing information on day-to-day activities like beer making are subject to a possible ban and these are usually about the passing of information which relates to crime but not information on the making of a natural and traditional food.

In the neighboring province of New Brunswick, you can apparently have the neighbor over to try your home brew as "a person who is not prohibited from consuming liquor may consume that wine or beer in that residence." But, as a person can only have 50 gallons on hand, you can have only so many neighbors over – could you provide for a large family gathering like a wedding or a reunion? Things are apparently freer in the far western province of British Columbia where a person may make beer in a residence for the person's own consumption or consumption at no charge by other persons. In British Columbia, sharing is good . . . or at least not illegal. In another western province, Saskatchewan, people may make and share home brew but they have to pay 10 dollars to display, convey and allow people to taste home-brew beer at a competition.

This degree of regulation is quite extraordinary given the possibility of a brewer's absolute autonomy from the point of view of production. A small-scale brewer with a little imagination and a larger garden patch can grow and malt the grain, grow the hops and maintain a yeast strain all without the need to walk beyond the borders of his or her property. It is perhaps one of the great examples of self-sufficiency, which is nothing more than the ability to provide oneself and one's family with the necessities and pleasures of life though the product of work. Yet that product has been effectively de-commoditized through law, prohibiting brewers from giving beer away or even sharing on that small garden patch that is the home.

These regulations also indicate that the provinces believe homebrewing to be an activity that is potentially harmful given the tight controls imposed. But what harm and to whom? Much of the regulation is framed to ensure that the free making of beer is not the basis of a barter economy, by imposing limits on quantity, sharing and transportation. The laws are not aimed at the making or consumption of beer, as any volume may be made and drunk. You just can't have a lot of home brew sitting around. It appears, then, that a primary goal of the law is to stop the commoditization of home-brewed beer. As we will see, that is a power still reserved in large part to the state instead of the commercial marketplace. In fact, when we come to consider the degree to which the government controls and receives revenue and taxation from the trade in beer, the tight regulation of homebrewing may not seem too odd at all, especially if dependency and reliance rather than autonomy is the governing principle behind such regulations.

Making Beer Commercially

After considering the simple dignity of homebrewing, we turn to the regulation of commercial brewing. Given that most beer is produced by large corporations, it may be no surprise that regulation is even stricter in relation to commercial brewing than to private homebrewing.

In some provinces, the very constitution of the beer is subject to law as is the place the beer is made. As a consumable, this may be expected in relation to health and safety but the rules in relation to beer go far beyond that. In Newfoundland a beer is not a beer under the liquor licensing regulations unless it is over 3% alcohol. In addition to strength, the ingredients of beer are also defined by law. In Saskatchewan, the lover of real ale would have great hope reading a law that stated:

> "beer" means an alcoholic beverage obtained by the fermentation of an infusion or decoction of barley, malt and hops in drinkable water . . .

Sadly, despite that legal limitation of the brew to four ingredients of barley, malt, hops and water, one expects as much brewer's corn sugar is dumped into the modern brewers' vats of Saskatchewan as anywhere else mass-produced beer is made these days. It is also interesting to note that yeast, the thing that actually makes the beer and gives it much of its taste when not subject to industrial processes, is not apparently part of the beer. Other provinces' laws are not as pure even if the actual industrial beer produced is likely much the same. Prince Edward Island and Ontario, for example, add the curiously open-ended "or of any similar products" to the list of accepted ingredients found in Saskatchewan's law. Is brewing sugar or the enzyme amyloglucosidase used in mass-produced light beer a "similar product"? One expects many things that are "similar" would make a real-ale lover shudder.

The Liquor Control Board of Ontario (LCBO) goes further in the control of the content of beer through its Quality Assurance Laboratory and its chemical analysis of each product sold in Ontario. The LCBO reports:

> All products sold by the LCBO and Beer Stores are chemically tested to comply with both federal and provincial standards. In fiscal 2003–2004, our lab conducted over 367,000 tests on more than 15,700 different samples.

These tests come at considerable expense and are in addition to the producer's testing. Their cost is also passed on to the consumer without any report as to the benefit of this form of risk management, no identification of the number of beers that are rejected or the causes for beer failure from a scientific perspective. It is also done without identification of the mischief that the testing avoids, the menace being sought out. Due to the cost and other obligations placed on the producer, the testing poses economic challenges to producers and importers that they may not care to take on. As a result, variety and consumer choice is restricted.

The restriction on choice is compounded by the legal definition of what beer is. By capping the minimum and maximum alcohol levels, weaker traditional styles like mild or ordinary bitter or stronger styles like barleywine may effectively be outlawed by regulators possibly unaware of their existence. The best of beer is all about craft. These rules, however, restrict the nature of the craftsman's expressive art as well as the audience's experience of that art. In this way, they also restrict our freedom in relation to beer through taking away the full range of available options.

Traveling with Your Beer

Reviewing the law of traveling with your beer is an encounter with another host of laws, ranging from those aimed at ensuring the government extracts its full share of taxation and profit to rules that imply you can't be trusted to be within an arm's length of a beer.

Anyone who has crossed into Canada from the United States is aware that the customs officers guarding our borders collect taxes and other fees in relation to purchases made abroad. In addition to the provincial and federal sales taxes and a further federal excise tax, the provincially owned LCBO levies a special fee which results in the monopoly that sells imported beer in the province receiving its lost profits for the beer it theoretically did not get to sell. Further, inquiries with customs officials indicate that the LCBO has restricted the amount of beer to be brought in by an individual to 120 bottles per crossing, *even with* full declaration and the payment of all required taxes and fees.

Even in light of the above, some provinces have an even more restrictive approach to interprovincial transit than has been established for international beer transit. Newfoundland also restricts interprovincial travel with beer to an amount "not exceeding those amounts that may be prescribed by the liquor corporation." The import of liquor into the province of Prince Edward Island, for example, is even more strictly regulated, with individuals only allowed to bring 24 bottles with them. Anything more has been described as smuggling even if it is bought in a neighboring part of the country from another control commission.

The movement of human and beer, however, is not just regulated as a billable event when crossing borders. Beer in motion itself is apparently a dangerous combination that requires the application of strict and complex law. Manitoba, for example, only allows unopened boxes of beer bottles to be transferred from one place to another as long as it "has not been opened since it was purchased from the commission." And that is not enough. The law has to tell you where in the vehicle it can be placed during transit. And this depends on what type of beer it is, as store-bought commercial beer can be "in that part of the interior, tonneau, or cab, of a motor vehicle" whereas home-brew beer has to be kept in the trunk.

There is a message underlying the taxation of and restrictions on beer movement. It is that the individual in a way doesn't really fully own beer like one owns a hammer or a loaf of bread. The beer buyer is there to be sold local beer and finding it from outside is an imposition on the government's right to control and make revenue from the public's demand for beer. The message that the law of the transport of beer can also be understood to be conveying is that we are weak and unprincipled and the mere presence of beer in the cab with the driver is cause enough to fear the breaking open of bottles by drivers throughout the land.

It is not enough to say that "thou shalt" not drink when driving or being driven. Some regulations state that individuals shall not crack the seal on the box the beer was in or have home brew even in sight because individuals cannot be trusted in the presence of beer. If we cannot be trusted and need a law placed between our acts and criminality, it would be fair to say that we Canadians are not being granted the dignity that one might expect in a free and democratic society. And if we cannot be trusted with such a minor thing, how could we be expected to participate as people blessed with dignity and independence in "matters that can properly be characterized as fundamentally or inherently personal" as the courts have declared to be the right of each Canadian? The paradox is strange.

Alan McLeod

Packaging and Advertising and the Public Experience

In addition to controlling the trade in and movement of beer, government regulation also controls our exposure to messages about beer. The risk to free decision making is evident in the way these messages affect choice. The individual's right to decide freely is being hobbled by these regulations.

We need laws about containers. In Manitoba, there is a ban on the sale of beer which is not placed in the packages specifically authorized by the commission. It is not only the information on the package that is at issue, though. The eastern province of Prince Edward Island goes so far as forbidding the sale of canned beverages including all beers, leaving it likely the only jurisdiction in North America which prohibits Guinness draft in a can. Even packaging restrictions can limit beer choice: in 2005 the US state of Connecticut temporarily banned Rogue Brewing's Santa's Private Reserve when the packaging was deemed insufficiently wholesome.

Such control is taken a further step in New Brunswick as holders of permits to sell beer are barred from exhibiting, publishing or displaying many themes in their advertising including:

> an advertisement that, directly or indirectly, depicts family scenes that in any way involve the use of liquor, including any group of adults accompanied by children.

This is clearly a matter of moral messaging as it makes no concession to the reality of a very large part of Canadian family life in which beer and family coexist. It also potentially raises issues of freedom of expression in that the public conversation about beer is being restricted by law. It is also interesting to note that misogynistic fantasies about sports and bikini-clad apparently under-aged girls is not so carefully regulated, if their popularity as beer advertising themes are any indication.

Even when you get into a seat in an establishment in some provinces, the hand of the state is still upon you. In Manitoba, the law restricts the amount of beer in every sale. You cannot be sold, served, given or supplied more than 500 ml of beer at any one time. Compare this to the concern for the local brewers in neighboring Saskatchewan where the Liquor Control Board can require bars to carry "one or more

118

of the brands or kinds of beer produced by each permitted manufacturer in Saskatchewan." Space must be made for the local product whether that is the beer you want or not.

It is important also to note that where you drink is restricted with great specificity as in Manitoba "no person shall consume, and no licensee shall permit any person to consume, liquor in a privy, lavatory, or toilet." It is testament to the fine drafters of this that they needed to clearly elaborate to ensure that the prohibition applies each to the privies, the lavatories and the toilets of Manitoba. Note also that this is may well include the privies in each home. One wonders about the grave threat posed by having a beer in the shower that required such legislation. Does a sauna qualify?

Some Canadian communities go so far as prohibit that experience altogether through banning the sale of the drink. Manitoba and some other Canadian provinces still allow for dry towns through the passing of local by-laws prohibiting beer sales. It is interesting to note, however, that this does not bar homebrewing or consumption, just the sale of strong drink through licensed establishments. And people are not barred from buying alcohol in the next wet town and bringing it home. They are just barred from having any bars and shops, notorious public places of beer consumption.

All these various forms of regulation layer upon the others described above to infuse the marketplace with various degrees of controlled communication. They go beyond informing the public about beer as each example of law also conveys a message about freedom of choice. Through pervasive control of how beer is described and displayed and even made available, the law tells us about the place of beer and teaches us that we are to keep it in its place. In doing so it also teaches that we are also to learn our place. And that is to listen to the law.

Wholesale and Retail: Taxes, Fees and Price

All this control serves one particular end: the almighty bottom line. The federal and each of the provincial governments not only tax beer heavily but also generate fees through the monopolistic control of stages of the beer trade. These fees and taxes artificially inflate the price paid for beer which usually dwarfs the actual costs of production. Some of the taxes imposed on beer in Canada include:

119

- general provincial sales tax of up to 10%
- general federal sales tax of 6%
- specific provincial tax (Saskatchewan has a special 10% tax on beer)
- federal excise tax of $15.61 per 1,000 liters of beer.

In addition to imposing taxes, provinces also control the wholesale and retail trade in beer through not only regulating it but also participating in it through government-controlled monopolies and licenses. Manitoba's law, for example, provides that a retail license for a beer vendor or a brewer's retail store authorizes the licensee to purchase beer from "the commission" only. Needless to say, buying through only one legal wholesaler is not likely to create the cheapest mechanism for whole-sale and interferes with the marketplace in that it bars craft brewers from selling. In 2003, Alberta's wholesaling commission marked up a liter of beer from a large manufacturer 98 cents, a fee which made up 15 to 20% of the total final retail price. On top of mark-up, brewers also face a listing fee to place the product on the monopoly's shelf.

And it does not stop there. The monopolistic commissions cannot be satisfied with just collecting taxes, charging wholesale fees and making retail profits. Some take it upon themselves to exercise their extraordinary power to alter the basic rules of free bargaining. For example, through its Supplier's Best Price policy the LCBO prohibits the sale of beer to itself at a price higher than that charged to any other provincial commission. If this happens, the LCBO demands the difference back. If a brewer does not pay it, its products may get struck. As a result, brewers are no longer free to bargain as they wish.

The result is artificially inflated prices for beer. This clearly is an imposition on purchasers, placing the cost of beer well in excess of a price that reflects its production for purposes apparently tied to ensuring government revenue. Yet it is still not the end of the matter. Prices have to also be kept above a certain level. Ontario has granted to the commission the power to create a fixed minimum price for beer and, in New Brunswick, minimum prices are set out directly in the regulations:

> No licensee and no employee or agent of a licensee shall sell or offer to sell draught beer at a price that is less than $0.11 per ounce or per 29.57 ml, tax inclusive.

In fact, New Brunswick even controls the gifting of beer, restricting the gifts of beer to customers to one 12 ounce serving of draught beer per day or one 12 ounce bottle of beer per day. Undoubtedly pure menace would be released upon society were a patron to receive a second glass of free beer. New Brunswick not only discourages this sort of free beer, but, in a display of regulatory schizophrenia, encourages it too through the very active giving of beer to those persons who are employed by the brewer or who comprise a social, professional, educational, occupational or athletic organization. In that case, the brewer may give an amount that is "reasonable" for consumption on the brewer's premises or in the form of vouchers. These powers granted to brewers, however, are clearly to create brand loyalty through generous sharing of locally produced free beer.

The most extreme characterization of relationship between the government and beer is found in the Liquor Distribution Act of British Columbia which has a section entitled "Government Acquires Title To Liquor." Under this provision, the province controls beer and other alcohols not only through taxation and other market impediments but through actually deeming all such beverages its own. It is clear that there is an exception for homebrewers to possess the beer they make but it is not clear that such possession actually equates with full ownership by the homebrewer of the beer he makes.

These examples illustrate how the liquor control commissions and the legislatures work together to assert complete financial control in relation to the market for beer. By doing so, the taxes and the price upon which they are based are maintained at an artificially high level without granting consumers recourse to the general marketplace and the consequent competition which would allow prices to reach their natural resting point. Combined with the general restriction on the trade in home brew and other restrictions on travel with and communication about beer, it is clear that we have an economic relationship with beer unlike any other class of normally acquired consumable product, and that relation is at odds with the vision of a robust democracy filled with citizens making autonomous decisions over matters of personal importance as selected by those citizens.

Conclusion

When we understand the Canadian law of beer, it is clear that our freedom to participate in that marketplace has become as tightly regulated as any part of society. The autonomous relationship we beer-loving citizens have with our brewing, our brewers and our beer is imposed upon and, as a result, so is the exercise of our right to communicate, associate, express and otherwise experience life in self-determined dignity.

These regulations impose pervasive state control and thereby undermine the commercial marketplace as well as the marketplace of ideas. Our autonomy in these areas is key to living in a free and democratic society as we Canadians are each defined more and more as consumers rather than citizens. Our exercise of freedom is tied up with our participation in the marketplace. And that marketplace largely consists of state-run monopolies.

That is very much at odds with the freedoms we assume are at the heart of our right to life, liberty and security of the person as provided for under section 7 of the *Charter of Rights and Freedoms*. Some provinces go even further, impinging upon rights which are fundamental to our relation with the state. For example, New Brunswick creates a reverse onus, overturning the key presumption of a person being innocent before the law until proven guilty:

> The burden of proving the right to have or keep or sell or give or purchase or consume liquor shall be on the person accused of improperly or unlawfully having or keeping or selling or giving or purchasing or consuming the liquor.

One might question the vision the state has of its own citizenry. The law of beer is used to redefine the marketplace, control communication, restrict mobility, and even dispossess the population in its relation to the otherwise commonplace product that is beer. And to what end? In large part it would appear only to sustain government control and the source of revenue it represents.

9

Another Pitcher? On Beer, Friendship, and Character

Jason Kawall

For no one would choose to live without friends, even if he had all other goods.
>Aristotle, *Nicomachean Ethics*

The end of drinking is to nourish and increase friendship.
>Plutarch, *De Moralia*, "The Banquet of the Seven Wise Men"

Most all of my good friends enjoy a drink or two. And of these, most all enjoy having a couple of beers in particular. To the extent that you are reading this book, the same may well be true of you, too. So should this be troubling to us? That is, is there something shallow or problematic in having friendships where a common joint activity is sitting down to share a pitcher? Do we have mere "beer buddies"? I will argue that, on the contrary, by appealing to widely accepted philosophical accounts of the nature and value of friendship we will find that such friendships will tend to be especially close and valuable.

It will help to begin with at least a rough characterization of friendship; we can use an account given by Bennett Helm:

> Friendship, as understood here, is a distinctively personal relationship that is grounded in a concern on the part of each friend for the welfare for the other, for the other's sake, and that involves some degree of intimacy.[1]

---

[1] B. Helm, Friendship. In E. N. Zalta, ed., *The Stanford Encyclopedia of Philosophy (Summer Edition)*, 2005, http://plato.stanford.edu/archives/sum2005/entries/friendship/.

123

We take friendships to be an important, indeed crucial part of a good life – as Aristotle suggests in the first epigraph to this piece, we would never choose to live without friends. A life without friends would be a terribly impoverished and cold existence. So what makes a friendship a close friendship, and why are close friendships so valuable to us?

The Pleasure and Utility of Friendship

We can begin with an obvious point, but one well worth stressing – we enjoy being with our friends, and we also enjoy drinking decent beer. The combination of the two would then seem likely to be enjoyable and valuable as such. We can consider this a bit further. Why exactly do we enjoy being with friends? At the very least, being with friends allows us to engage in pleasant activities we could not otherwise; we can play solitaire on our own, but it helps to have friends to play poker or to shoot pool. We can tell jokes, share stories, have a sympathetic ear to hear our woes, and so on. As to the beer – there is the hoppiness of a good IPA, the bright crispness of a pilsner, and so on. And of course there is alcohol in beer, and this certainly produces pleasant sensations (putting aside the abomination of so-called non-alcoholic "beers").

Still, recall that some might find friendships which involve time spent drinking beer together shallow. And we can now consider a possible source of the worry. If we are focused solely on pleasure – particularly the pleasure of drinking beer – then it seems that the supposed friendship is quite shallow. We could just drink with anyone. If so, there is no real friendship present, just an excuse to drink beer.

Here it will be useful to draw on one of Aristotle's insights into the nature and value of friendship. Aristotle distinguishes three kinds of friendship: those of pleasure, those of utility, and those of character. He describes the first two as follows:

> Those who love each other for utility love the other not in himself, but insofar as they gain some good for themselves from him. The same is true of those who love for pleasure; for they like a witty person not because of his character, but because he is pleasant to themselves.[2]

---

[2] Aristotle, *Nicomachean Ethics*. Translated by T. Irwin. Indianapolis: Hackett, 1985, VIII 3, 1156a11–14.

Thus it might seem that friendships where we often share a beer are mere friendships of pleasure, with no real concern for the other person. We can imagine the case of a barfly who sits with another simply as he finds the other one amusing. There is not a true concern for the well-being of the other for his own sake; rather, the barfly merely takes some pleasure in the antics of the other. And on the other hand, there might also be a worry that friendships where the friends frequently meet up for a beer are mere friendships of utility. We can imagine young students who spend time with an older student, not out of any particular enjoyment they take in this person's company, but merely because this person is old enough to buy alcohol for them. Or a person may be embarrassed to drink on her own – having someone to sit around and share a beer with may make her feel better. I think we can properly agree with Aristotle that these friendships of pleasure or utility are incomplete and hardly what we would hope for in a friendship. There is no real concern for the other for her own sake, and such "friendships" would seem to dissolve easily – as when the barfly no longer finds his companion amusing, or when the young students no longer need their older "friend" to buy beer for them.

But we need not endorse such friendships. We can begin to see our way past such cases if we focus instead on friends who do other things together (and enjoy doing them together), besides sitting down to a beer. If two supposed friends do nothing but meet to drink beer, we have good reason to suspect their friendship is defective. But if it is simply one aspect of a much broader, richer friendship with other shared activities and a genuine respect and concern for each other, these worries should be allayed; we would have a friendship of character. And note that the worry is not unique to those who enjoy having a beer together – suppose we have people who only ever meet to play golf, and do nothing together outside of this. We could well wonder about the value of such a supposed friendship. We certainly have grounds to suspect that it is a mere friendship of pleasure, or more strongly, that even the term "friendship" is too generous insofar as the participants are really only deriving pleasure from the game of golf, and not from each other's company.

Still, I have claimed that friendships might be particularly close and valuable where a common activity is sharing a couple of pints, while all that has actually been shown so far is that they are not necessarily defective – and there is a significant gap between not being defective and being especially valuable.

Consider the following attempt at showing a particular value to our beer-inclusive friendships: we might now plausibly claim that there is significant pleasure in spending time with friends, and in having a beer, and that the combination may be even more enjoyable than the sum of the individual activities. Suppose drinking a beer provides 5 units of happiness (whatever these amount to), while spending time with a friend provides 10 units of happiness. The proposal is that sharing a beer with a friend might produce 20 units of happiness (say), rather than just 15. The conversation with the friend flows that much more freely; you can share observations about the beer you are drinking, and so on – in these ways, the combination of time spent with friends and sharing a beer would have value greater than each of these activities taken individually; the whole could be more enjoyable and valuable than the sum of its parts. If so, such friendships may be particularly valuable for the greater amount of happiness they produce. This is plausible enough, as far as it goes, but then again this might be true of any combination of participating in any pleasurable activity with friends – golfing with friends could produce more happiness than the sum of the happiness produced by time spent with friends or time spent golfing taken individually. All friendships which include combinations of pleasurable activities shared with friends would end up creating substantial amounts of pleasure; we would not yet have distinguished beer-inclusive friendships. So where might we find an especial value in friendships in which we enjoy sharing a few beers together?

Self-Disclosure and Shared Insight

Another commonly recognized aspect of true friendships is that they involve some form of self-disclosure; we share aspects of ourselves which reveal more of our character and lives to our friends – and in turn, our friends disclose aspects of themselves to us. We come to know our friends much more fully than mere acquaintances – and they come to know us.

Why would such self-disclosure be valuable? First of all, by sharing aspects of ourselves with our friends they can better understand us, which in turn means they will be able to provide better advice to us, and perhaps better sympathize. As our friends come to know us, they may even be able to fill in blanks in our own self-understanding. They

126

might notice patterns in our behavior that we have overlooked ourselves, identify an issue for us that we have not suspected, or notice a virtue that we may not have recognized in ourselves. This can lead to improved choices in the future, and a more accurate self-image. Beyond this, we might even change our self-conception, goals, and aspirations in light of the interpretations we receive from our friends. Our friends can help to create who we are. In a similar vein, we might draw on Aristotle's claim that a friend can serve as something of a mirror for us – that we can see some of our own traits in our friends, and learn about ourselves in this way.

Second, we have the other side of this equation. We will also learn more about our friends – we will notice aspects of themselves and their lives that they might not have recognized; we will be better able to provide advice if they seek it from us insofar as we have more information. They may come to learn about themselves through their knowledge of us, given our similarities. As such, by engaging in such mutual self-disclosure, we will be better friends to our friends.

Third, we as a species commonly desire to share the events in our lives with those whom we trust. When we get good news we look forward to telling friends; similarly, it can help us to talk through difficulties with friends – we feel a burden is at least partially shared, even if a friend cannot help us in a particular case. As Simon Keller suggests,

> To share your thoughts and interests with a friend, and to take an active interest in hers, is to escape a little from your individuality, to reduce the intensity of being you; that, in part, is why it is good to share. To have a supportive friend is, or can be, to have someone who sees value in your projects and commitments, even when you – weary or self-doubting – do not.[3]

There is additional happiness in sharing good news, and at least some lessening of our suffering as we turn to our supportive friends in difficult circumstances.

How might meeting for the occasional Guinness – or Upper Canada Lager, for that matter – fit into all of this? Crucially, it is a practice or ritual that encourages self-disclosure and reflection. We could say that drinking a beer together is not merely drinking a beer together: it is

---

3   S. Keller, Friendship and belief. *Philosophical Papers*, 2004, 33, 329–51; passage from
    p. 343.

talking, planning, reminiscing, joking, advising, encouraging, and so on. It is a much richer overall ritual, in the same way that for many people a morning cup of coffee is not merely a method of obtaining caffeine – it is the smell of the coffee, time spent reading the newspaper, and so on. To ask someone to meet for a beer is a friendly gesture in our culture; to share a beer is to be in a social space with a certain openness – an openness that expands further with our good friends. So it is here that we begin to see the especial value of beer-inclusive friendships. They include a regular practice which encourages openness and extended conversation, a practice that will improve and deepen a friendship.

But why not just meet for a coffee instead? Clearly a friendship can gain many of the same benefits through meeting for coffee as through meeting for beer; there is no need to suggest that *only* sharing a beer together can provide space for conservation, self-disclosure, and reflection. Still, the ritual of meeting for a beer has aspects which make it particularly conducive to self-disclosure and reflection, particularly compared to meeting for a coffee. To begin with, meeting for a beer most frequently occurs in the evening, when work is done, and the participants are relaxed. It generally marks the end of the day, a relaxed and open space. Meeting for a coffee is somewhat more formal, and less open; we might need to return to work after a coffee; it is a common choice if we are meeting a person for the first time (particularly in a formal context). Meeting for a beer is a more friendly gesture, creating a different social space than meeting for a coffee. For example, many professors will often meet with students for a coffee; the same is not true of beer. This reflects the differences in the social spaces created by these activities.

We can also consider here a view that is commonly held, but which ought to be rejected. This is the view that when we interact with someone who has had a few pints we are seeing this person's "true self." The idea is that when a person is drinking we get a glimpse into her *real* personality, and that her true character shines through (and that this is perhaps hidden in other circumstances). If the person becomes more talkative, or raucous, or what-have-you, the true self view would claim that this is the person's true character emerging. Ultimately this is a mistaken view; we come to know our friends better while sharing a pitcher because more information is shared, but we need not see this as a result of us interacting with the friend's true self. To see the implausibility of the true self view, consider the following. There is a way a given person will act if she has not been able to sleep for 48 hours; there is a way she will act if given a hallucinogen; there is a way she will act if she has had 12 cups of coffee and recently received bad news; there is a way she will act if she has taken too much cold medication. Why is it that having a few beers would reveal the true self of the person, rather than any of these other circumstances? Why would it be privileged? It is much more plausible to hold that different aspects of our character would be exhibited under all of these different circumstances, but that none of them should be taken to be our true self, as somehow more fundamental to us than other aspects of our character. We may disclose more to our friends while sharing a beer, and in this sense, our friends may get a better sense of who we are – but this is quite different from holding that our friends get a better sense of who we are because they are somehow witnessing our true self. Finally, to see the strangeness of the true self view, consider that as a person drinks, her ability to drive and perform other activities becomes impaired. But would we really want to say that a person who drives very well when sober is ultimately, truly a bad driver, because if she has a few drinks her driving becomes so much worse? Surely this would be absurd, and illustrates the overall weakness of the suggestion that we see a person's true nature when she has had a few pints.

Shared Activity

Friends enjoy spending time together, and seek out opportunities to share activities. To the extent that we are far from a friend, or unable to spend time together, our friendship may suffer over time. At the very least, we would be happier if we could spend more time with our friend, and there is a risk of drifting apart (particularly as we are not together, and so do not influence and shape each other as we would otherwise).

When we meet our friends for a beer, we reinforce the friendship with shared activity. Again this is not unique to meeting for a beer – there are many activities in which people can participate and share time with friends. Still, when we share a couple of pints, we are typically engaged in a relaxed activity that allows time for reflection and conversation that can deepen the bonds of friendship. Sitting out on a porch with a few friends and a few beers as the sun goes down;

bundling up on a cold winter's night and meeting with a friend for a stout at the local tavern. These shared activities are pleasant in themselves, but also provide a space for joking around, catching-up on the events in each other's lives, and so on. Of course, friends will often watch a game at the bar with friends, or just sitting around someone's living room. There is value in appreciating a good beer in itself as an activity. The point here is that these shared activities as *shared* activities will deepen a friendship; and there is typically value in participating in these activities in themselves.

Narrative Content and Shared Stories

Now it sometimes happens that what was meant to be a couple of pints with friends turns into a couple more, and then a couple more, and eventually some rather interesting behavior may ensue . . . So, what should we say about those occasions where we have a few beers too many with friends – how should we understand their role in a friendship?

A plausible suggestion is that such occasions will often serve to provide shared stories that will further reinforce the bond between friends. Unusual, funny events – including amusing acts performed while a bit drunk – can punctuate a friendship, giving us touchstones to refer back to, the possibility of inside jokes, and so on. These can be events that friends will look back on and still laugh about years later. These sorts of episodes may be particularly valuable insofar as they are particularly memorable, and the friends involved will all tend to remember them; with other, less striking events, it is more unlikely that all of the friends will remember. Occasional episodes of beer-assisted silliness stand out, and the resulting shared stories can serve to unify a group of friends, and later bring smiles to their faces when they reminisce. The felt bond of the friendship will be strengthened.[4]

---

[4] In the background of this discussion there are legitimate concerns about truly unfortunate events happening. I will rely on the reader's good common sense to sort out what is appropriate and what is not. A person who is constantly drinking to excess, drinking and driving, or whose drinking is otherwise adversely affecting her life or the lives of those around her presumably has a drinking problem; this, of course, is not what is being endorsed.

Trust and Loyalty

Over time, through ongoing shared, enjoyable activities, and mutual self-disclosure, a friendship will deepen with respect to trust and loyalty. Of course, a gradual process may not be necessary for significant trust and loyalty to develop; people who share a particularly dangerous or otherwise significant experience might quickly develop a bond (think of soldiers thrown into battle – they may quickly develop a certain trust in each other). We can understand trust and loyalty as complimentary virtues – I can trust you because you are loyal to me, and you can trust me because I am loyal to you.

Why is trust, in particular, valuable? First, we can discuss matters of importance to us with a friend without fear of gossip, and without fear that the friend will use what we say against us. In a trusted and trustworthy friend we have a sounding board for our ideas, hopes, worries, and so forth.

Second, and relatedly, as our trust grows, we may also properly come to place greater trust in the interpretations of ourselves and the advice given by our friends. That is, we may come to trust the judgment of the friend – particularly with respect to her beliefs about us. As a result, we can feel more confident in taking her advice to heart. If you barely know someone, and she barely knows you, and you have no track record of how her advice comes out, you have little initial reason to trust her advice (beyond a basic trust we might have in all other competent adult humans). But with time and experience gained through a friendship, trust is developed.

Third, we can also come to trust our friends in the sense of relying on them to perform certain actions. Through their loyalty, you might expect that friends would help you with some task where you need a second set of hands; they might look after your place while you are traveling, and so on. You can also trust them to not perform certain actions – to not use various discussions against you, to not share personal information with others. When we share a beer we gain the benefits of mutual self-disclosure discussed above; but notice that in doing so we are also thereby creating further trust in each other. This, in turn, will allow for further actions grounded in and reflecting this trust.

We can now consider a final variation of the worry that beer-inclusive friendships are somehow shallow. The worry now is that any trust and loyalty developed while sharing a few pints would be false – that we would have merely chemically-driven, shallow imitations of genuine trust and loyalty. We might disclose more to others, and be more trusting when we share a pitcher, but this is simply due to the alcohol involved; it is not due to a genuine trust in our friends. And if this is correct, we would have reason to see beer-inclusive friendships as shallow and defective in their lack of genuine trust and loyalty.

Several points should be raised in response. To begin, even if a friend's sharing of information in a given case is in part a product of having had a few pints, this information will be incorporated into the friendship as a whole. That is, the information shared is not isolated – it will be there for the relationship in days, weeks, and years to come. The other friend can draw upon this information in giving advice, coming to understand and interpret her friend, and so forth (whether while sharing a beer or not). As such there is little basis for considering the trust that is ultimately generated to be false or non-genuine.

Beyond this, we make choices in what information we will disclose about ourselves in a conversation while sharing a beer or two. Merely having a beer does not turn a person into a blathering twit who will share any and all facts about herself with just any random stranger who happens to be present. True, if a person drinks a great deal she may be less inhibited in self-disclosure, but even here control can and typically will be exerted. More broadly, it is also important to keep in mind the broader ritual of sharing a pitcher. There is a difference between merely sitting next to a stranger who also happens to be having a beer, and meeting with a friend for a pint. The latter again involves a different social space, one which encourages openness and reflection. We should be careful not to overstate the role of alcohol here – it may influence a person, but this person still chooses what she wishes to disclose, and prior to that she chooses whether she would even like to have a beer with the other person. A major influence on what she will disclose is the company she is with, and the antecedent trust or friendliness she feels towards those with whom she is sharing a beer.

Finally, even to the extent that alcohol does play a role in self-disclosure and conversation, we need not see this as especially worrying. A comparison with love and attraction will be helpful here. Psychologists have discovered that people will often attribute the physiological excitement caused by (for example) a frightening movie or rollercoaster with a date or other individual. That is, they will experience excitement, with their hearts pounding due to the rollercoaster, but they will subconsciously associate these feelings of arousal with the other person, and they will feel more attracted to this person as a result. Or consider that the hormone oxytocin, associated with trust and bonding in mammals (including humans) is released during sexual activity. Similarly, there has been much discussion of the impact of pheromones on attraction.

One could claim that any feelings of attraction or bonding influenced by such factors are somehow false and problematic precisely due to these influences. But consider this more closely. Should we instead only interact with people in bare concrete rooms with a single light-bulb hanging down so as to avoid any outside influences on the relationship? Gas masks and strong ventilation would presumably also be necessary to avoid the impact of pheromones. Should we attempt to find methods to overcome the effects of dopamine, oxytocin, vasopressin and other hormones or neurotransmitters in the formation of monogamous bonds (so that our bonds are "genuine" and not influenced by brain chemistry)? Surely these proposals should strike us as absurd; indeed it is unclear that love could even exist in humans without the work done by dopamine and other neurotransmitters.

More broadly, our brains are chemical engines – there is no avoiding this – and what we eat and drink and a thousand other factors can influence them. But this does not reduce the value of our emotions or bonds. Regardless of the underlying chemical mechanisms, being in love still feels wonderful; being dumped much less so . . . That we are embodied creatures, and that our bodies play a key role in shaping who we are, how we act, and how we feel, is not something to be regretted or something we must overcome. Rather, we can embrace our embodiment as part of our nature and constitution as human beings. The external influence of exciting events can help us to fall and stay in love; the internal influence of a few beers can make us more open in conversation with our friends. When we share a few pints together our brain chemistry is influenced, but this is simply an aspect of human nature which, over time, has been incorporated into a rich ritual and open social space. Humans have been drinking together for thousands (if not tens of thousands) of years. This is who we are; there is no need to see such influences, and the trust to which they contribute, as foreign or false.

133

Jason Kawall

Summary

We are now in a much better position to assess the value of our beer-inclusive friendships. We have good reason to expect them to be particularly strong, close friendships insofar as they incorporate an enjoyable activity which encourages self-disclosure, further shared activities, unusual narrative content (i.e. shared stories), and trust. In participating in the practice of sharing a few pints together we place ourselves in an especially open social space with our friends, a practice that has been with us for centuries. Far from being shallow, those friendships which incorporate this practice may well be those that carry us through a lifetime.[5]

[5] Ultimately, I would like to thank everyone with whom I've bent the elbow over the years. But in particular I would like to thank those with whom I've discussed this paper: Colleen Baish, Lesleigh Cushing-Stahlberg (who insists on telling me just how important she thinks this paper is), Fitzsimmon Fuddnudler, Steve Hales, Christine Miller Kelly, Spencer Kelly, Jay Newhard, and Ben Stahlberg. A version of this paper was read at Bloomsburg University in April 2006; I would like to thank the students and faculty (especially Gary Hardcastle, Wendy Lee, Scott Lowe, and Kurt Smith) for their helpful comments.

134

Part III

The Metaphysics and Epistemology of Beer

10

Beer and Gnosis
The Mead of Inspiration

Theodore Schick

To the modern mind, beer is the most plebeian of alcoholic beverages; the balm of the workingman; the delight of fraternity brothers. To the ancients however, beer was a gift from the gods; a sacred libation; a holy elixir. As Stephen Harrod Buhner reveals in his book *Sacred and Herbal Healing Beers*, "In all cases where oral accounts still exist, the knowledge of fermentation was a gift of the gods, of the sacred, to humankind."[1] But not only did the ancients believe that beer was a gift from the gods; they believed that drinking it made them like gods, giving them a knowledge normally reserved only for divinities. Robert Gayre, for example, reports that mead, the honey-based brew of yore, is "the giver of knowledge and poetry, the healer of wounds, and bestower of immortality."[2] The Norse saga, the *Poetic Edda*, refers to this brew as "the mead of inspiration."

There is no question that beer is psychoactive because ingesting it alters our state of consciousness. But is it also revelatory? Does it give us a special sort of knowledge? The great American philosopher and psychologist William James thought so. Alcohol, he writes:

> brings its votary from the chill periphery of things to the radiant core. It makes [the drinker] for the moment one with the truth. Not through mere perversity do men run after it. To the poor and unlettered it stands in the place of symphony concerts and of literature; and it is part of the

---

[1] S. H. Buhner, *Sacred and Herbal Healing Beers*. Boulder, CO: Brewer's Publications, 1998, 72.

[2] R. Gayre, *Brewing Mead*. Boulder, CO: Brewer's Publications, 1986. Quoted in Buhner, *Sacred and Herbal Healing Beers*, 19.

deeper mystery and tragedy of life that whiffs and gleams of something that we immediately recognize as excellent should be vouchsafed to so many of us only in the fleeting earlier phases of what in its totality is so degrading a poisoning.[3]

Far from distorting our view of reality, James claims that drinking beer puts us in closer touch with it. To determine whether James is correct in his assessment, we'll have to examine the knowledge-giving power of beer in more detail.

The Blood of the Gods

So important was the knowledge of fermentation that many societies developed elaborate myths to commemorate its discovery. The story told in the *Poetic Edda* is one such. It seems that Odin's arrival is Aasgaard occasioned a war between the gods loyal to him – the Aesir – and those indigenous to the city – the Vanir. Neither was able to gain the upper hand, however, so they agreed to a truce which was cemented by both groups spitting into a bowl. From the contents of the bowl they created a new god – Kvasir – who traveled the world dispensing wisdom. Two dwarves who were envious of his knowledge invited Kvasir to their home and killed him. The dwarves drained Kvasir's blood into two jars and a kettle, mixed it with honey, and let it ferment, creating *Kvas* – the mead of inspiration. The dwarves later gave their store of Kvas to the giant Suttung in compensation for killing his mother and father. Sutting in turn gave it to his daughter Gunnlod for safe keeping.

Now Odin fervently desired the knowledge contained in Kvas, and after much machination was able to enter the cave where it was kept by turning himself into a snake and slithering through a hole made by Suttung's brother. Gunnlod was willing to give him a drink as long as he was willing to give her something in return – a night of lovemaking. Odin agreed and fulfilled his part of the bargain with gusto. After the first night, he downed an entire jar of Kvas. This only made him want more, so Gunnlod agreed to let him have another drink in exchange

[3] William James, *The Varieties of Religious Experience*. New York: New American Library, 1958, 297.

for another night of lovemaking. Odin was happy to oblige. After the second night, he consumed another jar of Kvas. His thirst for Kvas still unslaked, Odin asked Gunnlod to renew their bargain yet again, and she consented.

After Odin consumed all of the Kvas, he turned into an eagle and flew to Aasgaard as fast as he could. Sutting saw him leave the cave and gave chase, also assuming the form of an eagle. The Aesir became aware of the chase and created a fire just inside the walls of Aasgaard. Suttung flew into it, caught on fire, and burned to death. Odin in the meantime regurgitated all of the Kvas he had consumed into jars created by the Aesir. But some spilled on the ground, was discovered by men, and became the mead of inspiration. To drink this brew, the *Poetic Edda* suggests, is to drink the blood of the gods. And to drink the blood of the gods is to become like the gods.

Many indigenous cultures believe that to consume beer is to ingest something sacred. This view stems not only from the belief that certain ingredients of beer are associated with gods, but also that the ingredients themselves possess souls. Michael Aasved informs us that, "When the spirits of these plants are personified by a patron deity, the beverage becomes the blood or milk of that god or goddess which embodies all the life-giving virtues of the sacred substance."[4] For example, in South America, many different cultures use the manioc root to make a beer called "masato." According to one legend, the manioc plant sprang from the grave of the sacred child, Mani. According to another, Manioc, the daughter of the earth-mother Nungai, taught them how to grow manioc. For both of these cultures,

> Making and drinking the manioc beer is a re-creation of the sacred giving of the beer to humankind . . . When they take beer into their bodies, they also take into themselves the "house of transformation of Mani" and thus partake of her essence directly.[5]

For these people, drinking beer is a way of communing with god.

This communion, however, is often thought to give one knowledge of sacred realms. The African tribe known as the Twi, for example,

---

[4] M. Aasved, Alcohol, Drinking, and Intoxication in Preindustrial Society: Theoretical, Nutritional, and Religious Considerations. PhD dissertation, University of California, Santa Barbara, 1988, 781–2.

[5] Buhner, *Sacred and Herbal Healing Beers*, 116.

considers their palm beer to be an invaluable source of knowledge of the supernatural. Buhner explains:

> Tribal spirituality is concerned with understanding and learning to affect the non-material world, for it is recognized that material reality alone cannot explain the totality of human life. To affect the unseen, non-material world, power must be accumulated. Gaining such power involves an understanding of cosmology, the forces that affect the outcomes in the material world, and a knowledge of how to affect them. Alcohol enables the elders to temporarily access the spirit realm and communicate with the ancestors, who in turn speak to the gods on their behalf.[6]

The Twi believe that their palm beer gives them knowledge of a supersensible reality. Because this non-material reality directly affects the material world, knowledge of it is a valuable source of power.

The notion that altered states of consciousness give us access to realms that are normally beyond our ken is not one that is only found in primitive cultures. William James, for example, holds this view. He writes:

> our normal waking consciousness as we call it, is but one special type of consciousness, whilst all about it, parted from it by the filmiest of screens there lie potential forms of consciousness entirely different. We may go through life without suspecting their existence; but apply the requisite stimulus, and at a touch they are there in all their completeness, definite types of mentality which probably somewhere have their field of application and adaptation. No account of the universe in its totality can be final which leaves these other forms of consciousness quite disregarded. How to regard them is the question, . . . for they are so discontinuous with ordinary consciousness. Yet they may determine attitudes though they cannot furnish formulas, and open a region though they fail to give a map. At any rate, they forbid a premature closing of our accounts with reality.[7]

The dominant theory of knowledge in the West is known as "empiricism." It holds that sense experience is the only source of knowledge. But it doesn't indicate what state of consciousness we must be in to acquire knowledge. Ordinary waking consciousness may not be the

---

6   Ibid., 131.
7   James, *The Varieties of Religious Experience*, 298.

only state of consciousness that puts us in touch with reality. As James indicates, "For aught we know to the contrary, 103 or 104 degrees Fahrenheit might be a much more favorable temperature for truths to germinate and sprout in, than the more ordinary blood-heat of 97 or 98 degrees."[8] James's point is that since body chemistry plays a role in the production of all of our beliefs, we can't reject a belief simply because it can be shown to have an organic cause. If we did, "none of our thoughts and feelings, not even our scientific doctrines, not even our disbeliefs, could retain any value as revelations of the truth, for every one of them without exception flows from the state of their possessor's body at the time."[9] Therefore the fact that an experience is produced by a certain physiological state, can't, by itself, show that it's erroneous.

The English philosopher, C. D. Broad, agrees that altered states of consciousness may give us insight into hidden aspects of reality.

> Suppose, for the sake of argument, that there is an aspect of the world which remains altogether outside the ken of ordinary persons in their daily life. Then it seems very likely that some degree of mental and physical abnormality would be a necessary condition for getting loosened from the objects of ordinary sense perception to come into contact with this aspect of reality . . . One might have to be slightly "cracked" in order to have some peep-holes into the super-sensible world.[10]

If there are aspects of reality that are normally hidden from us, altered states of consciousness may give us access to them. To escape the confines of straight thinking we may have to get bent.

Author and activist Aldous Huxley agrees with James and Broad that altered states of consciousness may be a source of knowledge. He came to this conclusion, however, not by drinking beer, but by taking mescaline. Huxley was invited by a psychologist friend to take mescaline in a controlled laboratory setting. He chronicles his experiences in the book, *The Doors of Perception*. The title of his book is taken from a line by the poet William Blake: "If the doors of perception were cleansed, every thing would appear to man as it is, infinite." The rock

---

[8] Ibid., 30.

[9] Ibid.

[10] C. D. Broad, *Religion, Philosophy, and Psychical Research*. New York: Harcourt Brace, 1953, 198.

group, The Doors, allegedly took their name from the title of Huxley's book. Here's Huxley's theory of how minds are affected by drugs:

> Reflecting on my experience, I find myself agreeing with the eminent Cambridge philosopher, Dr C. D. Broad, "that we should do well to consider much more seriously than we have hitherto been inclined to do the type of theory which Bergson put forward in connection with memory and sense perception. The suggestion is that the function of the brain and nervous system and sense organs is in the main eliminative and not productive . . . The function of the brain and nervous system is to protect us from being overwhelmed and confused by this mass of largely useless and irrelevant knowledge, by shutting out most of what we should otherwise perceive or remember at any moment, and leaving only that very small and special selection which is likely to be practically useful . . ." To make biological survival possible, Mind at Large has to be funneled through the reducing valve of the brain and nervous system. What comes out at the other end is a measly trickle of the kind of consciousness which will help us to stay alive on the surface of this particular planet.[11]

James likens getting into an altered state of consciousness to lifting a veil. Huxley likens it to opening a valve. The function of our ordinary waking consciousness, he claims, is to reduce the amount of information we receive to a manageable level. Altered states open the reducing valve of consciousness and let in more of what's out there. Huxley apparently believes that the visions he had under the influence of mescaline were not, strictly speaking, hallucinations. Rather they were experiences of other aspects of reality normally filtered out by our waking consciousness.

Gruit: the Psychedelic Brew

Beer doesn't usually produce the sorts of visions that mescaline does. Perhaps it doesn't open the reducing valve quite as wide. However, beer hasn't always been as psychologically tame as it is today. Up until the fifteenth century, European beers contained all sorts of psychoactive herbs such as gale, yarrow, rosemary, wormwood, juniper berries, ginger, nutmeg, and cinnamon. Known as "gruit ales" or "gruit" for

---

[11] A. Huxley, *The Doors of Perception*. New York: Harper and Row, 1954, 22–4.

short, these brews were "highly intoxicating – narcotic, aphrodisiacal, and psychotropic when consumed in sufficient quantity."[12] They now are very difficult to come by.

Gruit was the beer of choice in Europe for over 1,000 years. It began to be replaced by hopped ale – what we now call beer – in the fifteenth century; not because hops were discovered to be a superior preservative, but because gruit production was strictly controlled by the Catholic Church. In many parts of Europe, gruit brewers had to buy their herbs from officially licensed monastic houses, giving the Church a virtual monopoly on the production of beer. Hops were not part of the gruit mix, so those producing hopped ale did not have to pay the gruit tax.

Hops are much less psychoactive than the herbs used in gruit. According to Buhner,

> hops possesses two characteristics notably different from the herbs they replaced. They cause the drinker to become drowsy and they diminish sexual desire – quite the opposite of the other herbs used in beer and especially those used in gruit production.[13]

Because hops contain chemicals similar in structure to the female hormone estrogen, excessive exposure to it can lead to a condition known as "brewers' droop" which results in the inability to maintain an erection.

Some believe that the fall of gruit was closely related to the Protestant reformation. In the fourteenth and fifteenth centuries, many Europeans began to look askance at the lavish and hedonistic lifestyle of many church leaders. Their promotion of the highly inebriating gruit was emblematic of their decadence. So the production and consumption of hopped ale not only undercut the Church's financial power, it also served as a protest against its depravity. As Buhner reports: "The historical record is clear that hops' supplanting of other herbs was primarily a reflection of Protestant irritation about "drugs" and the Catholic Church, in concert with competing merchants trying to break a monopoly and so increase their profits."[14] So the movement toward hopped ale was in part an anti-drug movement. The passage of the

[12] Buhner, *Sacred and Herbal Healing Beers*, 169.
[13] Ibid., 172.
[14] Ibid., 173.

German beer purity laws in 1516 which mandated the use of hops was a form of prohibition not unlike that passed by the US Congress in 1919.

Through Beer Goggles Darkly

Gruit may well have produced many more visions than the hopped ale we're familiar with. James, Broad, and Huxley would have us believe that these visions could be just as true as our ordinary experiences. If they are, however, they must pass the same sorts of tests that ordinary experiences do.

Even though James was open to the possibility that altered states of consciousness provide insight into the nature of reality, he was well aware that being in such a state did not guarantee the veracity of the perceptions produced. "To come from [an altered state] is no infallible credential. What comes must be sifted and tested, and run the gauntlet of confrontation with the total context of experience, just like what comes from the outer world of sense."[15] In other words, experiences produced by altered states of consciousness aren't self-authenticating. Although they may seem more real, more true than any other experiences we've had, they may not be. Just because something seems real doesn't mean that it is.

One test of the truth of an experience is agreement among those who've had it. If there is widespread agreement, there is reason to believe that those who had the experience actually experienced what they thought they did. In the case of beer-induced experiences, however, there is very little agreement about what is experienced. Some see god, some see ancestors, and some see pink elephants. Unless some way of resolving this disagreement can be found, there is little reason to believe that any of these experiences is true.

Disagreements about what has been experienced are usually resolved by gathering more information. Suppose that someone claims that the fruit in a bowl is real; someone else claims that it is plastic. To determine who is right, we would touch, smell, and perhaps taste the objects in the bowl. If they felt, smelled, and tasted like real fruit, we would be justified in believing that they are real. Disagreements about what's

---

[15] James, *The Varieties of Religious Experience*, 326.

experienced under the influence of alcohol can't be resolved in this way, however, because fellow drinkers do not usually have the same experiences. Without a method for distinguishing true beer-induced experiences from false ones, we are not justified in believing any of them to be true.

In fact, some believe that, far from sharpening our view of reality, beer distorts it. Recent scientific confirmation of the "beer goggles" effect seems to support this view. Those under the influence of beer often perceive ugly people as beauties. Researchers at Glasgow University and the University of Manchester recently quantified this effect. At Glasgow University, 80 students were shown 120 pictures of men and women and asked to rate their attractiveness on a scale of 1 to 7. Half of the subjects were given the equivalent of two pints of beer while the rest were given a non-alcoholic beverage. Those under the influence rated the members of the opposite sex as 25% more attractive than their more sober counterparts.

At the University of Manchester, researchers found that the beer goggles effect is due to more than just the amount of alcohol consumed. It's also influenced by the amount of light in the bar, the drinker's eyesight, and the smokiness of the room. They were even able to devise a formula showing the relative importance of these variables, β = the beer goggles effect. Let An = the amount of alcohol consumed, L = the luminance of the person of interest, Vo = visual acuity, S = smokiness of the room, and δ = the distance from the person of interest. The beer goggles formula, then, is:[16]

$$\beta = \frac{(An)^2 \times \delta(S + 1)}{\sqrt{L} \times (Vo)^2}$$

These scientists appear to have quantified the extent to which these factors distort our perception of reality.

James, Broad, and Huxley, however, would probably object to this interpretation of their findings because it begs the question in favor of ordinary waking consciousness. It assumes that the way things appear in our ordinary waking life is as they really are, and that may not necessarily be the case.

---

[16] BBC News, 2005. http://news.bbc.co.uk/go/pr/fr/-/1/hi/england/manchester/4468884.stm. Published: 2005/11/25 15:08:28 GMT.

For much of recorded history, the daily consumption of beer was much greater than it is now. In the absence of sanitary water supplies, beer was the safest form of liquid refreshment. The boiling and fermentation involved in its production make it relatively free of waterborne bacteria. The earliest known indication of per capita beer consumption can be found in Hammurabi's Code where he establishes a beer ration based on social standing. Workers were to receive 2 liters a day, civil servants 3 liters, and administrators and high priests 5 liters. The ordinary Babylonian, then, may well have had beer coursing through his veins almost all day long. In effect, he was fitted with a permanent pair of beer goggles. The way the world looked through those beer goggles would have been normal to him. Who's to say, James, Broad, and Huxley might ask, that that's not the correct way to view the world?

The Knowledge that Sets Us Free

Even if beer does not reveal any new facts about the nature of reality, it may still be a source of knowledge because factual knowledge is not the only sort of knowledge there is. We ordinarily claim to know many different types of things. We know, for example, that snow is white, how to ride a bicycle, and what it is to be in pain. In each case the object of our knowledge (what our knowledge is about) is different. In the first case, it is about a fact; in the second, a skill; and in the third, an experience. These three different sorts of objects correspond to three different sorts of knowledge.

The type of knowledge we have when we know that snow is white is known as "propositional knowledge" or "knowing that." A proposition is a statement that affirms or denies something and thus is either true or false. This is the sort of knowledge that most schools are in the business of dispensing.

The type of knowledge we have when we know how to ride a bicycle is known as "performative knowledge" or "knowing how." Anyone who has a skill has this sort of knowledge. Acquiring this sort of knowledge requires using the body as well as the mind.

The type of knowledge we have when we know what it's like to be in pain is called "knowledge by acquaintance" or "knowing what." Our knowledge of sensations and emotions is of this variety. If we've experienced anger, love, or hate, for example, we know what it is to be in those states. Yet what we know in these cases can't be translated into a string of propositions, no matter how long, because reading those propositions wouldn't give you full knowledge of what it is to be in those states. To fully know what it is to be in one of those states, you have to be in them.

Drinking beer is like that. To know what it is to have downed a few beers, you simply have to have downed a few. So drinking beer acquaints us with a particular state of consciousness and, as such, provides us with a "knowing what" kind of knowledge.

While being in this state of consciousness may not make us privy to any new facts, it may change our attitude to facts we're already aware of. It may alter the meaning we attach to those facts or the way we interpret them. James views this aspect of alcohol consumption as one of its main virtues. He writes:

> The sway of alcohol over mankind is unquestionably due to its power to stimulate the mystical faculties of human nature, usually crushed to earth by the cold facts and dry criticisms of the sober hour. Sobriety diminishes, discriminates and says no; drunkenness expands, unites, and says yes. It is in fact the great exciter of the Yes function in man.[17]

By altering our consciousness, beer may change our attitude toward things. While it may not give us a knowledge of new facts, it may give us a new way of seeing old facts. As the beer goggles effect illustrates, this new way of seeing may open up new possibilities and, indeed, excite the Yes function in man. In any event, beer puts us in a frame of mind that has been experienced by humans for thousands of years. Any serious student of human nature who wants to fully understand what it is to be human must knock back a few.

[17] James, *The Varieties of Religious Experience*, 297.

11

The Unreasonable Effectiveness of Beer

Neil A. Manson

THE CHARACTERS

Phil – philosophy graduate student, skeptic
Clem – autodidact, homebrewer
Demi – Ole Miss grad, townie, job-seeker

THE SCENE

The Long Shot Bar off the Square in Oxford, Mississippi.

Clem: Hey, Phil! Long time, no see. Can I buy you a beer?

Phil: Clem! I haven't seen you all summer. Welcome back! Sure, I'll take a beer. Have you tried out the new Southern Pecan? It's brewed in Mississippi.

Clem: No, but I'm always into something new. Two Southern Pecans, please.

Phil: Only two? What about your friend here?

Clem: Oh, sorry I didn't introduce you. Phil, this is Demi; Demi, Phil. And no, I'll only get two beers for now, even though she is my girlfriend. Demi isn't drinking tonight.

Phil: You don't like beer? You two won't last long. Are you a Baptist or something?

Demi: Or something. Actually, though, it's the football game. I want to be in shape for the Grove tomorrow, so I'm holding back on drinks tonight. And, by the way, nice to meet you, Phil. I've seen you around, but we've never been introduced.

148

Phil: Ditto. I knew you looked familiar. Well, Clem, I guess it's just the two of us. And look! There are our two Southern Pecans. What shall we drink to?

Clem: To God!

Phil: Um, well . . . since you're paying . . . to God! But whence this sudden religious fervor?

Clem: It's not emotion; it's rational reflection. Like Benjamin Franklin said: "Beer is proof God loves us and wants us to be happy." At least, I *think* he said it. All I *know* is that someone at this bar told me he said it. Anyway, I got to thinking. If God loves us, then He exists. And if He exists, then all praise is due to Him. After all, He is the supreme being. And what better way to praise Him than to use His gift of beer to toast Him?

Demi: Why do you keep calling God "He," Clem?

Phil: Because he's a sexist pig. That, and he's arguing to God from beer, not appletinis. Clem, you cannot really be suggesting that beer, wondrous as it is, provides some sort of scientific proof of God's existence?

Clem: Why not? The "intelligent design" idea is all the rage now. It's been in the news, on magazine covers even. People are trying to get it taught in high schools. Politicians take a stand on it. Lots of different Christian groups are in favor of it. I hear even the Pope is going to endorse it. The ID people say evidence of supernatural tinkering is all over the place, everywhere from the smallest micro-organism to the universe as a whole. Why not seek it in a nice, medium-sized object like a beer?

Phil: Yes, now I see it . . . if it weren't for the miracle of yeast, the sugars in malted barley couldn't be converted to alcohol – precisely the chemical that produces great pleasure in us! I find it hard to believe that in nature there just so happens to exist this array of components perfectly suited to making us happy! Yep, Clem, I'm sure you can make at least as good a case for God from beer as from irreducible complexity or cosmic fine-tuning.

Demi: Um, fellas . . . what the heck are you talking about?

Phil: Since Clem is buying, I'll fill you in and let Clem work on his drink.

Clem: [*slurp*]

Phil: OK, Demi, let me give you a brief history here. There is this thing philosophers and theologians call "the design argument" or "the teleological argument." That last word is from the Greek word *telos*, which means end or purpose. The basic idea is that there are strong signs that the universe and a lot of things in it were designed with an end or purpose in mind. Since there can't be design without a designer, we are supposed to conclude that some supernatural being exists that did the designing.

Demi: Gee, you know how to sound like a professor when you try! Yeah, I heard about this in my intro religion course once, but the teacher didn't really go anywhere with it. What are these signs you're talking about?

Phil: Well, historically – going all the way back to the ancient Greeks, at least – the signs were seen in organisms. The human body was seen as beautifully proportioned. Its parts were perfectly suited for various purposes – eyes for seeing things, hands for handling things. Animals had wings for flying. Fish had fins for swimming. The structures seemed too intricate and perfect to have arisen by chance. The most famous statement of this argument was from a British reverend, William Paley, a couple of hundred years ago in his book *Natural Theology*. He used the anatomy of the day to argue for design in biology, and said seeing these structures was like finding a watch in the wilderness. If you did, you'd know that it didn't just appear naturally, that it must have had a designer. He said that likewise, these biological parts must have had a designer.

Demi: Are you telling me he thought God just came down and said, "Presto! Let there be eyes and hands and wings"? Did he think it was just a big miracle?

Phil: He never said how, exactly, God did it, just that nature couldn't have done it. It's process of elimination: if no natural process did it, and if it is too complex to arise by chance, that only leaves design by an intelligence as an option. It's like labels on beer bottles. How, exactly, do they get there? Who knows? But they can't get there by luck, and glass doesn't naturally come with "Negra Modelo" stamped on it, so the bottlers must do it somehow. How does supernatural creation work? It beats me, and I guess it beat Paley, but he'd probably ask, "Do you have a better idea?"

Demi: Well, Darwin did, didn't he? Doesn't evolution explain all of this? I remember I took a biology course and we talked about the evolution of the eye from light-sensitive spots in a cell. I also remember how wings evolved just from flaps of skin, like with flying squirrels.

Phil: Yes, just about everyone accepts that Darwin's theory explains the things Paley was pointing out. In fact, Darwin was consciously trying to answer Paley's questions. If I remember right, there is even a section in *The Origin of Species* called "Organs of Extreme Perfection and Complication" where he talks about whether evolution can explain the eye. By the way, one of Darwin's most famous defenders nowadays, Richard Dawkins, wrote a book about evolution entitled *The Blind Watchmaker* in reference to the whole watch analogy. Dawkins says evolution produces these complicated organisms that look like they were designed, but evolution isn't planning ahead. It's blind.

Demi: I know the story. Your basic organism produces more offspring than the environment can handle. Due to random genetic mutations, they aren't all the same. The ones that are better fitted to the environment get selected by nature for the next round of reproduction. And the process just repeats itself, until eventually you get things like eyes and hands and wings. So what else is there to explain? Am I missing something? Why did you nod when Clem said this idea is "all the rage" nowadays? I thought only Creationists believed this stuff.

Clem: Hey Phil, do you want to try the Amberjaque now?

Phil: You're done? Man, you drink like a fish, Clem. I've barely started this other one. Well, get me one and I'll drink it when I'm done this one. What are these beers anyway? I've never heard of them.

Clem: They're from a brewery down on the coast . . . Lazy Magnolia, I think. It's Mississippi's first legal brewery. The Southern Pecan was a nut brown ale. This one is a light amber ale. Guess I should've reversed the order.

Demi: You guys still haven't answered my question. Why doesn't evolution explain all this?

Clem: Well – and you may not agree with this, Phil, but I'm sure you'd like to work on your beer so I'll say it anyway – I don't necessarily think the theory of evolution gives the whole story. I also don't think that makes me a Creationist, even though Phil likes calling me one. From what I've read, the "intelligent design" people don't say everything in the universe was created directly by God six thousand years ago in the exact order indicated in the Book of Genesis.

Phil: Good thing, too, since beer dates to the Sumerians at least eight thousand years ago. Come to think of it . . . that's about when humans started talking about these "god" things. Coincidence? You be the judge!

Clem: Hey, the ID people and I won't fight you on history. We agree that the universe is billions of years old, that there has been life on earth for at least a billion years, and that Darwin's theory explains a lot of what we observe in biology. But how about the origin of life itself? Darwin's theory doesn't explain that. Where did DNA come from? You need it to exist in order to mutate randomly, but where did this thing that randomly mutates come from? It is an extremely complicated molecule. No one has ever zapped a vat of primordial chemical goo and gotten DNA out of it. The ID people say the theory of evolution can't explain where DNA came from. If you say it got produced just by luck, well, that's a lot of luck! It would be like a tornado blowing through a Budweiser plant and a decent-tasting beer coming out.

Phil: Darn it, Clem, you're going to interrupt my beer drinking by making me correct you! Now you know as well as I do that the ID people are not just raising the origin-of-life issue again. How life first arose a billion years ago and whether it needed a miraculous kick-start is not the question. The ID people are saying that even after the evolutionary ball got rolling, there are still parts of organisms that are "irreducibly complex." They aren't just saying evolution doesn't explain the origin of life. They're saying it doesn't even explain life's subsequent history. Don't soft-pedal the ID position. They say Darwin was wrong, not just that his theory doesn't explain everything.

Demi: Irreducibly complex? What does that mean?

152

Clem: It's like a mousetrap. If you take away one of the parts it doesn't work anymore. If you take away any piece – platform, catch, spring, hammer, or holding bar – the thing isn't just less good at catching mice. It's no good at all. The ID stuff I've read says molecular biology shows that all sorts of cellular organisms are irreducibly complex.

Phil: Yeah, and if you take away the barley, you don't have any carbohydrates to work on. If you have the barley but can't malt it, you don't release the sugars. If you mash the barley but forget the yeast, then the sugars don't get converted to alcohol and carbon dioxide. And if you include all of that stuff but leave out the keg, you get a sticky puddle instead of a saleable product. So I guess, by that standard, beer is irreducibly complex – take away any part and you end up with something that either fails to deliver alcohol to us or is not even a drink at all. What does *that* show?

Demi: Yeah, Clem, what's your point?

Clem: Well, the ID people think that the irreducible complexity seen in various cells shows evolution could not have produced them, because any hypothetical ancestor of those cells just would not function. If the hypothetical ancestors of irreducibly complex cells are total duds in the survival game, then you can't explain irreducibly complex cells in terms of ancestors that underwent favorable mutations. The required ancestors couldn't possibly have survived to reproduce. Plus, sorry to shoot down your analogy, Phil, but unlike beer, cells in nature aren't supposed to have intelligent agents like human beings there to help them develop – not according to Darwinians, anyway.

Demi: You mean the ID people are saying there is no possible evolutionary path to these structures? You can't get here from there?

Clem: Right. So evolution can't explain irreducible complexity. And since the complexity is supposedly far too great to be a result of luck, an intelligence had to have designed those cells sometime in the history of life. But that would mean Darwin's idea – that all the features of all life can be explained in terms of developments from primitive life – is wrong.

Phil: That's crazy! What's the alternative? That God came down and directed evolution? That God pushes bio-molecules around to get micro-organisms just right? Actually, that *is* their alternative, and it's absurd. Anyway, I think it is nuts to say evolutionary biologists can't explain these things. First, it turns out that lots of the allegedly "irreducibly complex" bio-structures do, in fact, have good evolutionary explanations. I remember reading how the poster child for the ID people, the bacterial flagellum, is actually evolvable. But even if biologists can't explain right now how every one of the features the ID people fuss over evolved, that doesn't mean we should throw up our hands and say a miracle happened!

Clem: You're really getting worked up, Phil. Maybe you need to finish off that beer.

Phil: All I am saying is, give science a chance.

Clem: Hippie.

Demi: Clem, don't tell me you really believe this stuff?

Clem: [*belch*]

Phil: Whoops. You didn't know Clem was . . . kind of religious, did you, Demi?

Demi: Well, duh! I met him at church!

Phil: What? So why are you upset at the "intelligent design" idea?

Demi: Well, just because I believe in God doesn't mean I'm a Creationist. I don't think every word in the Bible is literally true. The Bible isn't even meant to be taken literally. God didn't write a science textbook. The Book of Genesis isn't competing with *Introduction to Modern Physics*. God inspired the authors of the Bible because He is trying to communicate with us spiritually.

Phil: You just called God "He."

Demi: Don't you have a beer to finish?

Phil: I guess I'm not the only one who gets worked up by this stuff.

Demi: I just don't see why anyone would think God is scientifically provable in the first place. My belief in God is a matter of faith. That's what God says it should be. If science could prove God, what would be the need for faith anyway? I'm just not comfortable with human reason putting God in a box. Any being that we could show exists just by reason – any being we could fully comprehend – wouldn't be supreme anyway. Divinity graciously shows itself to us by acting on our spirits. Without that, reason can tell us nothing about God.

Clem: That's a dangerous attitude. If it is all a matter of pure faith, and if we can't even say what God is like without Him telling us, then how is anyone supposed to communicate the truth about God to someone who doesn't already know it? How can you "spread the word" if there is no word to be spread in the first place? I don't like this idea that, when it comes to belief in God, you either get it or you don't. Why shouldn't there be a place for reason and arguments? What else are you supposed to provide when you want to convince somebody about God . . . a pint of Guinness? And if it's fine to use reason and arguments concerning God, what's wrong with looking to science for evidence?

Demi: Because once you say science can prove God does exist, the atheists will start using science against us. If God created life, then why is there bubonic plague? If God can push around bio-molecules, then why doesn't He eliminate tsunamis and hurricanes?

Phil: Exactly! Why didn't God make skunky beer impossible? Why doesn't He rig our bodies so that we never get hung over? I'd worship any god that saved me from worshipping the porcelain god.

Demi: I don't want to play the game of scientifically justifying the mysterious ways of the Lord. God created the whole world but lets it run its course. The important point is that He (or She, or It) wants to help us through the world spiritually. The world is a testing ground for us, for our souls. It's not God's set of tinker toys.

Clem: So you think God did everything at the beginning of time, but after that He doesn't interfere with the world except in the sense that He guides our spirits? Does that mean you're perfectly happy saying we weren't created, but evolved?

Demi: Sure. Why not? If that's how God wanted to do it – set up the universe and let it eventually produce us – what's the problem? That seems a lot more God-like to me than having to create people miraculously out of dust.

Phil: Not to mention it avoids the whole Eve-from-Adam's-rib thing. Bet you had a field day with that one in your women's studies class, eh, Demi? [*burp*]

Demi: I'm a Kappa Mu. We don't take women's studies classes. Anyway, Clem, it's not like God is in a big hurry to get to the part where we humans come around. God is eternal, remember?

Phil: Good point. You're a sensible woman, Demi. [*burp*] Why are you with Clem?

Demi: All this shouting over the music . . . honey, let me have just a little sip. [*slurp*] Mmmm . . . tastes like Newcastle.

Phil: Are you sure you don't want one?

Demi: No, I'm being good tonight.

Clem: OK, so you believe in God *and* evolution. You're what I call a "theistic evolutionist" – someone who thinks God created the universe so that evolution would eventually produce beings capable of knowing God.

Phil: Wow! Maybe God didn't even have *homo sapiens* in mind. Any old intelligent sci-fi alien would do. But that would mean . . . why, that would mean we humans aren't really that special! Oh, the horror!

Clem: But what about the whole universe, from the very beginning of time? If I said that the Big Bang itself looked designed, would you hate that idea, too?

Phil: Uh-oh . . . here comes the fine-tuning stuff again.

Demi: What's fine-tuning?

Clem: It's the fact that the basic laws of physics themselves need to be just right if there is even to be a process of evolution. You think the universe was created by God to produce us by evolution. Well, modern physical cosmology shows the universe is extremely well-suited to do that. For example, if the masses of the basic parts of atoms – neutrons and protons and electrons – had been just a little bit different, then chemistry as we know it would be impossible. There would be no carbon atoms, no carbon-based biochemistry, and no life. Or if you go right back to the Big Bang, the rate at which the universe expanded had to be just right. If it had been just a little bit different, either the universe would have collapsed in on itself after a very short time, or it would have flown apart and matter would have been too diffuse to form galaxies, stars, and planets. There is no life without stars, because it is in stars where all the chemical elements are made.

Phil: Hey, I love life. Barley is a kind of life. So are hops and yeast. Come to think of it, I'm alive! So if the universe weren't set up just right, then there would be no beer and no people made happy by it. Therefore God exists, and He loves beer. QED.

Clem: Snide retorts are no substitute for serious replies. Look, Demi, do you see the argument? Do you see why the physicists talk about "fine-tuning"? It is like a radio dial that needs to be on just the right setting to get reception.

Demi: How "just right" are we talking about here?

Clem: Some of the calculations are hard to imagine. I remember for some of the values, the physicists said if they were different by something like a billion billion billionth of a percent, any form of life in the universe would be impossible.

Demi: And that's just the way the universe was set up in the first place? Even if evolution can produce all life, you couldn't get life without fine-tuning?

Clem: Yes.

Phil: That would be real impressive, Clem, except for all the assumptions you make. First, you assume there is only one way for there to be life: through the biochemistry that *we* know. Who's to say that in some other sort of universe, there wouldn't be some other kind of chemistry that led to life in some other way? Maybe on Alpha Centauri they sit around the bar lapping up silicate gels. It doesn't really matter to God whether the beings are made of carbon or silicon or some totally alien stuff anyway, because whatever their physical form, God can just endow them with souls. Second, there's a better explanation of fine-tuning. Cosmologists have models of the Big Bang where it is the result of a quantum-level fluctuation event.

Demi: What the heck is that?

Phil: Actually, I don't really know. [*belch*] But what they say it means is that there are lots of other universes – maybe even an infinite number of other universes – and they are all different. So however fine-tuned our universe might look, there is bound to be a universe out there that is just right for life. Of course, that is the universe we will observe. If it weren't just right for life, we wouldn't be around to observe that it is . . . just right for life!

Clem: Hmmmm . . . sounds pretty speculative to me! Let's keep track here. When you can't explain an irreducibly complex system, you tell me to be patient, that an evolutionary explanation is on its way. When you can't explain why the universe is just right for life, you say there has got to be some other unknown way for there to be life with some radically different laws of physics. When you can't explain fine-tuning, you expect me to believe there are a kazillion other universes out there to make the problem go away. Looks like I'm not the only one around here with religious commitments!

Phil: You know me . . . I'll say anything to stomp out that stupid God meme. It's only good for superstition, repression, war, and, worst of all, alcohol prohibition.

Demi: Let's be nice, boys. Can't we just talk about something we can all agree on? How about beer? Both of you love beer.

Phil: Yeah, Clem, you still haven't done what you said. You still haven't shown how beer proves God exists. C'mon, give it a shot. The beer is starting to kick in, so my rigorous standards of argumentation are weakening.

Clem: I've been thinking about it. I can't say I've done the scientific research to show how the divine finger is manifested in the brewing process. To make beer, you have to mash barley to get it to produce sugars. Then those sugars get turned into alcohol and carbon dioxide through the action of yeast. That process is called glycolysis. Is there anything about glycolysis that shows design? I'll have to ask my friend in the chemistry department. Who knows? Maybe yeast is irreducibly complex!

Phil: So God actually goes out of His way to design infectious agents?

Demi: See, Clem, I told you to watch out for atheists turning the tables on you.

Clem: OK, scratch that idea.

Demi: Yuck!

Clem: I was thinking of something more abstract anyway – not about beer per se, but about our unnatural capacity to enjoy it.

Phil: Unnatural? What could possibly be more natural than to enjoy beer?

Clem: Well, think about it this way, Phil. You believe all life is the product of blind evolutionary forces, right?

Phil: Now you're talking!

Clem: So every biological feature in the world is the result of natural selection?

Phil: Yes.

Clem: Including every feature of human beings?

Phil: Yes, yes, everything – emotion, reasoning ability, bipedalism, you name it.

Clem: And with natural selection there's no peeking, right? I mean, nature can't anticipate what is coming up in the future, can it? So you can't explain a biological feature in terms of the effects it will have in the future, can you? If you did, you would be giving a goal-based explanation – a teleological explanation – rather than a purely Darwinian, natural-selection explanation, right?

Phil: Yes, yes, we've already covered this. The process of natural selection is blind; it doesn't have a goal in mind. That's the whole basis of the theory. Without that, it isn't really scientific anymore. So what's your point? Where are you going with this?

Clem: Well, I was just thinking – you said earlier that beer was discovered eight thousand years ago. But if the evolutionary story about human beings is true, then the *capacity* to enjoy beer was in humans a long time before that. If the anthropologists are right, modern humans – *homo sapiens sapiens* – date to at least a hundred thousand years ago. So if you could take your time machine back a hundred thousand years ago with a few bottles of Three Philosophers . . .

Demi: What's Three Philosophers? Us?

Clem: No, it's a beer! From the Ommegang Brewery, which I believe is in upstate New York somewhere. It's a mix of Belgian dark ale and Lindeman's Kriek. What a terrific beer!

Phil: Then why waste it on cavemen?

Clem: Well, if you *were* to take this beer back in time, then the people then *would* be able to enjoy it just as much as we do.

Phil: Excuse me, Clem, but are you totally drunk?

Clem: My point is, evolution didn't see beer coming. The process of natural selection could not know more than a hundred thousand years ago that eventually a human being was going to produce this substance we call "beer." Now we all agree beer is a wonderful thing. It unleashes creative thought. It makes us happy. It provides a sanitary form of liquid sustenance. In medieval times, that last one was a necessity.

Phil: I suppose you're going to say making women look beautiful is another necessity.

Demi: Maybe up north, but not in this town.

Clem: So isn't it a little mysterious that we have a capacity to enjoy beer when there is no way that capacity could have been selected for before the invention of beer?

Demi: I'm not following you, Clem.

Clem: It's like mathematical ability. Where would we be without it? We wouldn't be able to construct equations to express the laws of physics, and so we wouldn't be able to do science. Without the ability to do math existing somewhere in the human gene pool a hundred thousand years ago, there would be no technology, no books, no bridges, no modern medicine, nothing advanced. But what good was it in hunter-gatherer societies a hundred thousand years ago to be able to do abstract mathematics? Those people were too busy hunting mastodons and scratching out a living for mathematical ability to do them any good. So shouldn't natural selection have eliminated mathematical ability from the gene pool if it is useless? How can evolution explain the arrival of this biological feature – the ability to do abstract mathematics – if the feature is only useful a hundred thousand years after it emerges?

Phil: So you're saying evolutionary theory can't explain the human propensity to enjoy beer, because the propensity existed well before beer ever came along?

Clem: Yeah. It's like . . . imagine humans had an extra finger sticking out of their hips. Imagine that this extra finger had been a feature of the human body plan for the past hundred thousand years. And it turns out this finger is absolutely useless – it has no function at all – until the last thirty years. Then it becomes perfect for changing the channels on remote controls while humans sit on the couch. You couldn't explain the finger as being an adaptation for channel-changing, because remote controls weren't around when the extra finger came to be. So either you have to say the existence of the extra finger is completely dumb luck, or you have to say there was some intelligence guiding evolution – a being with the foresight to know remote control devices lay in humanity's future.

Demi: My God, you're drunk.

Clem: Don't you see the problem? [*burp*] If the capacity to enjoy beer predates the actual existence of beer, isn't that unexplainable by evolution?

Phil: Well, that's an interesting theory! Here's a better one. Receptivity to beer is a happy accident. By trial and error, humans eventually hit upon the substance that activates whatever extra pleasure receptors evolution fortunately provided us. If, by the wanderings of evolutionary development, it happened to be that seaweed activated our pleasure receptors, stimulated our creativity, and protected us from sickness, we'd be sitting here sampling twenty varieties of miyok-kuk.

Clem: What are you saying, Phil? That beer is not good in itself? That beer is only good relative to its effects on us? That there is nothing intrinsically special about beer?

Phil: Well, I guess I am.

Clem: I don't know you anymore.

Phil: What do you think, Demi?

Demi: I think I need a White Russian.[1]

---

[1] A conversation very loosely based on David Hume's *Dialogues Concerning Natural Religion* (Edited by N. K. Smith, Indianapolis: Bobbs-Merrill, 1979; first published 1779), with a lemon slice of inspiration from Eugen Wigner's "The unreasonable effectiveness of mathematics in the natural sciences" (*Communications in Pure and Applied Mathematics*, New York: John Wiley, 1970, 13(1)).

12

What's a Beer Style?

Matt Dunn

Ah yes, California. The wester the weirder is what I've heard. And it's hard to get much further west than Solana Beach. It's perched on the Pacific Ocean just north of San Diego, so things get pretty weird there. It was at the Pizza Port Brewing Company in Solana Beach during the fateful spring of 2004 that Tomme Arthur fermented a beer with 100% *Brettanomyces anomalus*. It was called Mo Betta Bretta and I have no idea what style it is.

Of course my wester-is-weirder rule has exceptions. Take, for example, Delaware. Strange business law in Wilmington and strange brewers in Rehoboth Beach (maybe it has something to do with the sea). In 2002 Dogfish Head Brewing Company released one of the most unexpectedly delightful beers I've ever tried: Aprihop. It shows the bold, signature Dogfish Head hop character but it's all smoothed over with the fruity, velvet, subtle, sweetness of apricots. In 2004 this beer won a gold medal at the World Beer Cup in the rather nebulous Specialty Beer category. Of course most beers are far more pedestrian. But as we'll see, there are no clear-cut rules for classifying them either.

Instead of wild yeast and apricots, most beers tend to be made from water, grain, hops, and good old-fashioned brewer's yeast. Even when we restrict the list of variables to these four, the possible variation is still bewildering. Beer varies in color, in alcoholic strength, in bitterness, in any number of properties. There are black beers and white beers and every shade between. There are strong beers, weak beers, hoppy beers, and sweet beers. It seems as though there is a continuum of beer: black blends imperceptibly into brown, roast malt character into caramel, stout into porter, citrus hops into herbal. Yet we break up this continuum into more or less distinct things that we call beer styles. But what kind of a thing is a beer style?

In this chapter I will discuss the philosophy of classification. Classifications are dictated in part by the *metaphysical status* of the things being classified. In other words, the *kind of thing a beer style is* dictates the way we classify beers. Perhaps beer styles are like the elements of the periodic table? If so, we might call them natural kinds. And if they're natural kinds, then there is only one natural way to group them into styles and we're in pretty good shape. But what if beers are more like books? There is no one natural or true way to classify books in the library. The Dewey decimal system and the Library of Congress classification are equally right, which one you choose depends on what you want the classification to do for you. I'll argue that beers are more like books. Therefore, the debate about beer styles is a debate about what we want beer styles to do for us. Because we can't always agree on this, we're kind of up the creek.

Broadly speaking, classifications can be of two different types: (1) those that are constructed for pragmatic reasons and (2) those that are constructed to capture the actual structure of the world. These two types of classification can be called *conventionalist* and *realist* classifications respectively. A conventionalist about a particular set of things would say that every grouping is just as correct as any other. The realist, on the other hand, would say that there are right and wrong ways to group things into kinds, and, in the extreme, there is only one correct grouping of things into kinds, the way that accurately represents real distinctions in the world. Of course these two types of classification are not mutually exclusive. Sometimes a realist classification is also convenient. In fact, often the reason why realist classifications are desirable is because they are the most convenient or conducive to our needs. For example, knowing the actual structure of matter as elucidated in the periodic table has better allowed us to manipulate the world. Yet the fact that the two types of classification are related in this way does not mean they do not have important differences.

Let's first look at conventionalist classification in more detail. Take, for example, the library. If libraries did not classify books in some way, finding a particular book would prove daunting. However, there are many equally correct ways to classify books. They could be classified by their color, their weight, the number of words in them etc. If we always went into libraries knowing which book we wanted, libraries could just assign a place on the shelf for each book and keep an alphabetical list indicating their locations. But of course we need more from a library. We rarely go to the library with a particular book already in mind. Rather, we go to the library with a topic that we're interested in learning more about. So we need the library to classify books by at least subject and location. And there are many ways to do this.

Conventionalist Classification

The classification of beer styles can be interpreted as conventionalist. For example, one popular way of conducting a beer competition, particularly in the US, is to judge beers "to style." This format is intended to minimize the influence of the individual judges' personal tastes, to make the judging as objective as possible. In such a competition, styles are formulated in terms of their properties that are accessible by the judges through their senses so that they can evaluate the beers and compare them with the style description. The entrant that most closely matches the style definition is the winner. Take, for example, the description for Classic Irish-Style Dry Stout from the American Brewers Association style guide:

> Dry stouts have an initial malt and light caramel flavor profile with a distinctive dry-roasted bitterness in the finish . . . emphasis of coffee-like roasted barley and a moderate degree of roasted malt aromas define much of the character . . . slight acidity may be perceived but is not necessary. Hop aroma and flavor should not be perceived. Dry stouts have medium-light to medium body. Fruity esters are minimal and overshadowed by malt, high hop bitterness, and roasted barley character. Diacetyl (butterscotch) should be very low or not perceived. Head retention and rich character should be part of its visual character.

This description makes it possible to have a beer competition. For example, a beer in the competition that showed medium diacetyl would score lower than one that showed no diacetyl.

The reason why this is seen as conventionalist doesn't necessarily have to do with the fact that the style is used for pragmatic purposes. It's conventionalist because the boundaries between, for example, Dry Stout and Oatmeal Stout might be less than precise. An Oatmeal Stout that employed more roasted barley than is typical would probably be indistinguishable from an Irish Stout. The one blends imperceptibly into the other. They are vague. Vague concepts do not allow for qualitative distinctions. For example, how many hairs does one have to lose before one is bald? This question has no determinate answer because the concept the term "bald" refers to is vague. There is no clear, natural distinction between bald and not bald. Similarly, how dry and roasty does a Sweet Stout or Oatmeal Stout have to be before we call it a Dry Stout? But just because we can't draw a qualitative distinction between two styles doesn't mean that we can't draw a line at all. So the lines are drawn where they will capture most of the examples likely to be encountered, thus making beer judging easier. Some boundary cases might be placed in either of two similar styles, but such is life. There is a trade-off between economy and trying to have the most precise styles possible.

Other kinds of style illustrate the point about conventionalist classification without relying on the notion of vagueness. Take the wood- and barrel-aged beer style. The wood-aged style is not a result of the imprecise boundaries between wood-aged beers and, for example, beers aged in stainless steel. There is, for all intents and purposes, a clear and distinct boundary between wood and stainless steel. This style is a result of our desire to be able to assess the relative merits of *any* style of beer aged on wood. For some reason, we think this is important to do. It's something we value. I don't think anybody believes that an American Pale Ale aged in a barrel and an Imperial Stout aged in a barrel belong naturally together in a group. More to the point, a Pale Ale aged in a wood barrel would be more naturally grouped with Pale Ales not aged in barrels rather than with the wood-aged Imperial Stout. In fact, before about 1930, pretty much all beers were aged in wood, so wood-aged would be a useless criterion to employ. A brewer in the 1800s would think you daft if you said wood-aged was a style.

Realist Classification

Now let's consider realist classifications, where the goal is describing the actual, interest-independent structure of the world. Take, for example, the periodic table. The periodic table is a way of classifying

165

types of matter. There are many different ways that we could classify matter. For example, by the monetary value of each element in the table. But this type of classification, while possibly useful in some contexts, might be said to be "artificial" or, using our terminology, conventional. But why? Because what makes gold valuable is its rarity. But its rarity is not what makes gold what it is, it does not pick out gold as a particular kind of thing in the world. There are a lot of other things that are rare that are not gold. Similarly, if gold were abundant and therefore not of any great monetary value, we would still consider gold to be gold. In other words, scarcity is neither a necessary nor sufficient condition for being gold. What is gold, then?

Chemists have a theory about the fundamental components of matter. They believe that matter is composed of protons, neutrons, and electrons. Furthermore, their theory describes how the different number of protons, neutrons, and electrons cause certain elements to have certain properties like their color, density etc. Thus the classification of matter is based on these fundamental components, in particular, the number of protons an element has, its atomic number. So gold is the element, and the only element, with atomic number 79.

Natural kinds

One reason to think that the chemical elements are amenable to a realist classification is because they are *natural kinds*. Matter is naturally divided into elements. We do not make the divisions, we simply describe the divisions nature gives us. Different kinds of books, on the other hand, are not natural kinds. They are artifactual kinds, categories that are artifacts of the particular needs we have as humans when dealing with books. But what makes something a natural kind? One influential account of natural kinds, and the one I was implicitly drawing on in my discussion of the chemical elements, is due to the twentieth-century American philosopher Hilary Putnam.

This is Putnam's theory of natural kinds as stated in his 1970 paper, "Is semantics possible?":

> A natural kind term . . . is a term that plays a special kind of role. If I describe something as a lemon . . . I indicate that it is likely to have certain characteristics . . . but I also indicate that the presence of those characteristics . . . is likely to be accounted for by some "essential nature" which the thing shares with other members of the natural kind.

What the essential nature is is not a matter of language analysis but of scientific theory construction. (Putnam, 1975, pp. 140–1)[1]

The similarities between Putnam's lemon example and the chemical elements should be clear. The atomic number of an element is its "essential nature" and its essential nature accounts for the various characteristics of the element that we can, roughly speaking, ascertain with our senses. For example, gold is yellow, shiny, malleable, etc. Furthermore, the reason we believe that gold and lemons are natural kinds is because of the scientific theories produced by chemistry and biology. (There are many reasons to think that lemons and gold are not natural kinds, but for our purposes, let's assume this is not problematic.)

Ale and lager

We might think of ale and lager as natural kinds on Putnam's account. Ales are fermented with ale yeast, *Saccharomyces cerevisiae*. Lagers are fermented with lager yeast, *Saccharomyces uvarum*. Ale yeasts tend to impart different characteristics to beer than lager yeasts, ales tend to have a more complex fermentation character. *S. cerevisiae* produces many different types of chemicals during fermentation: esters and phenols for example. These impart distinctive characters to the beer: banana, butter, clove, strawberry, tropical fruit, pepper etc. *S. uvarum*, on the other hand, typically has a less expressive fermentation profile. While lager yeast may produce some of the same chemicals during fermentation as ale yeast, it does so in different proportions and with slight variations. The resulting beer typically is of a different character than ale. Lagers are described as clean and crisp, typically not fruity. Some may exhibit subtle sulfur and sweetcorn notes and Budweiser is particularly famous for its green apple, but in general they have a much more restrained fermentation profile.

The distinction between ale and lager yeasts has been implicit for at least the last 200 years. Brewers in Bavaria and Bohemia had noticed that their yeasts tended to stay at the bottom of the fermenting vessels during fermentation. British brewers noticed that theirs rose to the

[1] H. Putnam, *Mind, Language and Reality: Philosophical Papers*, vol. 2. Cambridge: Cambridge University Press, 1975.

167

top. But these brewers didn't know what yeast was. It wasn't until Pasteur's work in the 1860s and 1870s that the biological basis of fermentation was firmly established. And it wasn't until a decade later, through the work of Danish microbiologist Emil Christian Hansen, that the pure culture fermentation technique was developed. This allowed for the isolation of a Bavarian yeast, imported from the Spaten brewery in 1845, and its successful deployment in the Carlsberg brewery in 1883–4.[2] This yeast was of a constant type and different from the British top-fermenting variety and thus, because Hansen's work was conducted at the Carlsberg Laboratory near Copenhagen, came to be dubbed *Saccharomyces carlbergensis*, later incorporated into the species *S. uvarum*. Recent work in evolutionary taxonomy has further supported the claim that *S. uvarum* is a distinct species.[3]

Thus it appears that we have two good examples of a Putnam-style natural kind. Lagers and ales fall into two natural categories delimited by their underlying "essential nature," the yeast that is used to ferment them, which was discovered through scientific research. One potential problem with this analysis immediately presents itself. It is actually the two yeast species that are natural kinds. They were the things existing out in nature. The beer was man-made. This objection is not fatal, however, for two reasons. First, the yeast itself was actually man-made, in a sense. *S. uvarum* is thought to be the result of a hybrid speciation event between *S. cerevisiae* and another species of yeast, probably during beer fermentation before the development of pure culture techniques. Furthermore, there is good evidence that hybridization events occur frequently between different strains of yeast involved in the same fermentation.[4] This doesn't, however, cast doubt on the species status of *S. uvarum* for a variety of reasons I won't detail here. Secondly, there are several chemical elements that do not exist "naturally." They can only be created in the lab. But only certain kinds of elements can be created, not any willy-nilly combination of protons, neutrons, and electrons. Thus it seems there are natural

2   M. Teich, Fermentation theory and practice: the beginnings of pure yeast cultivation and English brewing. *History of Technology*, 1983, 8: 117–33.

3   H.-V. Nguyen and C. Gaillardin, Evolutionary relationships between the former species *Saccharomyces uvarum* and the hybrids *Saccharomyces bayanus* and *Saccharomyces pastorianus*; reinstatement of *Saccharomyces uvarum* (Beijerinck) as a distinct species. *FEMS Yeast Research*, 2005, 5: 471–83.

4   Ibid.

constraints, laws of nature if you like, that allow only certain kinds of elements to exist. It would seem that if we are willing to grant einsteinium, for example, natural kind status, we should be willing to grant *S. uvarum* and the beer made by it, natural kind status as well. Either way, let us assume that ale and lager are natural kinds in order to see how far Putnam's account can get us in understanding how beer is classified.

One way in which the classification of beer may be seen as natural or realist is if the ale–lager distinction is employed in delimiting styles. Now of course beers are either of the ale or lager kind. This much, I believe, is not controversial. But there are some cases where the distinction between ale and lager may play a slightly more interesting role in delimiting beer styles. For instance, if the classification of beer were completely conventional, we would expect that all beers exhibiting the same relevant characteristics would be placed in the same kind, the same conventional kind. Yet this is not the case. There are several styles of beer that are brewed with one yeast, but taste as if they were brewed with the other. California Common, also called Steam Beer, is one well-known example. Anchor Steam, made by the Anchor Brewery in San Francisco, is fermented with a lager yeast but tastes very much like an American Pale Ale. Altbier and Kölsch, beers hailing from the cities of Düsseldorf and Köln respectively, in the Rhenish region of Germany, also come to mind. They are both fermented with ale yeast, but taste very much like lager beer. They employ special varieties of ale yeast, though they are certainly varieties of *S. cerevisiae*. Fermentation is conducted at lower than typical temperatures for ale yeast and they are cold-conditioned for long periods of time much like lagers. Both types of beer are clean, crisp, and refreshing with very minimal fermentation character.

Let's look at Kölsch in more detail. We'll compare it with the lager-style Dortmunder Export that's associated with the German city of Dortmund. The descriptions given by the American Brewers Association for these two styles are virtually identical. Kölsch is "golden to straw color," Dortmunder is "straw to deep golden." Both have "medium bitterness." In a Kölsch, "caramel character should not be evident," in a Dortmunder, "malt flavor . . . should not be caramel like." In a Kölsch, "fruity esters should be minimally perceived, if at all . . . chill haze should be absent," in a Dortmunder, "fruity esters, chill haze, and diacetyl should not be perceived." The similarities persist, albeit

169

to a slightly less perfect degree, in the more technical characteristics such as original and final gravity, alcohol content, and bittering units. My point here is that these beers are not distinguishable by their characteristics alone. They overlap almost completely, much more so than, say, Oatmeal Stout and Dry Stout. The reason why they are considered to be different beer styles is because one is fermented with an ale yeast and the other with a lager yeast. Here, the classification seems to be taking into account the essential nature of the two beers. Now, one might object that what is actually being taken into account is the geographical origins of the styles. Lagers are typically from southern Germany while ales predominate in the Rhineland. While this is something I will discuss below, this objection does not hold for Kölsch and Dortmunder. Both Köln and Dortmund are in North Rhine-Westphalia and Dortmund is only slightly further from Düsseldorf than is Köln.

Descriptivism

The fact that two beers with identical characteristics should be recognized as different natural kinds is related to Putnam's argument against another influential account of natural kinds: *descriptivism*. Descriptivism can be characterized as the claim that the meaning of a natural kind term is just the description of the observable properties of that kind. For instance, gold's description, as we've seen, is shiny, yellow, malleable, etc. This position is most famously associated with the seventeenth-century British philosopher John Locke. Descriptivism was taken up in many forms by various subsequent philosophers and Putnam was arguing against the position as it had evolved in the late nineteenth and early twentieth century. The basic issue Putnam has with descriptivism is that it requires that psychological states determine the extension of natural kind terms. What this means is that the objects in the world, the extension that our description refers to, are determined by the description itself. In other words, what I *mean* when I say gold is just "the stuff that's shiny, yellow, malleable, etc." One problem with this kind of a position is that it's possible for our description to be wrong without affecting the object we are referring to, without affecting what we *mean* when we say such and such. For instance, if I believed mistakenly that Sam Adams Triple Bock is just a year's worth of sludge from the bottom of Sam Adams fermenters, I would still be referring to the beer Sam Adams Triple Bock when I used the term "Sam Adams Triple Bock." My description of an object does not necessarily affect what I *mean* when I say "Sam Adams Triple Bock."

Putnam offers a similar reason to think that the descriptivist account of natural kind terms fails. It fails because it would not locate where the meaning of the terms "Kölsch" and "Dortmunder" come from in the example we've been discussing. Naturally, Putnam's own account of natural kinds succeeds in this example. That's why we're using it. Putnam's argument for why this is the case involves a thought experiment about a place called Twin Earth. It was presented in his 1975 paper, "The meaning of 'meaning'." For our purposes, I will retell the story in terms of our example.

Imagine a place called Twin Köln. It is exactly like Köln in every way except that in Twin Köln, the beer they call Kölsch is actually fermented with a lager yeast, it's actually Dortmunder. It's indistinguishable from Kölsch except for the fact that it's made with a lager yeast. Now imagine that in Köln, there lives a famous beer writer named Michael Jackson. In Twin Köln, there lives his doppelgänger, Twin Köln Michael Jackson. Further imagine, and this may be harder to do but try anyway, that both Michael Jackson and Twin Köln Michael Jackson have no idea how Kölsch or the beer called Kölsch in Twin Köln are made. One day, Michael Jackson visits Twin Köln and finds that the word "Kölsch" has the same meaning in Twin Köln as it does in his hometown of Köln. It just means *a straw to golden colored beer with no caramel malt character, no fruity esters, etc.* But then he learns how the beer called Kölsch is brewed in Twin Köln. He therefore corrects his former belief that the word "Kölsch" has the same meaning in Twin Köln as it does in Köln. He now believes that in Twin Köln, the word "Kölsch" actually means beer fermented with a lager yeast. Now imagine that Twin Köln Michael Jackson travels to Köln and experiences with Kölsch everything Michael Jackson experienced in Twin Köln with the beer called Kölsch. Twin Köln Michael Jackson would ultimately come to believe that in Köln, the word "Kölsch" actually means beer fermented with an ale yeast. Let's also assume that Michael Jackson and Twin Köln Michael Jackson never run into each other because that would just be weird.

So far so good. In this story, the term "Kölsch" simply has two different meanings, one in Köln and one in Twin Köln. Now roll back the clock to, say, the year 1800. Nobody in Köln or Twin Köln knows anything about the distinction between lager and ale yeast. Their particular yeasts perform in exactly the same way (the top vs bottom fermenting distinction isn't perfect), but in Twin Köln, they were using what would come to be called lager yeast, while in Köln, they were using what would come to be called ale yeast. They were brewing beer in the same way then as they do now (more or less). Now imagine Michael Jackson's great-great-grandfather and Twin Köln Michael Jackson's great-great-grandfather. The first lived in Köln, the second in Twin Köln, as we might have expected. They were exactly alike in every single possible way. It's particularly important to point out that they both had exactly the same beliefs about the word "Kölsch." When they thought about or used the word "Kölsch," their brains were in exactly the same state. But in Köln, "Kölsch" referred to Kölsch and in Twin Köln "Kölsch" referred to Dortmunder. So Putnam claims that Michael Jackson's great-great-grandfather and Twin Köln Michael Jackson's great-great-grandfather each understood the term "Kölsch" differently from the other in 1800 *although they were in the same psychological state*, and although, given the state of science at the time, it would have taken their scientific communities about 100 years to *discover* that they understood the term "Kölsch" differently.[5] In other words, even though they didn't realize it at the time, they meant different things when they said "Kölsch."

So now we have seen that it is plausible to think of at least some beer styles as natural kinds. If it's plausible to think of *all* beer styles as natural kinds then we can end disputes about style and simply devote our energies to discovering the essential nature of each beer and group them accordingly. Done and done. Unfortunately, this won't do. It won't do because, as we'll see, it's not clear that any two examples of a single style share any sort of essential nature that uniquely identifies them as of that style. Just like two books on beer don't share any essential nature. The books could be printed on different kinds of paper or with different fonts. One could just be code on a computer.

A Mixed Bag

The bottom line is that we use a rather mixed bag of criteria when formulating beer styles. And in general, the essential nature of a beer

---

[5] Putnam, *Mind, Language and Reality*, 224.

is trumped by other criteria, and for good reason. For one, it's not clear that aside from ale and lager, beer has any particular thing we could call its essential nature. Perhaps we could use the chemical constituents of a beer as its essential property? Unfortunately, every single batch of American Pale Ale ever made probably has a different chemical composition no matter how closely breweries doctor their water, select their hops and grains, and control fermentation temperature. Every American Pale Ale ever brewed may very well have a different essential nature. Yet this is to pour our beers too finely. We can't have the Sierra Nevada Pale Ale Batch #9,546 style – we recognize most American Pales as such *in spite* of their differing essential natures.

Secondly, a beer's geographical origin is often important in determining which style it falls under, despite what I said above about Kölsch and Dortmunder. Consider the Baltic Porter style. This style would arguably include such beers as Okicim Porter from Poland, Aldaris Porter from Lithuania, and Carnegie Porter from Sweden. The thing is, these beers are different. The Okicim and Aldaris are a deep, translucent mahogany. They are rather sweet, syrupy, and strong, 8.3% and 6.8% abv (alcohol by volume) respectively. Carnegie Porter, on the other hand, weighs in at only 5.5% abv. It is a shade darker than Okicim and Aldaris. It's drier on the palate with more of a roasty dimension. I would say that Okicim is more similar to a German Dopplebock like Spaten's Optimator or even to a strong lager like Samichlaus than it is to Carnegie. Similarly, Carnegie is much closer to some kind of English Stout or Porter than it is to Okicim. Arguably, the difference between Carnegie and Okicim is greater than the difference between a Sweet Stout and a Dry Stout. So while it is the geographical origins of a beer that sometimes indicate its style, it seems unlikely that geographical origins qualify as a type of essential nature. Furthermore, we should also note that some Baltic Porters are made with ale yeast while some are made with lager yeast. Baltic Porter doesn't fare well as a natural kind.

Yet why is the geographical origin of a style important? Why should we include it in our criteria for beer style-hood rather than focus exclusively on, for example, the yeast used in fermentation? The reason I think it's important is because I value tradition. I find traditional ways of brewing to be aesthetically pleasing in many different respects. Of course I love a screaming double IPA hopped to the hilt with 30% alpha acid Demon Snuffer hops brewed in a state-of-the-art

Steinecker brew house with a Stromboli internal boiler system as much as the next person. But while brewers continue to innovate, I want to remember the roots. I want to highlight the traditional and regional aspects of beer. And I'm certainly not alone in this. Look at the success of the Campaign for Real Ale, CAMRA. This organization has steered British brewers back towards their traditional method of cask-conditioning. Thus I would claim that it's important to at least try to represent all the possible ways a beer might be brewed in the Baltic region. Moreover, identifying them all as Baltic is important. Should Aldaris and Okicim be identified as Baltic while Carnegie isn't?

So it appears that the classification of beer into beer styles reflects the diverse desires of the beer-brewing and beer-drinking community. This classification is conventional, the natural kind status of a beer is just one of many criteria that are used to classify beer. Therefore, I claim that disputes about classification are inevitable. One reason why this is the case is because there's no consensus about how much any one criterion should be used. Nor does there seem to be a definitive way to answer this question anyway. There is just no clear way to quantify how much a criterion affects the diagnostic characteristics of the style. If we say that 10% of each beer style should represent historical origins and 20% should reflect the yeast used, what would this even mean?

There is another, more fundamental reason why disputes over beer styles will persist. They will persist because disputes over conventional classifications take a rather different form than disputes over realist classifications. In the latter case, all the disputants typically agree on the best way to classify things. For the periodic table, at least in modern chemistry, it's by atomic number. Disputes arise over whether or not it has been clearly shown that such and such element has such and such atomic number. Not whether atomic number is the relevant thing to worry about. The empirical and conceptual dispute over whether or not some element has a particular atomic number seems far more tractable than the dispute over whether atomic number is the relevant criterion in the first place. The empirical and conceptual debate, at least on one philosophical interpretation, has clear standards of adjudication, namely, empirical test and the rules of logic. If something has an essential nature, it's just a matter of time and effort before we discover it, or so the story goes. This is, or was, Putnam's story. I say it "was Putnam's story" because he famously renounced his belief in scientific realism on which he based his theory of natural kinds. On the other hand, the debate about what the proper criteria are in the first place is a debate about values. I value some sort of geographical or historical component while others might value a purely sensory, characteristic-based, criterion. As we've seen, it's hard to accommodate both in the same classification.

Conclusion

Unfortunately, debates about values are notoriously fraught with relativism. How does somebody with a particular set of values convince somebody else with a different set of values that they are wrong? Well, it's not clear how this would happen. In fact, it's not clear that it's even possible. We can't point to values out in the world and say, "See, that's why you're wrong." Typically, some dynamic equilibrium is reached amongst the members of a community. It is an unsteady compromise, with certain values winning sometimes, but ceding ground at other times.

Now some people might argue that the empirical and conceptual debate is similarly fraught with relativism. Some would say that standards of evidence and logic are male-biased, western, or bourgeois. Of course there is neither time nor space to address this issue here. Suffice it to say that I think chemists have made more progress on the periodic table than we have on the classification of beer styles because they aren't arguing over which criteria are appropriate. And we need to remember that even when they were, because the elements are more amenable to a natural kind interpretation than are beer styles, it was at least possible for chemists to find *the right* criteria. With beer, on the other hand, it doesn't seem possible for there to be a "right criteria." Beer is simply the wrong kind of thing for that.

If the debate about beer styles is irreducibly a debate about values, I value a weirdness criterion, a measure of the distance a style departs from others. In other words, I'm putting Mo Betta Bretta in the Mo Westa Weirda style. I'm not quite sure what to do with Aprihop yet.[6]

---

6 I would like to thank Brian Hood and Steven Hales for helpful discussion. The ideas in this essay were influenced by the following sources not cited in the text: J. Dupre, Natural kinds and biological taxa. *The Philosophical Review*, 1981, 90: 66–90; S. Gross, Natural kind terms. In E. K. Brown, ed., *Encyclopedia of Language and Linguistics*. Boston: Elsevier, 2005; S. Schwartz, Putnam on artifacts. *The Philosophical Review*, 1978, 87: 566–74; E. Sober, *The Philosophy of Biology*. Boulder, CO: Westview, 2000.

Part IV

Beer in the History of Philosophy

13

Drink on, the Jolly Prelate Cries

David Hilbert

Tar-Water

The recipe

A curious letter appeared in the *Dublin Journal* for May 8–12, 1744. It is titled "Directions for the making and using tar-water" and the author credit is "By the author of Siris." It begins with a recipe:

> To prevent mistakes in the making tar-water, the public is desired to take notice that Norway tar, which is liquid and of a brown colour, is fittest for this purpose. Four quarts of cold water having been poured on a quart of this tar, and strongly stirred together with a flat stick for three or four minutes, must, after it has stood eight and forty hours to settle, be poured off and kept for use either in bottles or other vessels corked up. The same tar will not do well a second time, but may serve for other uses. Water drawn off the tar the second or third time, if long stirred, may be as strong as the first water, but has not that spirit, and is more disagreeable to the stomach.

It finishes with a description of the point of making this disgusting concoction:

> Of tar-water one pint a day may do in chronical cases, drunk on an empty stomach either at two or four doses, to wit, night and morning and two or three hours after dinner or breakfast; but to children it should be given in less quantity. It may be drunk cold or warm, as anyone likes best, but in acute cases, as fevers of all kinds and pleurisies, it should be drunk warm and in bed, as much and as often as the patient

can bear. For instance, half-a-pint or even a whole pint every hour, which will be made easy by the heat and thirst of the patient. I never knew it fail in the most threatening fevers. For outward fomentations or for beasts to drink, it may be made much stronger by infusion of warm water. I am persuaded tar-water may be drunk with great safety and success for the curing of most diseases, particularly all foul cases, ulcers and eruptions, scurvies of all kinds, nervous disorders, inflammatory distempers, decays, etc.

The mission

The author of this eccentric missive, as most readers of the *Dublin Journal* would have known, was George Berkeley, Anglican Bishop of Cloyne, an obscure diocese in the south of Ireland. Berkeley was Ireland's most distinguished philosopher but he was also an enthusiastic amateur physician. Much of his energy in later life was devoted to promoting the virtues of tar-water which he considered capable of curing an amazingly wide range of illnesses. Berkeley's interest in tar-water was obsessive. He wrote one long book of philosophy, several poems and innumerable letters promoting its use and extolling its virtues. He was an enthusiastic consumer of tar-water himself and inflicted it on his family, friends and those unlucky inhabitants of his diocese whose ills happened to come to his attention. For one brief example of how enthusiasm can cloud judgment, consider the opening lines of the best known of the poems:

On Tar

Hail vulgar juice of never-fading pine!
Cheap as thou art, thy virtues are divine.
　　(*On Tar*. George Berkeley (1744).
　　Dublin printed, London re-printed,
　　for W. Innys, C. Hitch, and C. Davis.)

The poem continues on for another 28 lines dragging God, Nature and the Great Chain of Being into the description of the virtues of water infused with congealed pine sap. Although the writings on tar do reflect Berkeley's philosophical interests and sophistication, his interest in tar-water was intensely practical. He wanted to reduce the amount of human suffering in the world and he thought he had found a cheap and effective means of doing so.

Changing the subject

Tar-water is not an altogether pleasant subject to contemplate. A reasonable simulation of its flavor, although not its yellowish color, can be obtained by diluting turpentine with tap-water. (Only trained philosophers should undertake this experiment since turpentine is toxic and experienced beer drinkers will understand the dangers of drinking undiluted water.) Its central importance in Berkeley's personal health regimen was the relief of constipation. Fortunately for us, Berkeley himself offers a more appealing alternative. In a letter to his good friend Thomas Prior, Berkeley makes an interesting and revealing observation. He claims:

> The virtues of wood-juices shew themselves in spruce-beer, made of molasses and the black spruce-fir in the northern parts of America; and the young shoots of our common spruce-fir have been put to malt liquor in my own family, and make a very wholesome drink.

Berkeley shows himself here not just as a quack, but in addition as a homebrewer and someone who finds malt liquor "wholesome." It is Berkeley the master of obscure lore about the brewing habits of Americans and the consumer of beer for medicinal purposes that we will focus on, leaving the purveyor of toxic alternative medicine behind.

The Problem of Successful Drinking

Berkeley's other mission

Berkeley's desire to benefit mankind was not restricted to the concerns of the body. His first, and best known, humanitarian mission was directed towards philosophical and spiritual concerns. As a young man still in his teens, Berkeley became concerned with the skepticism and atheism that he saw as characterizing the intellectual culture of his times. As Berkeley saw it, the accepted philosophy led to the absurd consequence that the sight of a mug of ale gave no reason to believe that any beverages were present and that this doubt led to the even worse practical consequence that one never had a reason to reach out

181

one's hand for a brew. Added to this was the further claim that one had no reason to thank God for creating a world containing malt and hops, since there is no reason to think that there is a God. In other words, the principles of the philosophers stood in the way of both the pleasures of the tavern and the consolations of religion. Philosophers, according to him, were in the unfortunate position of ". . . doubting of those things which other men evidently know, and believing those things which they laugh at, and despise" (*Dialogues*, preface).[1] This struck the budding philosopher as both wrong and harmful. Fortunately, Berkeley thought he had a solution to these problems. To understand his solution, however, we need to look a little more closely at the problem Berkeley was attempting to address.

Grabbing a brew

Consider the following scenario. You are sitting at a bar with a fresh glass of Guinness in front of you. Wanting a sip of beer you reach out your hand, grasp the glass and bring it to your lips. If all goes well you will be rewarded with a creamy mouthful of stout. This basic pattern is displayed many times over on a good day. We are so familiar with the sequence; want something, do something, get what you want; that we rarely reflect on what a complicated affair this actually is. We'll leave to one side for now the problem of how it is that our wants are actually within our grasp and focus on how it is that we know what to do in order to satisfy those wants. Exactly what you need to do in order to get your beer depends on where it is in relation to you. If it is in front of you, you will need to extend your arm forward. If it is to the side you will need to reach to the side. We've all had the experience of watching others, who may have enjoyed one too many, miscalculate and fail at this essential task. In order to succeed at your goal, taking a drink of your beer, you need to know that there is a beer on the bar and exactly where it is in relation to you. If you are wrong about where it is you will miss the glass (or worse, knock it over). If you are wrong about what is on the bar you may succeed in grasping it and bringing it to your lips but you could end up gagging on a mouthful of Chablis instead of enjoying your stout.

---

[1] George Berkeley, *Three Dialogues between Hylas and Philonous*. Indianapolis: Hackett Publishing, 1979. First published 1713.

There is no mystery, at least prior to the intervention of philosophers, about how you find out that it is stout, not Chablis, and that it is in front of you, not to the side. You know what is there and where it is by looking. In general, it is by using our senses that we gain the knowledge that we need in order to successfully drink (or do anything else). Success in obtaining a drink depends on the properties and relations of the things around us and it is perception that gives us knowledge of those properties and relations. Without perception we could not intelligently guide our behavior and, even in a target-rich environment like your neighborhood tavern, random reaching movements are unlikely to procure your desired beverage (and if you are unlucky may lead to terrifying results such as drinking diet pop). Fortunately we are equipped with senses that provide us with the information about the world around us that we need in order to behave in ways that are likely to lead to the results that we desire. We can summarize this explanation of why we often succeed in obtaining what we want in two principles:

1   The success of our actions depends on the properties and relations of the things around us – for example, where the mugs, bottles and glasses are and what's in them.
2   Our senses give us knowledge of the properties and relations of the things around us.

If both principles are true, then what we need for successful drinking is knowledge of what kind of drinks are where and our senses provide us with this knowledge. Unfortunately this simple explanation of our successful imbibing has satisfied very few philosophers. In particular, the truth of the second principle has been doubted by troublemaking, wine-drinking, philosophers since antiquity.

The relativity of perception

A variety of reasons have been given for doubting that the senses provide us directly with accurate knowledge of the world, but most of these reasons fall into two basic categories. First, there is the undeniable fact that what the senses tell us about the world can change even while the relevant parts of the world remain unchanged. My beer looks darker viewed through the green or amber glass of the bottle allow for the ordering of sensory content – they are not part of the content itself. The analogy with a painting was pretty helpful, but now, instead of a painting, think of *experiencing* the sun shining on a Kentish hopfield. I see the sun above me shining down on the hops in front of me and at the same time I smell the strong aroma of hops wafting in the air. I see the picking basket full of hops next to me just after I heard it being placed on the ground to my left. Before I hand the exhausted picker an empty basket from my right, I offer her a refreshing pint of IPA from one of the kegs behind me. Above, below, left, right, next to, in front of, behind, before, after, at the same time as – my experience is run through with spatio-temporal relationships. I think we can see that the other elements of the experience are ordered in space and time, but are space and time really so different from the other elements such as the sun, hops, air, aromas, baskets, pickers, IPA, etc? Well, yes they are.

Notice how the situation differs with regard to space and time and the other elements of experience. Take away the IPA and the experience is cruelly transformed into one with exhausted but unrefreshed hop pickers. Take away the hop pickers (refreshed or unrefreshed) and the experience is transformed into one with the sun shining on an unharvested hopfield. The elements may change, but experience remains. Removing specific elements of content would simply transform one experience into another. This is true even for something that seems as ubiquitous as air. Remove the air from our Kentish hopfield and the experience is transformed into a *very short* experience of the sun shining on a Kentish hopfield in a vacuum. Take away space and time, however, and the experience isn't simply transformed – it is obliterated. Think for a moment about all the sensory content, both outer and inner, that you have ever experienced, are currently experiencing, or ever will experience, and then take away space and time. What would your experience of that sensory content be like? There would be all the same sensory content, but no spatio-temporal framework to order it – no before, no after, no same time as, no top, no bottom, no left, no right, no next to, no tall, no short, no etc. Without the spatio-temporal relations that provide structure for the sensory content, the best we would be left with would be unordered sensations and not an experience at all. Thus, space and time (or perhaps some alternative sensory form – but more on this later), are required for the possibility of having any experience at all.

198

than it does after being poured into a clear mug. The flavor of my beer changes depending on exactly which delicacies I've consumed from the bowl of munchies on the bar. Second, there are "unusual" situations in which the senses generate obviously false information. Hallucinations and other gross disturbances of our perceptual faculties are examples of this kind of situation. Other, much more common, examples are the double vision and the spinning sensation that afflict those who over-imbibe.[2] One important influence on Berkeley was the great French philosopher René Descartes who discusses these arguments in his book, *Meditations on First Philosophy*. Berkeley, himself, has an extensive discussion of these kind of considerations in his most widely read book, *Three Dialogues between Hylas and Philonous*.[3] Both agree that these considerations lead to the conclusion that the senses don't provide us with any direct contact with an independently existing world outside our minds. Berkeley, unlike Descartes, further argues that the senses do not provide evidence of any kind regarding the existence or nature of a world outside our minds. What we learn from the smooth cold feel of the bottle in hand concerns only our *experience* of the bottle and not the properties of objects that exist independently of us. The experience of the insipid flavor of Knickerbocker Natural Light informs you only of the experience and provides no reason to believe that there is such a travesty of the brewer's art that exists independent of your experience.[4] If what we need to know in order to act sensibly concerns the properties and relations of things that exist external to us then, according to Berkeley, the senses will be no help. Philosophical reflection has led us into a dead end by offering us an explanation of the possibility of successful action and then undermining one of the crucial components of that explanation.

---

[2] A more subtle example that crosses categories is the undeniable fact that the more beer one drinks the better it tastes. This basic case is, of course, closely related to the (temporary) increase in conversational brilliance and physical attractiveness that is directly correlated with the number of brews consumed.

[3] Berkeley, *Dialogues*.

[4] My bachelor party focused not on strippers or pornography but rather on cheap beer. Paradoxically, the beer I remember best out of a thoroughly detestable lot was the Knickerbocker Natural Light and what I remember is its truly amazing lack of flavor. Fill a glass with beer, pour out the beer and, without rinsing, fill it with water. You will have created a liquid indistinguishable in taste from Knickerbocker Natural Light. I have never understood the point of this beverage.

Berkeley's Solution

The beer is in the mind

Fortunately for tavern owners everywhere, Berkeley had a solution to the problem of successful drinking. The solution is in one sense very simple. Berkeley denies that bottles and cans (and the beer contained in them) exist independently of being perceived. Your idea of lager and the stuff itself are the very same thing. This solves our problem because our experiences and ideas are perfectly known by us. It may be possible to doubt that there is anything in the external world that corresponds to the sight of a freshly filled glass of Guinness (extra chilled) with foam running down its sides but it is not possible to doubt that it looks that way to me. By moving the Guinness inside your mind, Berkeley eliminates the possibility of error. The glass of Guinness is, according to Berkeley, neither more nor less than an idea in your mind and like all of your ideas it exists whenever you have it and it is exactly as it seems to you. Berkeley's fundamental insight is so simple that he managed to express it in a three-word Latin slogan: *Esse est percipi* (to be is to be perceived). The problem of perceptual error flows from the gap between our knowledge of the nature of our experiences and the world that exists independently of being experienced. Berkeley solves the problem by denying that there is a world that exists independently of being experienced. The prevailing philosophical view in Berkeley's time held that there are two basic kinds of stuff in the world, mind and matter. Matter was unthinking while mind was immaterial and did the thinking. Berkeley denies the existence of unthinking stuff, matter, and claims that all that exists is minds and their ideas. There are bottles of beer but they exist only as ideas in some mind or other. The beer that you drink is in your mind in the same way that your idea of the taste of a perfect pale ale is in your mind. Both exist because they are perceived and both are exactly as you perceive them to be. What is much more complicated is to understand how an apparently sane young man could have taken this idea seriously.

I refute it thus

When Berkeley published these ideas the initial reaction was, to put it mildly, hostile. His theory was not so much refuted as ridiculed and it

185

is easy to see why. The central objection was vividly put by Samuel Johnson, a noted British intellectual and the compiler of the first real dictionary of English. Johnson, on having Berkeley's solution to the problem of perceptual error explained to him, walked over to a large rock and kicked it hard enough that he bounced backwards saying, "I refute it thus." Johnson's point being, presumably, that ideas are not the sort of thing that one can bounce backwards off. We can put the point slightly differently. When I grab the glass before me, it resists the pressure of my hand. When I tip it into my mouth the amber liquid flows down my throat. After my second or third glass my conversation becomes more animated. Mere ideas cannot resist pressure, flow down my throat and cause me to become intoxicated. Beer that existed only in the mind would be beer that failed to do any of things that beer does. The difference between ideas and the objects with which they are associated is that objects cause effects on us and other things while ideas are merely the passive contents of our minds. Berkeley, perhaps under the influence of spruce beer, has made a serious philosophical blunder. His solution to the problem of perceptual error leaves us without any account of successful drinking. What I want, after all, is not to have ideas of beer but to have the effects of beer. I want not only to experience it visually but I want to be able to act on the basis of that experience to accomplish my goals. If what I see is something that exists merely in my mind how can I use what vision tells me to pick up the beer and get a drink. I can't grab ideas and I certainly can't drink them. What is the point of the error-free perception of beverages that Berkeley guarantees if it doesn't allow me to drink them?

The possibility of successful drinking

To see why we cannot just dismiss Berkeley's solution to the problem of perceptual error as silly we need to look again at what is involved in successful action. In every case when you desire a drink of beer there is some situation that you are in. In some of those situations reaching out your arm and performing a coordinated set of movements of your mouth, hand and arm will result in a refreshing drink of fine malt beverage. In other situations that same sequence of movements will result in a disgusting mouthful of Red Bull and vodka. In yet other situations you will be merely making a pointless sequence of motions that results in nothing entering your mouth. In some situations reaching a little to the right or in others reaching a little to the left will result in the desired drink. Depending on which situation you are in the very same action can produce any of a variety of results and any of a variety of actions can produce the desired result. In order to achieve your goal you must know which of these situations you are in; how results are connected to actions. In other words, what you need to know are action–experience connections. If I perform one movement I will experience the taste of Pilsner Urquell, if I perform a different movement I will experience the taste of white Zinfandel. If I know the prevailing action–experience connections I can get the experience of a smooth, although slightly bitter beer and avoid the cloying sweetness of the wine. If I don't know the prevailing action–experience connections then I will be fumbling about at random with no idea how to get what I want nor any means to predict what I get.

According to Berkeley, perception tells us what the prevailing action–experience connections are. The sight of a tall glass of amber fluid with white foam on top allows me to predict the experience I will have if I reach out my hand and bring it to my mouth. The sight of a small glass full of pinkish liquid allows me to predict a different experience from performing the same action. Although, according to Berkeley, both glasses are merely ideas in my mind they serve as signs of the prevailing connections between movements and future experiences. The beer that I see does not cause the taste that I experience, since ideas don't cause anything, but that doesn't matter as long as it is a reliable sign of the drinking experience I will have as a result of grasping the glass and bringing it to my mouth. As long as my perceptual ideas are a reliable guide to the results of action then it doesn't matter that the things that I perceive are ideas in my mind rather than objects that exist independently of being perceived.

And perception is a reliable guide to the prevailing action–experience connections. Although Johnson may have been correct that the idea of a stone didn't cause him to rebound backwards, the perception of a stone is a reliable indicator that the situation is one in which forceful kicking movements will produce the experience of pain and falling backwards. Berkeley's point is that as long we can successfully predict the results of our actions then we don't need to know their causes. Perceiving a bottle is a sign that we learn to interpret, a sign that predicts the results of various courses of action. What is important is that there be regular connections between perceptual experiences, actions, and future experiences. As long as those connections – which Berkeley calls the laws of nature – exist, then we can happily go about our drinking. That the signs are merely ideas in our minds is not a problem as long as the signs do their job.

The divine bartender

There are two problems that still face Berkeley's theory. First, not all ideas are alike. Stuck at the college reception forced to choose between apple juice and sparkling water, I imagine instead that there is a cold bottle of Goose Island on the table. When I imagine the bottle of beer it exists as a bottle in my mind. But this is the only way any bottle of beer exists according to Berkeley. The imaginary beer and the "real" beer are exactly alike in this way: both are nothing more than ideas in my mind. But the beer that I see is a useful guide to the action–experience connections, while the beer that I merely imagine is not. Reaching out for imaginary brews, even at a college reception, does not quench one's thirst and can produce an unfortunate reaction from onlookers. Since both beers exist according to Berkeley, he can't account for the difference between them in terms of which one is really there and which is not.

This problem suggests a second, even more pressing one. We have seen that perception often is a good guide to the prevailing action–experience connections, but it seems that Berkeley can offer no explanation of this fact. The common sense solution, that the consequences of action are determined by the properties and relations of the objects around us, is not available to Berkeley. He cannot explain why drinking from a glass filled with beer tastes different from drinking from a glass filled with milk by appealing to the nature of the contents of the two glasses. The glasses, being mere ideas, have no contents and thus can't be the cause of the taste sensations we experience. Berkeley instead appeals to the regular connection between seeing glasses filled with amber fluid, the action of drinking, and the taste of beer. Yet why is there this regular connection?

The last piece of Berkeley's puzzle provides his solution to both these problems and finally allows us to see the future Bishop's philosophical framework completed. The missing piece is the existence of an all-powerful, all-knowing being who always acts to produce the best possible result, i.e. God. We won't concern ourselves with Berkeley's attempts to argue that God exists but instead examine the role God plays in Berkeley's explanation of action and perception. Consider again the difference between the imaginary brew and its real counterpart. When I imagine the cold bottle in my hand what I imagine is up to me. If it is Guinness I want it is Guinness I get. If I prefer Foster's then it is an oversized can in my hand. If I wish to avoid Lucky Lager then I can do so. Other ideas I have are not up to me. When I look at the container on the table in front of me, I don't get to decide what I see. The ideas of sense are not under my control and if Lucky Lager is my fate then it is Lucky Lager that I see, no matter how much I wish it were Guinness. These ideas, the ideas that come from the senses, are caused by God, not by me. It's God that sets the rules for what I see, touch, hear, taste and smell. It's also God that determines the action–experience connections which obtain in any circumstance. Because God is benevolent, wants only the best, He causes ideas in us according to certain regular patterns. When we see a bottle and reach for it we will get one kind of touch experience. When we see a can and reach for it we will get a different kind of touch experience. By establishing regular connections among experiences, actions, and further experiences, God makes it possible for us to engage in successful action. By choosing based on the signs given to us by God, we are able to predict the future experiences we will have. God underwrites the associations between ideas that allow for successful action, and the ideas of real things are the ideas caused in us by God. As Berkeley puts the point:

> The ideas of Sense are more strong, lively, and distinct than those of the imagination; they have likewise a steadiness, order, and coherence, and are not excited at random, as those which are the effects of human wills often are, but in a regular train or series, the admirable connexion whereof sufficiently testifies the wisdom and benevolence of its Author. Now the set rules or established methods wherein the Mind we depend on excites in us the ideas of sense, are called the laws of nature; and these we learn by experience, which teaches us that such and such ideas are attended with such and such other ideas, in the ordinary course of things.
>
> This gives us a sort of foresight which enables us to regulate our actions for the benefit of life. And without this we should be eternally at a loss; we could not know how to act anything that might procure us the least pleasure, or remove the least pain of sense. That food nourishes, sleep refreshes, and fire warms us; that to sow in the seed-time is the way to reap in the harvest; and in general that to obtain such or such

189

ends, such or such means are conducive – all this we know, not by discovering any necessary connexion between our ideas, but only by the observation of the settled laws of nature, without which we should be all in uncertainty and confusion, and a grown man no more know how to manage himself in the affairs of life than an infant just born. (*Principles*, 30–1)[5]

God serves the drinks, but does so in response to our orders and according to a menu established by him. Our job is to use the hints he gives us to figure out what is on the menu so that our orders will satisfy our desires.

Successful drinking at last

All the elements to Berkeley's solution to the problem of successful action are now before us. The problem of perceptual error is solved by getting rid of matter. Beer, and everything else that we perceive, exists only as an idea in the mind and not independently of the mind. Since we know our ideas perfectly we also know that the beer is just as we perceive it to be. A new explanation of successful action is now necessary and Berkeley supplies it. Successful action depends on knowledge of action–experience connections and not the properties of material things existing independently of us. The action–experience connections are guaranteed by God and he causes in us sensory ideas that serve as signs of the prevailing action–experience connections, signs that we can learn from experience. Here's how it works in a more concrete case. I want a drink and I walk to the kitchen and open the refrigerator. God causes in me visual ideas of the contents of the refrigerator. He gives me the idea of a can of diet root beer on the top shelf. He gives me the idea of bottle of Beck's on the bottom shelf. I have learned from experience that one sort of reaching motion will procure the root beer and a different sort of reaching motion the Beck's. Depending on which action I perform He will then give me either the idea of grasping a can or a bottle. Further actions will result in experiencing either the taste of artificial sweeteners or the taste of beer. Although the beer *is* in the mind, that is no obstacle to obtaining and drinking it. In fact, according to Berkeley, this account of action is the only workable

---

5 George Berkeley, *A Treatise Concering the Principles of Human Knowledge*. Oxford: Oxford University Press, 1998. First published 1710.

one and if only it were to be adopted great benefits of all kinds would be obtained. In one of his more grandiose moments he describes the benefits to mankind that will follow on acceptance of his theory:

> If the principles, which I here endeavor to propagate, are admitted for true; the consequences which, I think, evidently flow from thence, are, that atheism and skepticism will be utterly destroyed, many intricate points made plain, great difficulties solved, several useless parts of science retrenched, speculation referred to practice, and men reduced from paradoxes to common sense. (*Dialogues*, preface)[6]

We don't need to share his enthusiasm, he was a very young man when he wrote this, but we can still appreciate his cleverness and ingenuity in pursuing his mission.

Conclusion: Berkeley's Missions

Berkeley saw no conflict between his practical interest in brewing beer and improving health and his speculative interest in convincing philosophers that the concept of matter was unhelpful (and incoherent). Although the only things in the world are minds and ideas we can still eat and drink and cure illness. Berkeley recognized that it seems odd to say that "we eat and drink ideas and are clothed with ideas" (*Principles*, 38).[7] As Berkeley points out, however, sounding odd is not an obstacle to truth. As I take a bite of my liverwurst and onion sandwich which I wash down with a drink from my tall glass of weissbier I would not think to describe what I am doing in Berkeley's terms. There is hardly anything in the world less ethereal, with the possible exception of tar, than a liverwurst and onion sandwich and to say that it is an idea seems odd indeed. Berkeley's ideas, however, can be just as pungent as liverwurst or just as smooth and tart as weissbier. To eat liverwurst and drink weissbier is just to have some sensory ideas and adding independent existence doesn't make the sensory experience any more vivid or concrete. Once the importance of action–experience connections is properly understood then my later bad breath and mild buzz are also adequately explained. And if we can explain bad breath

6 Berkeley, *Dialogues*.
7 Berkeley, *Principles*.

David Hilbert

in this way then we can also explain the healthful effects, if any, of tar-water in the very same way. As long as God is around to impose appropriate punishments (the smell of liver and onions) for misguided culinary decisions and appropriate rewards (lack of pain in the gut) for drinking disgusting concoctions, there is no need for matter in the world. God and ideas we can't deny but matter is unnecessary, and indeed, the idea of it is intellectually harmful. A world without matter is according to Berkeley, just the world as we experience it. Although it may seem odd to say that we eat and drink ideas there is nothing odd at all about actually eating and drinking ideas. Whenever you munch a pretzel or chug a brew you are doing nothing more nor less than eating and drinking ideas.

14

Beer Goggles and
Transcendental Idealism

Steven M. Bayne

Some beer drinkers have reported a remarkable side effect of drinking beer – their drinking partners become more beautiful. Typically, such reports are made only in retrospect. It is not until the next morning, when Fiona once again gazes on her drinking partner, that she is prone to report that he was a lot cuter the night before. Well, actually Fiona's report is most likely to simply take the form of an exclamation – something like "Oh my God, what was I thinking!" for example.

Now, it is unlikely that anyone would accuse philosophers of letting a lack of evidence stand in the way of an interesting discussion, so it probably does not matter whether there is anything more than anecdotal evidence for the beer goggles effect, but it may be worth noting that there does appear to be more than just anecdotal evidence. In their 2003 article, psychologists from Glasgow University and the University of St Andrews found that heterosexuals between 18 and 26 years old who had drunk the equivalent of one half to three pints of beer within a three-hour period rated faces of the opposite sex as more attractive than those faces were rated by people who had not had anything to drink.[1] Furthermore, the psychologists found no beer goggles effect when heterosexual subjects rated either the attractiveness of faces of members of the same sex, the distinctiveness of faces of either sex, or even the attractiveness of objects other than human faces. So there is some experimental evidence that beer goggles do in

---

[1] B. T. Jones, B. C. Jones, A. P. Thomas, and J. Piper, Alcohol consumption increases attractiveness ratings of opposite-sex faces: a possible third route to risky sex. *Addiction*, 2003, 98 (8): 1069–75.

193

fact exist, but do they have the effect of making our drinking partners more *beautiful*?

Subjective versus Objective

When Fiona retrospectively reports the effects of beer goggles by exclaiming something like "Oh my God, what was I thinking!", it should be clear that Fiona doesn't believe Dwayne actually was cuter last night, but that somehow last night he only *seemed* to be more attractive. In other words, Fiona realizes that her beer goggles did not affect Dwayne himself, but only the way he appeared to her. Drinking a couple pints of Sam Smith's Oatmeal Stout did not change how attractive Dwayne was, but it only affected how attractive Dwayne seemed to Fiona. As many of us are inclined to do, Fiona is here distinguishing between subjective and objective elements of cognition – that is, those elements of cognition that are due to our own constitutions versus those that are due to the constitutions of objects.

Cognitions dealing with taste are regularly taken to be ones that are due to our own constitutions rather than strictly the nature of the object. So for example, when I brew a steam beer I use Wyeast American Lager yeast rather than their California Lager yeast, because I find that the California Lager yeast produces an unpleasant taste. To me it tastes way too citrusy – almost like someone left a grapefruit in my beer. On the other hand, someone else may find the taste of the California Lager yeast to be perfectly delicious – actually not just someone, but apparently lots of someones as it seems to be the standard yeast to use in steam beer. After running across enough people who seem to like the taste of steam beer produced with California Lager yeast, I (mostly) gave up on the idea that there was simply something in the taste of the beer that I was able to detect but everyone else was missing, and I came to believe there is just something about my subjective constitution that makes the yeast's taste disagreeable to me. It's not that I've stopped thinking it tastes unpleasant, it's just that I have now come to attribute this to my sense of taste rather than to the beer itself.

Of course not all cognitions of the beer work this way. For example, if I am not concerned with how California Lager yeast tastes, but with its being a bottom-fermenting yeast, this doesn't seem to have anything to do with my own constitution. That is, although the construction of my sensitive and cognitive faculties may be responsible for the way the beer tastes to me, it does not affect whether the yeast ferments on the bottom or at the top. Let my senses and intellect be ever so different than they are (or even non-existent), California Lager yeast will still be a bottom-fermenting yeast.

It may not be surprising that the taste of something turns out to depend not simply on the characteristics of objects, but also on the construction of our sense faculties. Traditionally, however, philosophers have counted other qualities as subjective that ordinarily we might think of as being objective characteristics of objects. For example, one such quality is color. The deep dark brown color of the roasted barley I use in my toasted oatmeal stout, for example, is something I take to be more like the characteristic of being a bottom-fermenting yeast than the case of an unpleasant taste – that is, I attribute the deep dark brown color to the roasted barley itself rather than to my subjective constitution. Philosophers, however, have traditionally considered color, just like taste, to be a *secondary* quality – that is, dependent on our subjective constitutions.

In his *Essay Concerning Human Understanding* (1690), John Locke explains that primary qualities are ones such as solidity, size, shape, motion, and quantity while secondary qualities are ones such as color, sound, taste, warmth, or cold. Primary qualities are characteristics objects have in and of themselves, independent of our perceptions of them. Secondary qualities, however, are "nothing in the objects themselves, but powers to produce various sensations in us by their primary qualities" (Locke, *Essay*, bk. II, ch. VIII, 10).[2] Consequently, on one standard interpretation of the primary–secondary quality distinction, since tastes, colors, sounds, etc. are due to our own constitutions, if there were no human cognizers, there would be no tastes, colors, sounds, etc. Yet even if there were no human cognizers, the solidity, size, shape, motion, and quantity of objects would still remain the same. Without any human cognizers, that freshly poured pint of Bell's Amber Ale that is now located on the bar would have no taste, it would have no color,

---

[2] John Locke, *An Essay Concerning Human Understanding*. London: Penguin, 1974. Originally published 1690.

it wouldn't have any aroma, it wouldn't make a sound, and it would be neither warm nor cold.

Space, Time, and the Subjective Constitution of our Mind

Some of you may be willing to accept that beer-goggles-enhanced attractiveness and characteristics such as tastes, colors, sounds, etc. do not exist in the objects themselves, but instead are characteristics that only arise because of our own cognitive constitutions, but how far are you willing to go? In the late eighteenth century, Immanuel Kant also recognized the distinction between qualities that are due to the constitutions of objects and those that are due to our subjective constitutions. He doesn't mention beer goggles specifically, but he does write in his *Critique of Pure Reason* that "we ordinarily distinguish quite well between that which is . . . valid for every human sense in general, and that which . . . is valid . . . only for a particular situation or organization of this or that sense" (A45/B62).[3] "And so," Kant continues, "one calls the first cognition one that represents the object in itself, but the second only the appearance of it." Basically, size, shape, motion, and quantity (spatio-temporal qualities – qualities that are consistent for all human perceivers) are the ones we attribute to the objects themselves, while tastes, colors, sounds, odors, warmth, cold (qualities that are limited to only one sense or can vary from perceiver to perceiver), or even more variable qualities such as beer-goggles-enhanced attractiveness (qualities that we only experience sometimes under special conditions) are the ones we attribute only to the way the objects appear. Kant tells us that although we commonly stop here, we should not. That is, according to Kant, although the spatio-temporal qualities are consistent and universal for all human perceivers, they still cannot represent objects as they are in themselves, because space and time themselves "belong only to . . . the subjective constitution of our mind" (A23/B38).

According to Kant, there are two elements in the objects we perceive: matter (or content) and form (or structure). Neither element by

---

[3] Immanuel Kant, *The Critique of Pure Reason*. Edited and translated by P. Guyer and A. W. Wood. Cambridge University Press, 1998. First published 1781.

itself is complete. Matter must have structure in order to be an object. On the other hand, without matter, there would be nothing to have structure in the first place. Think about a painting. The paint is the matter and the canvas is the form. In order to have a painting, bits of paint must be spread out on some sort of canvas – paint by itself doesn't make a painting anymore than a canvas by itself does. A painting of the sun shining on a Kentish hopfield can't be made with paint by itself. Of course the paints are the raw materials for the painting, but without some sort of canvas, how would we be able to relate the bit of paint that is supposed to represent the sun to the bits of paint that are supposed to represent the hop flowers? For that matter we even need some sort of canvas in order to arrange the bits of paint that represent the sun or hop flowers individually – if there is no canvas of any kind, then all we have are paints and not a painting of the sun shining on a Kentish hopfield at all.

In the case of a painting it is relatively easy to recognize the elements of form and content. In the case of a painting, although in the finished product we see form and content mixed together as one, since we often see the painting process from start to finish, we regularly see the elements of form separated from the elements of matter – the form separated from the raw materials – the canvas separated from the paints. This makes it easy for us to distinguish between the elements of form and the elements of matter in a painting. In the world we experience through our senses, however, it is a very different case. Kant argued that we commonly don't realize that in sense experience, "even in the deepest research into its objects" (A45/B62), we never experience the raw materials separately from the form. Everything we experience is already a combination of form and content. As a result, we ordinarily don't recognize that there are both material and formal elements to the objects we perceive. So, what are the formal elements within our sensory experience? According to Kant, they are space and time.

We don't ordinarily think of space and time as being any different than any other objects in our sensory experience, but Kant wants us to realize that space and time are not just ordinary objects – instead space and time are what make our experience of objects possible in the first place. Just as bits of paint require a canvas in order to be a painting, in order to be sensory experience, sensations (the raw materials of sensory experience) require some form or structure in which they can be ordered. According to Kant, space and time are the forms that

197

Space and time may be prerequisites for experience by being the forms in which sensory content is ordered, but how does this lead us to the conclusion that they only belong to the subjective constitution of the human mind? Well, according to Kant, if the form that provides structure and order for sensory content were itself part of that sensory content, it would itself stand in just as much need of structure and order as the sensory content it is supposed to provide order for. According to Kant, space and time are the forms of human sensibility and as such they have their source in the constitution of the human mind, not in the constitution of things as they are in themselves.

The Reality of Space and Time

If space and time belong only to the subjective constitution of our mind, does this mean space and time are no more real than the added attractiveness produced by beer goggles? The short answer is no. We can see this in an ordinary sense by remembering that we experience the beer goggles effect only in special circumstances. Fiona perceived Dwayne to have enhanced cuteness only after drinking a couple of pints. When she realizes that special circumstances are required for perceiving this enhanced cuteness, Fiona also realizes that this enhanced cuteness is not an objective or real characteristic of Dwayne. The same is true for secondary qualities such as the unpleasant taste I experience with beers made with California Lager yeast. Although I experience this unpleasant taste whenever I drink such a beer (and not just when I am in special circumstances), since other people drinking the same beers do not experience an unpleasant taste, I conclude the unpleasant taste must not be an objective or real characteristic of the California Lager yeast – after all, I reason, if it were a real characteristic of the yeast, wouldn't other people taste it too? On the other hand, the cylindricality of Fiona's "Drink 'till he's cute" insulated beer can holder is perceived by anyone who perceives the holder. I don't just perceive the cylindricality after I've had a certain amount to drink, but I perceive it whenever I experience the holder. I'm also not the only one that perceives it – everyone else does too. Since the perception of the cylindricality neither occurs only in special circumstances nor varies from person to person, we conclude that cylindricality is an objective or real quality of the beer can holder. In an ordinary sense, then, it is plain that particular spatio-temporal qualities are more objective or real than qualities such as beer-goggles-enhanced attractiveness or secondary qualities.

Furthermore, if we think about space and time in general and not just the objectivity of particular spatio-temporal relations in particular cases, we can see that on Kant's view the reality of space and time is very different to the reality of beer-goggles-enhanced attractiveness, secondary qualities, or even particular instances of spatio-temporal qualities. Each of the latter three apply to our sensory experiences only contingently. That is, we may or may not experience the beer goggles effect, we may or may not experience a taste as being unpleasant, and the beer holder we experience may or may not be cylindrical. Space and time, however, necessarily apply to our sensory experiences. Remember that on Kant's view, space and time are the forms of human sensibility – they make human sensory experience possible. Therefore, every sensory experience we have must be a spatio-temporal experience. As a result, Kant asserts that his position "teaches the *empirical reality* of [space and] time, i.e., objective validity in regard to all objects that may ever be given to our senses" (A35/B52). How much more real do you want? Oh, you want space and time to have reality *outside* the framework of human cognition (this is what Kant would call having *transcendental reality*). Well, you can't have it.

According to Kant, space and time are *transcendentally ideal*. That is, outside the framework of human cognition space and time are meaningless – they are real "only from the human standpoint" (A26/B42). We humans are prone to project our perspective onto other thinking beings and even onto the world as it is in itself. Space and time are the canvas we humans must use to structure our sensory content, but there is no way to know whether other types of thinking beings use this very same canvas to organize their sensory data. For all we know they may use klaatu, barada, and nikto instead of space and time. Although space and time would be meaningless for such beings, klaatu, barada, and nikto would have as much empirical reality for them as space and time do for us. Neither form for structuring sensory data, however, has transcendental reality – that is, neither is valid for things as they are in themselves independent of the constitution of cognizers. Outside the framework of human cognition, space and time have no more reality than the added attractiveness perceived through beer goggles.

200

If space and time are empirically real, but transcendentally ideal, what can we say about the reality of the spatio-temporal objects themselves? Well, remember that freshly poured pint of Bell's Amber Ale we left on the bar a few pages ago? Well, I think it probably has warmed up enough now for us to be able to taste the flavor of the malt, so go ahead and take a taste . . . What? You've already finished yours? Well all right, go ahead and imagine another freshly poured pint – just make sure you imagine it being served at the appropriate temperature this time (it's a good thing we are trusting imagination here and not American bars and restaurants). Speaking empirically, there are many things we can say about this ale – we can talk about its copper color, the aroma of its hops, the flavor of the malt, the characteristic flavor of the yeast, the sound of the bubbles bursting as they surface, etc. Even if you choose to join with those who attribute such secondary qualities to our subjective constitution and not the beer itself, speaking empirically there is still a lot we are able to say about it. We can talk about its location on the bar, the volume it takes up in the glass, the motion of its bubbles, the location of the yeast's fermentation, the length of time it took to ferment, etc.

If, however, we were to accept the transcendental ideality of space and time, but we were not satisfied only speaking empirically, what could we say about the beer as it is in itself? Let's start with things we couldn't say. We clearly cannot say it has been freshly poured – *freshly poured* makes reference not only to a temporal relation (*freshly* signifying that the pouring was a recent event), but also to a spatial relation (*poured* signifying a change in location from one container to another). Clearly we also cannot talk about the beer's being a pint, for talking about a *pint* of something refers to its taking up a certain volume of space. You might think we could talk about its being an ale, but, alas, *ale* refers to a beer that is made with a top-fermenting yeast – of course *top* signifies a spatial relation, while fermentation is a process and these involve temporal relationships between the parts of the process, so we can't even talk about its being an ale without making reference to space and time. Of course it should be obvious that it wouldn't make sense to talk about the beer's being an extended substance without space and likewise about its being an enduring substance without time. So, if we can't talk about something in such basic terms as its being a process, an extended thing, or an enduring thing without space and time, then what can we say about things as they are in and of themselves, independent of our cognitive constitutions? In short, nothing. Kant tells us that "what may be the case with objects in themselves and abstracted from all this receptivity of our senses remains completely unknown to us" (A42/B59).

Arguments for Kant's Position

Reactions to Kant's theory may vary, but you may be inclined to wonder why you should accept it. In the case of the beer goggles effect we have experiential evidence. We believe in the beer goggles effect because like Fiona we can wake up the next day to gaze upon our drinking partners when we are not wearing our beer goggles (of course, they also get that same opportunity with us). It is because we are regularly able to compare our experiences of our drinking partners while we are wearing beer goggles to our experiences of them when we are not wearing our beer goggles, that we are able to conclude that the enhanced beauty is due to a change in our constitution rather than our partner's constitution. Yet we shouldn't expect any proof for Kant's position on space and time that is quite so dramatic as Fiona's "Oh my God, what was I thinking?" Since space and time are prerequisites for our having any experiences at all, we can't very well expect to have an "Oh my God, that's what things are like without space and time" experience. If we can't have a proof like this, why should we believe space and time are due to the constitution of the human mind rather than to the constitutions of things in themselves?

First of all, remember that Kant argues there are two elements in our experience or cognition: matter and form. Our sensations are the matter, while space and time are the forms in which they are ordered. Kant argued that space and time must have their source in the constitution of our mind because they could not be the means by which our sensory content is structured if they themselves were part of that very content. If they were themselves part of that sensory content, they would stand in need of ordering just as much as any other element of sensory content. If space and time stood in need of structure and order themselves, how could they in turn provide structure and order for our sensory content? Whatever serves as the form for sensory content cannot have its source in that sensory content itself. Thus, this form (space and time in our case) must have its source in the constitution of the mind.

Kant's second argument for identifying the human mind as the source of space and time concerns the consequences of denying this claim. In particular, Kant believes that if space and time were part of the matter or content of experience, there would be unacceptable consequences for the science of mathematics – namely, it would turn out to be an experimental science just like sciences such as physics, chemistry, biology, or even zymurgy. According to Kant, the subject matter of mathematics is space and time. If space and time, however, were part of our sensory content (rather than the form by which the content is ordered), this would mean that we would need to gain our mathematical knowledge in the same way that we gain knowledge of the rest of our sensory content – that is, through experience. In other words, we wouldn't learn, for example, the Pythagorean Theorem by means of some process of abstract reasoning, but instead we would need to learn it experimentally. We would learn it in much the same way that we learn, for example, that two ounces of Northern Brewers hops adds the same amount of bitterness to a beer as about three and a half ounces of Kent Goldings hops. In the case of the hops, we would add different amounts of the two types of hops to different batches of the same beer until we discovered at what point the different hops have an equal bittering effect. In the case of the Pythagorean Theorem we would have to go and measure the lengths of the sides of various right triangles in order to see whether the square of the hypotenuse does in fact equal the sums of the squares of the other two sides. Now I think you will agree that we don't normally see mathematicians roaming around measuring the angles of various right triangles or doing experiments in a lab, but you might find yourself wondering why exactly it is supposed to be such a bad thing if mathematics were an experimental science of this kind. Well, the truths of mathematics are supposed to be absolutely certain and necessary, but the things we learn from experience are neither. Usually when I substitute three and a half ounces of Kent Goldings hops for two ounces of Northern Brewers hops, I get approximately the same bitterness in the finished beer, *but there are no guarantees*. Are we willing to settle for the same thing with mathematics? Are we willing to settle for a claim such as *usually* 7 + 5 = 12, *but there are no guarantees*? Kant believes the answer to these questions is absolutely not. According to Kant, the only way to avoid this result and maintain the certainty and necessity of mathematics, is to deny that space and time are part of the content we take in through sensation – instead they must have their source in the human mind.

The Reality of Beer-Goggles-Enhanced Attractiveness

We have seen that with his position on space and time, Kant takes to a new level the distinction between those characteristics of our experience that are due to the subjective constitution of our minds and those that are due to the constitutions of objects themselves. Not only are the enhanced attractiveness we perceive in our drinking partners while wearing beer goggles, the unpleasant taste I find in beer fermented with California Lager yeast, and the amber color of a Dogfish Head 60 Minute IPA all characteristics that have their source in the subjective constitution of the mind, but so are spatio-temporal qualities such as being located in a glass on a bar, being a pint in volume, or being freshly poured. Outside the framework of human cognition, none of these types of qualities have any reality. Yet we have seen that for Kant, despite their source in the subjective constitution of the human mind, some of these qualities – the spatio-temporal qualities – do have empirical reality, that is, they are real qualities of the objects we experience. So what do we say about the beer-goggles-enhanced attractiveness of our drinking partners? Some of you may be tempted to conclude the very same thing. That is, despite its source in the constitution of the mind, the enhanced attractiveness we perceive after having a pint or two is a real quality of our drinking partner. After all, you might argue, when Fiona has her beer goggles on, she experiences Dwayne as being cuter – isn't that all it takes for him to be cuter? I think, however, most of us will recognize the problem with ascribing reality to beer-goggles-enhanced attractiveness – namely, tomorrow morning. When Fiona wakes up in the morning she no longer perceives the enhanced attractiveness in Dwayne that her beer goggles produced the night before (clearly an unfortunate turn of events for Dwayne). What would Fiona conclude when she realizes that Dwayne's added attractiveness comes and goes with her beer goggles? Well, it seems to me this realization would lead her to conclude that the added attractiveness is due to her beer goggles rather than to any feature of Dwayne. As a result she would deny the reality of the attractiveness she thought she perceived in Dwayne last night. Nevertheless, if you are truly committed to holding that the beer-goggles-enhanced attractiveness is a real quality of Dwayne, you might be inclined to argue that Fiona's morning-after realization should instead lead her to a more practical conclusion such as *it's time for another pint of Sam Smith's Oatmeal Stout*! Well, now who could argue with that?

15

Beyond Grolsch and Orval
Beer, Intoxication, and Power in Nietzsche's Thought

Rex Welshon

It's a truism that everyone in Germany likes beer. Friedrich Nietzsche concurs. But Nietzsche – perhaps the most trenchant critic of German character ever – despises the Germans for it, and he blames beer-loving Germans for "the alcohol poisoning of Europe, which has hitherto gone strictly in step with the political and racial hegemony of the Teutons" (*Genealogy of Morals*, III 21).[1] Why does Nietzsche have such hostility toward beer and alcohol? It's not that he is a prude. Although he admits in his autobiography *Ecce Homo* that a "single glass of . . . beer in one day is quite sufficient to turn my life into a vale of misery," he claims later in the same section that, "in spite of this extreme vulnerability to *small*, strongly diluted doses of alcohol, I almost become a sailor when it is a matter of *strong* doses" (*Ecce Homo*, "Why I Am So Clever" 1).[2] Nor does Nietzsche have deep moral or religious objections to the psychological states associated with intoxication or to the peculiar behavior intoxication sometimes causes. Indeed, from his early *Birth of Tragedy* to the late *Twilight of*

---

[1] Friedrich Nietzsche, *On the Genealogy of Morals*. Translated by W. Kaufmann and R. J. Hollingdale. New York: Random House, 1967. In this paper, I use the versions of Nietzsche's books given in the footnotes, on occasion altering translations.

[2] Friedrich Nietzsche, *Ecce Homo: How One Becomes What One Is*. Translated by W. Kaufmann. New York: Random House, 1967.

the Idols, he contrasts two great forces in human life, the rational and the creative, and steadfastly celebrates the intoxication found in the latter. Just in case we fail to get it, Nietzsche even gives the creative force a name. He calls it the "Dionysian," named after the Greek god of alcohol, Dionysus. Dionysus' followers (and those in Rome, where the name is changed to Bacchus) are well known for devilry, pranks, excess, and madness. To the bitter end of his sane life, Nietzsche continued to side with Dionysus; indeed, as he slipped into madness, Nietzsche started to sign letters "Dionysus."

Nietzsche is more than simply fond of Dionysian intoxication. His later thought is inconceivable without admiration of intoxication, for he praises artists and others who create, and he thinks that "for art to exist, for any sort of aesthetic activity or perception to exist, a certain physiological precondition is indispensable: *intoxication*" (*Twilight of the Idols*, "Expeditions Of An Untimely Man" 8).[3] Still, Nietzsche insists that he "cannot advise all *more spiritual* natures earnestly enough to abstain entirely from alcohol" (*Ecce Homo*, "Why I Am So Clever" 1). We get a glimpse of Nietzsche's reasons for this antagonism in *Twilight*. In a section called "What the Germans Lack," he complains that Germany has for a thousand years "deliberately made itself stupid" by abusing the two great "European narcotics," Christianity and alcohol, specifically beer. "How much dreary heaviness, dampness, sloppiness, how much *beer* there is in the German intellect!" he claims (*Twilight of the Idols*, "What the Germans Lack" 2). It is, then, neither intoxication nor neurotic bias that explains Nietzsche's distaste for beer, but the damp degeneration that increases with every beer.

Understanding Nietzsche's disdain for beer and praise for intoxication is our task. First, we discuss what Nietzsche calls "pathological intoxication," which is his generalized name for chemically induced states of intoxication. Second, we contrast pathological intoxication with Dionysian intoxication, going on to examine how Nietzsche developed from this his own preferred form of Dionysian intoxication, that which attends cultivating the will to power.

---

3 Friedrich Nietzsche, *Twilight of the Idols*. Translated by R. J. Hollingdale, in *Twilight of the Idols and The Anti-Christ*. New York: Penguin, 1968; see also *Untimely Meditations*. Translated by R. J. Hollingdale. Cambridge: Cambridge University Press, 1983.

Pathological Intoxication

It is a curious facet of Nietzsche's writing that, again and again, he both condemns and praises the same phenomenon. This infuriating feature is as true of Nietzsche's comments about intoxication as of any other. As we have just seen, Nietzsche is prone to saying both that intoxication is a form of narcotizing decadence and that a great life without intoxication is impossible. Unless narcotizing decadence is required for a great life, there is some kind of tension between these two views.

Here, for example, is one of numerous critical passages:

> The man of the people at least has to hold out to [the people] the prospect of conquests and grandeur: perhaps they will then come to believe in him. They always obey, and do more than obey, provided they can at the same time become intoxicated! . . . This mob taste, which *prefers intoxication to food*, by no means originated in the depths of the mob: it was rather transported and transplanted thither, and is only growing up in there most persistently and luxuriantly, while it takes its origin in the highest intellects and has flourished in them for millennia. The people is the last *virgin soil* in which this glittering weed can still thrive. – What? And is it to them that politics are to be entrusted? So that they can make of them their daily intoxication? (*Daybreak*, 188)[4]

This is typical Nietzsche, the venomous Nietzsche people expect to find when they read his books. In contrast, other passages extol the benefits of intoxication. Here, for example, is one of Nietzsche's notes:

> The condition of pleasure called intoxication is precisely an exalted feeling of *power* – The sensation of space and time are altered: tremendous distances are surveyed and, as it were, for the first time apprehended; the extension of vision over greater masses and expanses; the refinement of the organs for the apprehension of much that is extremely small and fleeting; *divination*, the power of understanding with only the least assistance, at the slightest suggestion: "intelligent" *sensuality* –; strength as a feeling of dominion in the muscles, as suppleness and pleasure in movement, as dance, as levity and *presto*; strength as pleasure in the proof of strength, as bravado, adventure, fearlessness, indifference

4 Friedrich Nietzsche, *Daybreak: Thoughts on the Prejudices of Morality*. Translated by R. J. Hollingdale. New York: Cambridge University Press, 1982.

to life or death – All these climactic moments of life mutually stimulate one another; the world of images and ideas of the one suffices as a suggestion for the others: – in this way, states finally merge into one another. (*Will to Power*, 800)[5]

It's hard to imagine a more interesting description of intoxication than that found in this passage. I'll discuss it at greater length later.

Were Nietzsche to have no good reason for distinguishing between kinds of intoxication, we could simply dismiss him as being inconsistent. In fact, however, he has a principled distinction, one based on the different causes of intoxication. He claims that "there are two sources of intoxication: the *over-great fullness of life* and a state of *pathological nourishment* of the brain" (*Will to Power*, 45, my italics). The latter of these – pathological intoxication – is of immediate interest to us. People have been drinking for thousands of years, more often than not for a very simple reason: it makes us feel good. Realized in an astonishingly diverse number of ways, intoxication is the result of imbibing, ingesting, or injecting chemical compounds – ethanol, caffeine, nicotine, opiates, hallucinogens, amphetamines, barbiturates – that are rapidly absorbed into the bloodstream, travel to the brain, and there cross the blood-brain barrier to affect neuronal signaling.

Occasionally, we find references to narcotics in Nietzsche's work. He is, for instance, fascinated by Indian and Asian gurus who use stringent vegetarian diets and narcotics to prompt hallucinatory visions. Despite such comments, Nietzsche has little patience otherwise for pathological intoxication, primarily because most examples of it are the result of alcohol, which in turn is affiliated with the regimes of self-deception, resentment and decadence characteristic of the herd. This psycho-social category, the "herd," and its constituent attributes of resentment, decadence, and self-deception, lie at the core of Nietzsche's psychological and social thought, so it is worth our time to unpack them.

According to Nietzsche, all of us seek to be powerful – psychologically strong, intelligent, goal-directed, creative, disciplined, unique, rich in contradictions – but only a few of us ever achieve it, for such a life is difficult, lonely, idiosyncratic, and characterized by suffering.

---

[5] Friedrich Nietzsche, *The Will to Power*. Translated by W. Kaufmann. New York: Random House, 1967. (*Will to Power* is more accurately described as a collection of *Nachlass* notes under the title of *Will to Power* than as a book entitled *Will to Power*.)

In comparison to those who succeed, the rest of us are to varying degrees failures. The vast majority of us are weak, narcissistic, dissolute, neurotic, undisciplined, and boring. We are indistinguishable members of a great herd of bleating animals. Consciously, but more typically unconsciously, we resent the better examples of humanity and hate ourselves because we know ourselves enough to recognize our insignificance.

In such declining lives one finds all kinds of perverse consolation strategies, excuses, stories, and explanations apologizing for and offering rationalizations of our lack of success. These strategies, which convert weakness into strength, failure into success, defeat into victory, are the strategies of *decadence*, a technical term meaning something that is against life. In the topsy-turvy world of the decadent, sickness is health and health is sickness:

> Where does one not encounter that veiled glance which burdens one with a profound sadness, that inward-turned glance of the born failure which betrays how such a man speaks to himself – that glance which is a sigh! "If only I were someone else," sighs this glance: "but there is no hope of that. I am who I am: how could I ever get free of myself? And yet – I *am sick of myself!*"
> It is on such soil, on swampy ground, that every weed, every poisonous plant grows, always so small, so hidden, so false, so saccharine. Here the worms of vengefulness and rancor swarm; here the air stinks of secrets and concealment; here the web of the most malicious of all conspiracies is being spun constantly – the conspiracy of the suffering against the well-constituted and victorious, here the aspect of the victorious is *hated*. (*Genealogy of Morals*, III 14)

We latch on to any framework according to which our failure is acceptable and adopt only those evaluative schemes according to which we failures are exemplary. If our decadent explanatory and evaluative schemes also entail laying low the powerful, well, so much the better.

Nietzsche calls decadent evaluative schemes the "slave revolt" in morality because the character traits dismissed by the nobility as base, rude, and barely worth mentioning are elevated by the herd to be exemplary standards against which everyone, not just themselves, is measured. For Nietzsche, religion is the most important social institution for spreading herd morality, and as essential for the herd of slaves it is the most offensive curse ever inflicted on humanity. Religion offers a diagnosis of the nature of human suffering, a psychological explanation of its causes, and a moral cure to rid us of it. Religion claims that the source of suffering is not, as Nietzsche has it, our recognition of ourselves as plebeian or the self-hatred which that recognition engenders. Nor is our suffering the result of the frustration we feel at our unrealized dreams or our envy of the powerful. Rather, our unhappiness is, according to religion, caused by our being power-desiring creatures. It is because we have passions in the first place that we suffer. The religious person moralizes passions as sin and offers a one-size-fits-all prescription to cure us: extirpate drives and passions altogether! For Nietzsche, this is asinine: "To *exterminate* the passions and desires merely in order to do away with their folly and its unpleasant consequences – this itself seems to us today merely an acute form of folly. We no longer admire dentists who *pull out* teeth to stop them hurting" (*Twilight of the Idols I*, "Morality as Anti-Nature" I). Even if we succeed at this game, doing so is against life itself.

This decadent world is the psycho-social context and moral environment in which Nietzsche criticizes pathological intoxication, for the above description is, he thinks, a description of *us*, we moderns. Inheritors of two thousand years of inverted and deceptive psychology and morality, we don't even comprehend our own decadence. One might be tempted to think that, given this state of affairs, Nietzsche would *praise* pathological intoxication, not as a cure for decadence, but at least as a respite from the astringency religion and morality impose. It's something of a surprise, then, to realize that for Nietzsche pathological intoxication is not opposed to but goes hand-in-hand with the herd psychologist, the slave moralist, and religion.

Unlike religious hysterics and moralizing prudes, Nietzsche thinks that pathological intoxication is neither morally wicked nor evil. After all, pathological intoxication indirectly reveals something important about human life, for it relaxes inhibitions and, at least temporarily and blearily, reveals the passions. However, whenever pathological intoxication occurs in the beaten-down herd, we interpret it according to our decadent self-understanding. Thus, pathological intoxication is an artificial and transient pleasure, self-destructive, embarrassing, and finally shameful. We enjoy ourselves Saturday night, but Sunday morning comes again and we slather another coat of moral goop over our enjoyment. Incessantly swinging between indulgence and guilt helps to convince all of us that the pendulum reflects an enduring tendency in the psyche, a tendency that psychology needs to explain and religion and morality must counter. We would, we tell ourselves, *like* to be stronger, better, more upright, but we can't because we're *weak* and unable to resist temptation (recall Oscar Wilde: "I can resist anything except temptation"). We think we must struggle against the passions and that the extent to which we lose the struggle is a barometer of weakness. But this gets things sideways: it's not the passions that must be fought, but the belief that the passions must be fought that must be fought. Under the influence of several pints, we access, albeit hazily, a world that is healthy, but then, thinking that whatever is so glimpsed must be rejected, we reject the passions rather than the combination of decadence and alcohol that distorts them like a fun-house mirror.

Some of us cannot forget the pleasures of pathological intoxication and become addicts or libertines, going on lewd rampages of self-gratification, destroying ourselves and those around. Nietzsche thinks nothing else should be expected. After all, since addicts and libertines are decadents, there is nothing there but a "multitude and disgregation of impulses" (*Will to Power*, 46), each one of which demands instantaneous satisfaction. It never occurs to us that even our desperate attempts to escape decadence are doomed so long as we acquiesce to the decadent prescription that no middle ground exists between indulgence and extirpation. Either way, we lose: either we lose ourselves to indulgence or we repent and are "saved." The former leads to despair, the latter to God.

When we turn to God, everything gets turned upside down. Entirely natural activities get reinterpreted as doing God's will on earth. We devise rituals of being born again in the spirit to signify repudiation of natural life. We construct the causes and effects of sin, redemption, and grace to explain how God can realize forgiveness on earth. Feelings of power are reinterpreted as arrogance, the essence of sin. Self-abasement is reinterpreted as humility before God. Our routine abilities to care for others and to forgive and forget are reinterpreted as God's miraculous gift of grace, miraculous since, given our sin, it is inexplicable otherwise. Since it knows no constraints, there is no end to the phenomena that religious psychology can reinterpret. It is an enormous sail kept aloft by its sheer size, getting more buoyant as it gets larger.

For Nietzsche, all of these rituals, rites, and practices are healthy displays of drives, admirably sublimated drives and passions, but put to the decadent end of defusing those very drives and passions. None

212

of them work for the goal they purport to serve, because they mistake symptom for cause, get causality backwards, and prescribe cures where there is no sickness. We make ourselves sick and addict ourselves to religion's anaesthetizing balms, which only make us sicker. It's this *deadening* of our passions and drives that gnaws at Nietzsche. Were we not decadents, alcohol could be an interesting diversion or be put to some festive ritual use, such as is found in the ancient orgies of Dionysus/Bacchus. As it is, however, our alcoholic indulgences do little more than offer us a chance to escape from ourselves long enough to confirm our decadence.

Dionysian Intoxication

The decadent regime of confusion, deception, and inversion must, Nietzsche thinks, be rejected. The key to overcoming it is acknowledging in the face of the decadent that some suffering can be eliminated, some is harmful, some foolish, and some beneficial. We should then reject the recommendation that we eliminate all the passions so as to prevent some of the suffering they cause. For cultivating some of the passions results in a kind of intoxication essential to a good life.

Early in his career, in the *Birth of Tragedy*,[6] Nietzsche suggests direct encounters with what he calls the Dionysian. The Dionysian is for Nietzsche a natural, rowdy, and boundless creative energy that mirrors psychologically the anarchic chaos of the world of becoming. Dionysian states of intoxication, frenzy, enthusiasm, ecstasy, even madness, permit intoxicants to relinquish their distinctness and experience this anarchy. Such an experience is, Nietzsche claims, shattering because realizing there is no order whatsoever in the world of becoming leads to nihilism, which is Dionysian wisdom. Particular kinds of music are especially likely to inflame eruptions of chaotic emotions, which in turn open the door to intoxication wherein we may abandon ourselves to the Dionysian. In these reflections, Nietzsche repeatedly affirms the benefits and dangers of Dionysian intoxication. This is why, at least in *Birth of Tragedy*, he is so interested in the mystery cults of Greece and in the Greek sense of the tragic. Art that blocks the

---

[6] Friedrich Nietzsche, *The Birth of Tragedy*. Translated by W. Kaufmann. New York: Random House, 1967.

preconditions of Dionysian states falsifies reality and is unhealthy, but tragedy, various kinds of music, and certain other rituals that result in intoxication embrace change and growth and are, therefore, healthy.

In his later work, Nietzsche de-emphasizes the alleged benefits of submerging oneself in states of Dionysian intoxication, and he admits that the views presented in *The Birth of Tragedy* are superficial, dependent upon and a romantic distortion of a more fundamental principle: the will to power. So, without actually abandoning the word "Dionysian," Nietzsche incorporates it into the will to power, a comprehensive view to which he devotes himself in his last 10 years. And of all of the facets of the will to power, arguably the most plausible is that which serves as a governing principle in psychology. This facet is directly relevant for understanding Nietzsche's mature appreciation of intoxication.

A tempting interpretation of Nietzsche takes us to be consciously aiming at power all the time. But this gets Nietzsche wrong and it is false anyway, for power is not the only possible goal. Happily, Nietzsche's views do not require that power is always a conscious, or the only, goal. However, if power is one of many different goals and if there are *other* drives and motivations as well, then power seems to recede from importance. This sits ill with virtually everything Nietzsche ever says about power. We can defend Nietzsche, but doing so requires digging deeper into the way power functions in psychological contexts.

The fundamental psychological unit for Nietzsche, and that to which he attributes will to power, is a drive, where a drive is an event with a subject, a goal, and a relation between subject and goal. Nietzsche insists that at every level of explanation higher than the inorganic, power is internally related to both *form-giving* and *self-overcoming*. In the organic and animal domains, form-giving is "the spontaneous, aggressive, expansive form-giving forces that give new interpretations and directions" (*Genealogy of Morals*, II 12). Form-giving is a modification of the energy we discharge in realizing the goal of a drive or, alternatively, the manner in which we undertake the activity that enables us to realize our goals. If we like, we can say that form-giving in psychological contexts is taking the activity imposed by any desire, drive or passion and cultivating that activity in a focused, organized, disciplined, and inventive manner so that engaging in that activity gives new shape and structure both to the goal, to itself as activity, and to the subject who has the desire. Concerning self-overcoming,

Nietzsche urges us to remember that "all great things bring about their own destruction through an act of self-overcoming; thus the law of life will have it, the law of the necessity of 'self-overcoming' in the nature of life" (*Genealogy of Morals*, III 27). In psychological contexts, this amounts to overcoming and going beyond our drives in the act of reaching the goals they provide.

Consider a concrete example. Suppose that we are climbers. We first learn the rudiments of safety and technique and practice them to become competent. In cultivating the activity of climbing, our technique becomes nuanced and subtle, matching moves to rock with increasing refinement until our movement occurs without overt intention, until the goal of *learning* to climb is absorbed into and disappears in the *activity* of climbing. Then the activity of climbing becomes its own end and we are transformed from a novice into an adept climber. This is what Nietzsche has in mind by claiming that a drive is an opportunity for form-giving, for expressing power. Power thus enters into psychological explanations as a particular mode of a drive's activity. Competent climbers regularly report that things change further for them. In becoming adept and then expert, the goal of climbing becomes overlain with consequences that would never have been experienced without climbing but which were neither foreseen nor intended when it was first taken up. Once experienced, these unforeseen and unintended consequences become their own goals and sometimes replace the goals we had when we started climbing. The initial goal overcomes itself and becomes the means to some other goal.

Self-overcoming is like that in general: in realizing a goal, the activity itself, if cultivated in a form-giving manner, results in overcoming our goal. This happens not because the goal is either discarded or becomes a stepping-stone, although both certainly occur. Rather, the original goal is incorporated and synthesized by engaging in the activity required to achieve it, thus altering it, the activity, and the subject so completely that none are the same as they once were. Thus, power is having and trying to realize a drive in a particular way, engaging in the activity constitutive of the drive in a form-giving and self-overcoming manner, infusing the drives we already have in a transformative way.[7]

---

[7] I have, in developing this view of the way in which will to power works in psychological contexts, learned from the work of John Richardson, as found in his *Nietzsche's System*. New York: Oxford University Press, 1996.

As we move from being novice climbers to being adept climbers, moments when "everything comes together" occur increasingly often. When muscular exertion is no longer tiring but energizing, the mind clears, fears disappear, hand-holds become huge, a feeling of fluid motion engulfs the body, and we feel a sense of liberation. Such moments are small-scale intoxications: physiologically invigorating, existentially liberating, and aesthetically revealing. Again, when we move from adept to expert, these moments stretch out, both in duration and intensity. The intoxicating experiences become self-induced, new possibilities reveal themselves, more complex pleasures occur. Although Nietzsche does not need to commit himself to the idea that intoxication occurs with mundane activities such as crossing one's legs or twiddling one's thumbs, an enormous range of human actions can be accompanied in this way. Whether it's soccer, skiing, brewing beer, cooking, sex, intellectual activity, connoisseurship of any kind, or simply walking (of which Nietzsche was fond), intoxication is a possible, and desirable, accompaniment.

Intoxication of *this* sort is possible even while drinking beer. Nothing is inconsistent if Nietzschean intoxication accompanies one's own beer drinking or beer drinking in the company of other beer-drinking friends and intimates. There is no reason for Nietzsche to oppose lifting a few pints to enjoy the free flow of conversation with friends. Indeed, he can even acknowledge that the connoisseurship found in beer culture (the kind of specialization humans love to exploit) is liable to induce intoxications of *his* kind. But if such intoxications are accompanied by beer, Nietzsche would insist that they should not be reduced to the neurophysiology of alcohol.

Most intoxications are trivial, but some are fondly recalled, some are sufficiently significant that we are prepared to suffer to experience them again, some are disturbing, some are sublime, and a few are profound. All episodes of intoxication share certain features, of varying intensity. Let's look at them, returning to the note from Nietzsche's *Nachlass* quoted earlier:

> The condition of pleasure called intoxication is precisely an exalted feeling of *power* – The sensation of space and time are altered: tremendous distances are surveyed and, as it were, for the first time apprehended; the extension of vision over greater masses and expanses; the refinement of the organs for the apprehension of much that is extremely small and fleeting; *divination*, the power of understanding with only the least

assistance, at the slightest suggestion: "intelligent" *sensuality* –; strength as a feeling of dominion in the muscles, as suppleness and pleasure in movement, as dance, as levity and *presto*; strength as pleasure in the proof of strength, as bravado, adventure, fearlessness, indifference to life or death – All these climactic moments of life mutually stimulate one another; the world of images and ideas of the one suffices as a suggestion for the others: – in this way, states finally merge into one another. (*Will to Power*, 800)

Note the many facets of intoxication. At its most basic, intoxication is the feeling of power, but how this feeling of power is experienced includes changes in spatio-temporal perception; increased sensitivity in sensory organs for details; cognitive flashes in which confusion is replaced with an incorporating and resolving insight; experiencing one's body as a graceful animal; sensual pleasure; levity; strength; bravado; adventure. Clearly, intoxication has numerous dimensions, not just physiological and perceptual, but cognitive and affective as well.

Intoxication's multi-dimensionality explains why it is affiliated with art and artists. The explosion of perception, cognition, affect, and physiological well-being characteristic of intoxication compels artistic creation, for the feelings of abundance and generosity therein spill over in the artist as the impetus to create. What initially "delights the artist's will to power" is, of course, beauty, something in which "opposites are tamed . . . without tension; . . . violence is no longer needed; . . . everything follows, obeys, so easily and so pleasantly" (*Will to Power*, 803). That intoxicating aesthetic experience compels the artist to create:

> In this state one enriches everything out of one's own abundance . . .
> The man in this state transforms things until they mirror his power –
> until they are reflections of his perfection. This *compulsion* to transform
> into perfection is – art. (*Twilight of the Idols*, "Expeditions of an
> Untimely Man" 9)

While artists are Nietzsche's favorite exemplar of intoxication and its consequences, they are not the only, nor in many ways even the best, example. Especially in *Beyond Good and Evil*,[8] *Genealogy of Morals*,

---

[8] Friedrich Nietzsche, *Beyond Good and Evil*. Translated by W. Kaufmann. New York: Random House, 1966.

217

Gay Science,[9] and *Twilight of the Idols*, he variously discusses philosophers (Heraclitus), military leaders (Napoleon), writers (Goethe), poets (Heine), and even religious figures (Jesus, Mohammed, Buddha) as others whose experience of power is intoxicating. Their intoxication is of a most extraordinary and elevated kind, not just a transient episode that goads us to other attempts, but a level of superior self-knowledge and surpassing achievement that for the rest of us is baffling and unattainable.

When Nietzsche discusses not particular individuals but *types* of healthy, flourishing human lives, it is the free spirits, geniuses, and new philosophers who, more than any other type, exemplify his kind of psychological health. These unique individuals sometimes become walking intoxicants. For instance, here he describes genius:

> The genius – in work, in deed – is necessarily a prodigal: his greatness lies in the fact that *he expends himself* . . . The instinct of self-preservation is as it were suspended; the overwhelming pressure of the energies which emanate from him forbids him any such care and prudence caution. One calls this "sacrifice;" one praises his "heroism," his indifference to his own well-being, his devotion to an idea, a great cause, a fatherland: all misunderstandings. He flows out, he overflows, he uses himself up, he does not spare himself – with inevitability, fatefully, involuntary, as a river's bursting its banks is involuntary. (*Twilight of the Idols*, "Expeditions of an Untimely Man" 44)

And here, a great human being:

> A strong, highly cultured human being, skilled in all physical accomplishments, who, keeping himself in check and having reverence for himself, dares to allow himself the whole compass and wealth of naturalness, who is strong enough for this freedom, a man of tolerance, not out of weakness, but out of strength, because he knows how to employ to his advantage what would destroy an average nature; a man to whom nothing is forbidden, except it be *weakness*, whether that weakness be called vice or virtue. (*Twilight of the Idols*, "Expeditions of an Untimely Man" 49)

Far from the dissipation of decadents who must be instructed to *eliminate* their passions and drives to avoid doing damage to themselves

---

9 Friedrich Nietzsche, *The Gay Science, with a Prelude of Rhymes and an Appendix of Songs.* Translated by W. Kaufmann. New York: Random House, 1974.

and others, great human beings, by *cultivating* their passions and drives in particular ways, reach a point of imprudent generosity, constitutional tolerance, and boundless willingness to present humanity with the yield of their unique talents. Great human beings *give* to the rest of us because their intoxication implies it and prevents them from doing otherwise.

In this way, the most spiritual and sublime intoxications are Dionysian, conceived as the ability to affirm all and deny nothing:

> A spirit *emancipated* stands in the midst of the universe with a joyful and trusting fatalism, in the *faith* that only what is separate and individual may be rejected, that in the totality everything is redeemed and affirmed . . . But such a faith is the highest of all possible faiths: I have baptized it with the name *Dionysus*. (*Twilight of the Idols*, "Expeditions of an Untimely Man" 49)

Finally, more than any other psychological state, power-induced intoxication opens the door to something Nietzsche considered integral to a good life, *amor fati*, the willingness to affirm everything, including one's own and others' shabbiness. As a result, intoxication, in addition to being generous and tolerant, is merciful.

Conclusion

For all of its excesses, self-centeredness, mistakes, and embarrassing rants, Nietzsche's work repeatedly reveals his conviction that humans are an extraordinarily lucky throw of the dice. As we come to understand how capable Nietzsche thinks humans are, his weariness with us also becomes understandable: so many more of us *could* be so much more than we actually *are*. Instead, we fritter our lives away, undone by chance, laziness, resentment, and decadence. No doubt it's too much to expect as much from ourselves as Nietzsche finds in the great exemplars of humanity. However, given that he actually identifies such human possibilities and finds that intoxication is integral to describing their greatness, it can be no surprise that he disdains the intoxication afforded us in beer and alcohol as diluted and depressing.

Beer will never be the great enemy – that honor goes to religion and morality – but in the hands of decadents and their handlers, nothing does more than beer to aid and abet the enemy. That's not the fault of beer, but of the decadents who drink it. Were we not decadent to begin with, beer could be a prompt to interesting psychological transformations. Yet, here, in the conclusion, we may say something more. If we recall states of intoxication prompted by imbibing without also subjecting them to decadent interpretation, or if by imbibing we are familiarized with a state that persuades us that decadence may indeed be rejected, then beer can also indirectly induce us to do something better with our lives. We should be careful not to read too much into this, of course, since any number of other things can also induce us to do something better with our lives. But we should not read too little into it either, since of all such things, beer is one of the most readily available. And it is certainly the most delicious.

Your Thinking Companions
on the Bar Stool next to You

Steven M. Bayne is Assistant Professor of Philosophy at Fairfield University. Steven has written the action-packed thriller *Kant on Causation* (2003), among other best-sellers. But mostly he kant get enough of that wonderful Duff. Steven recommends reading *The Critique of Pure Reason* only when wearing beer goggles.

Sam Calagione is the President and founder of Dogfish Head Craft Brewing. He is the author of *Brewing Up a Business* (2005) and *Extreme Brewing* (2006). A prophet of experimental beer, Sam has made Mesopotamian-style ale, IPAs with massive amounts of hops, stouts with 22% alcohol by volume, and invented a system for running finished beer through fresh hops right before drinking it. He is widely recognized as one of America's most innovative brewers.

Matt Dunn is completing a PhD in the History and Philosophy of Science at the University of Indiana at Bloomington. Prior to pursuing philosophy, Matt wrote a biology master's thesis on brewer's yeast and evolution. This was a practical question for him, as he is a home-brewer of long standing (or long kicking back?). Matt is also working on topics in the philosophy of biology like speciation and population genetics.

George Gale is Professor of Philosophy at the University of Missouri at Kansas City. His scholarly interests began with Leibniz, moved into explanation theory and modern cosmology, and now reside in the viniculture of the French Languedoc. George has just completed a

221

decade of being the Executive Director of the Philosophy of Science Association, which explains his increasing interest in (and need for) wine and beer.

Steven D. Hales is Professor of Philosophy at Bloomsburg University. Prior to the book you have in your hands, his scholarly endeavors involved various issues in metaphysics and epistemology, with a little Nietzsche thrown in. Currently his favorite beer is Ommegang's Three Philosophers, although he is prepared to subject this preference (frequently!) to the experimental method. Steve looks forward to receiving effusive praise for *Beer & Philosophy* at hales@bloomu.edu.

David Hilbert is Associate Professor of Philosophy at the University of Illinois at Chicago. He has published various books and articles on perception and color, both of which have clear connections to beer. An occasional homebrewer, Dave once made a spruce beer based on George Berkeley's recipe. Don't try this at home, kids. Remember: Dave is a trained philosopher.

Michael Jackson is one of the world's foremost authorities on beer. He has hosted the *Beer Hunter* television series, and has written numerous books on beer, beer styles, and how to taste and evaluate beer. A frequent keynote speaker at beer festivals, Michael is the leading force behind the enthusiasm for Belgian-style beer in the United States.

Dale Jacquette is Professor of Philosophy at the Pennsylvania State University. He spends at least half his time in Europe finding new beers to sample, particularly in countries where they speak German. Dale still manages to write five articles and publish one book every year, and has been a Distinguished Fulbright Fellow in Venice and a Research Fellow at the Netherlands Institute for Advanced Study in the Humanities and Social Sciences.

Jason Kawall is Assistant Professor of Philosophy at Colgate University. His official academic interests are animals, ethics, and the environment, and he has published widely in these areas. Unofficially he is interested in British ales and single-malt scotches, topics he is diligently researching in Scotland, although the terms of his grant apparently say something else . . .

Michael Lynch is Associate Professor of Philosophy at the University of Connecticut. He spends most of his thinking time on beer, but most of his writing time on truth, about which he has published three books and several articles. Michael is affiliated at the University of St Andrews as an Associate Arché Fellow, but that's mostly an excuse to drink Belhaven at the Central Pub.

Peter Machamer is Professor of History and Philosophy of Science at the University of Pittsburgh. In addition to numerous books and articles on matter, space, time, neuroscience, and Galileo, Peter is a devoted gourmet, and has lectured on wine, beer and food for various groups and restaurants around the country. In addition he was the wine, beer, spirits and food writer for *Pittsburgh Magazine* and wrote a weekly wine (and why not beer!?) column for 13 years for the *Pittsburgh Post-Gazette*.

Neil Manson is Assistant Professor of Philosophy at the University of Mississippi. Neil has published on philosophical theology, the design argument for God, the fine-tuning argument, and various other things. While originally more of a whiskey and gin man, he is coming to appreciate the excellence and diversity of beer. Neil can drink more than you.

Alan McLeod is Senior Legal Counsel for the City of Kingston, Ontario, Canada. That's his day job, anyway. His alter ego is the owner and proprietor of *A Good Beer Blog* (http://beerblog.genx40.com/). Alan is also a homebrewer and inveterate taster and collector of exotic beers from around the world.

Garrett Oliver is the brewmaster at Brooklyn Brewery and the award-winning author of *The Brewmaster's Table: Discovering the Pleasures of Real Beer with Real Food* (2003). He has appeared on numerous television programs to discuss beer, has been profiled in the *New York Times* and *Gourmet*, and is a regular judge at major beer festivals. Garrett has hosted hundreds of beer tastings and dinners, writes regularly for beer and food-related periodicals, and is internationally recognized as an expert on traditional beer styles and their affinity with good food.

223

Theodore Schick is Professor of Philosophy at Muhlenberg College. Ted is author of books with titles like *How to Think About Weird Things* (2004), and likes to think about weird things after a couple of Weyerbacher Blithering Idiot barleywine-style ales. He is also an old-school guitarist in a band called Doctors of Rock.

Martin Stack is Associate Professor of Management at Rockhurst University. His dissertation examined the historical development of the American brewing industry, and he has published in a number of scholarly journals. Martin has also published several encyclopedia articles on beer, breweries, and the US brewing industry, and he is currently at work on a project examining how historically defined consumer preferences affect the way multinational breweries expand into new markets.

Rex Welshon is Associate Dean of Letters, Arts, and Sciences and Chair of the Philosophy Department at the University of Colorado at Colorado Springs. Rex writes on Nietzsche and the philosophy of mind when he doesn't have to go to pointless meetings. Rex also enjoys hiking, canyoneering, horseback riding, skiing, and the imbibing of comestibles.

Index

This index was compiled by Greg Kenenitz and Ryan Wanttaja while drinking Ommegang Abbey-Style Ale, Ommegang Hennepin, Guinness Extra Stout, Ruddles, Victory St. Victorious Dopplebock, Victory Weizenbock, Victory Sunrise Weissbier, Arcadia Scotch Ale, Sam Adams Winter Lager, Weyerbacher Double Simcoe IPA, Yuengling Porter, and Dale's Pale Ale.